"A practical guide for living an authentic life in the ministry. Lee and Fredrickson generously share from their own experiences and introduce the major areas of life in ordained ministry. That Their Work Will Be a Joy is a wise companion for ministers and the congregations who love them."

—JEANIE M. THORNDIKE, PRESBYTERY OF LOS RANCHOS

"Anyone who has served as a pastor knows there is joy in serving the Lord in the local church. The authors underscore the joys, but also paint a realistic picture of the challenges: relational demands, conflict, expectations, overwork, burnout, and other critical issues . . . Not only is the book realistic; it is also practical. It provides insights and sound advice about how pastors can exercise self-care, and how congregations can effectively undergird their pastors."

—REGGIE THOMAS, GOLDEN GATE BAPTIST THEOLOGICAL SEMINARY

"Out of the tension between the ideal and the actual, the authors have forged five principle-based habits or patterns that, if shared by pastors and their congregations, would create new life and effectiveness in any church. Each chapter's postscripts—written for pastors, congregants, and seminarians— are alone worth the cost of the book."

—MICHAEL B. ROSS, THE PASTORS INSTITUTE

"Written in accessible language for congregational leaders, pastors, and seminarians alike, this book is full of tangible content, concepts, and insights that will spark the kind of deeper understanding needed for effective partnership. Of value to the individual, I particularly recommend its use for group study, bringing together clergy and lay leaders."

—GARY WALTER, THE EVANGELICAL COVENANT CHURCH

"Though pastoral ministry is one of the most fulfilling calls a Christian can have, it is inherently challenging and stressful. I know of many colleagues who have left the church or wanted to leave, but felt trapped and unsupported. That Their Work Will Be a Joy is written for both clergy and laity to understand the pressures pastors face, and the proactive steps that can be taken to develop and maintain healthy lives and congregations."

—WAYNE WALTERS, FULLER THEOLOGICAL SEMINARY

That Their Work Will Be a Joy

That Their Work Will Be a Joy

Understanding and Coping
with the Challenges of Pastoral Ministry

Cameron Lee *and*
Kurt Fredrickson

CASCADE *Books* · Eugene, Oregon

THAT THEIR WORK WILL BE A JOY
Understanding and Coping with the Challenges of Pastoral Ministry

Cascade Books
An Imprint of Wipf and Stock Publishers
199 W. 8th Ave., Suite 3
Eugene, OR 97401

www.wipfandstock.com

ISBN 13: 978-1-60899-762-6

Cataloging-in-Publication data:

Lee, Cameron

That their work will be a joy : understanding and coping with the challenges of
pastoral ministry / Cameron Lee and Kurt Fredrickson.

xiv + 264 p. ; 23 cm. Includes bibliographical references.

ISBN 13: 978-1- 60899-762-6

1. Pastoral Theology. 2. Pastoral Care. I. Fredrickson, Kurt. II. Title.

BV4010 T33 2012

Manufactured in the U.S.A.

Contents

Foreword

by Wayne Cordeiro

WAYNE CORDEIRO IS THE senior pastor of New Hope Christian Fellowship in Honolulu, Hawaii, and the author of *Leading on Empty: Refilling Your Tank and Renewing Your Passion* (2009).

I wish this book had been written sooner.

I was not prepared for the rigors of ministry, but I had a love for God and for people. Weren't they enough?

It was like John Lennon's 1967 hit song that promised, "All You Need Is Love." That's exactly what any young couple would love to hear. According to the song, you didn't need a job (too stressful), or money for insurance (too expensive), a budget for a mortgage (too constricting), a savings account for unexpected setbacks (that's what parents are for), or anything else that resembled reality.

All you needed was love . . . or so we thought.

Today, the USA suffers from an unprecedented number of couples divorcing or abandoning marriage and family altogether.

And they thought all they needed was love.

That was good enough for me. Love, I mean. I loved God. I loved the ministry, and I loved the eternal difference I could make. The very thought of giving my life for something that counted was thrilling. What could be better? It was everything a young, ardent follower of Christ would hope for that would propel him into an adventure of a lifetime.

But I didn't read the small print. It read: *Jump now, pay later*.

Paul said, "*Let us not grow weary* in well doing, for in due time, we will reap if we do not grow weary" (Gal 6:9) because he knew all too well the possibility of us indeed becoming weary in serving the purposes of God. Our faith is not bulletproof, nor is it invincible. It is fragile and susceptible to growing weary. How often have I seen men and women serving with a faith that was once vibrant and adventurous, but now are weary? What was once a faith described as total commitment is now cautious and calculating.

They're still serving, but they are weary, and the tide is rising.

According to the American Baptist Press, North America has approximately 350,000 churches, and every year 1 percent of them die. This totals 3,500 congregations that at the end of the year will no longer exist. Even more sobering is, if you do the simple math, in this next decade a staggering 35,000 congregations will become extinct. In another recent poll, I was surprised to find that 1,500 ministers leave the ministry every month due to various reasons. It could be retirement or job loss, but there is a staggering amount of ministers that are burning out and need to end their ministry for health and family reasons.

Recently, I completed a book by the title *Leading on Empty*. I had given this message at a Willow Creek Leadership Summit several years prior, and it quickly became the leading message of the conference. The topic hit an open nerve that many were struggling with.

Part of my story is unpacked in the second chapter of the book you're holding. My struggle did not come from sin or neglect. It was overconcern for others and not enough concern for my own emotional balance. But I felt selfish when I thought of myself, so I sacrificed more than was healthy. In the process, I couldn't distinguish between the call of Christ and the consumerism of Christians. The malady I may have suffered from was not service to Christ but service to triviality.

Since the book was released, I have received hundreds of letters and requests to meet with ministry leaders across the country that are wrestling with emotional depletion. These letters, I'm sure, represent only a fraction of those who are grappling with struggles that cannot be shared with their congregations. The battles are internalized but sporadically surface at home. If they remain unresolved, their congregations soon feel the brunt of the effects.

I recently met with a pastor in our city that was struggling with his own emotional balance and frustrated with the unwillingness of the people to change and improve. He tried for several years to rally the church, but the people were settled in their ways. Yet the congregants remained dissatisfied about the low attendance and the constant financial shortfalls. He labored under his lack of self-worth and effectiveness. It wasn't long before he felt like an utter failure.

Two days ago, I received a copy of a letter that same pastor sent to his congregation. It reads in part:

> The current news about our congregation is not encouraging. We will be voting in two weeks on the recommendation of the Church Council to follow through with closing the church. There seem to be only a few months left for our congregation.

The pastor's lack of personal well-being affected not only the pastor but the future of the seventy-five-year-old church. This is our city's second closure in the past year, signaling a rise in churches falling into the fateful one percent of ministries becoming extinct.

Tomorrow's church will not suffer from a lack of leaders. It will suffer from an overabundance of underdeveloped leaders. It will suffer from a plethora of ministers who are defeated on the battleground of their own hearts, their own homes, and in their own emotions. They remain cautiously engaged but with the flag of faith flying at half-mast.

But here's some promising news.

Exponential Conference, the largest gathering of church planters, reports that there are 3,000 new churches being planted each year. That signifies we are on the upswing of a new generation of leaders that have a calling and a conviction. However, the replacement rate still will not keep up with the attrition rate of 3,500 churches closing and 1,500 ministers leaving each year.

And will history repeat itself? How many of these 3,000 will enter the 1 percent of closures in a few years? How many of these young, ardent followers will become "weary in well doing?"

Watch successful people. They don't do a myriad of things in passing ways. Instead, you'll discover that they do a few intentional things over and over again. These practices have transferable benefits to every endeavor, but their foundations can be discovered in a few basic, non-compromising disciplines. Like the importance of scales to a world-renowned pianist, there is a regimen of priorities and practices that are common to all successful leaders.

What you are about to read is a healthy remedy to the current epidemic. Cameron Lee and Kurt Fredrickson offer us wise and time-tested principles that, if heeded, will bring healing to those caught in the cross currents of ministry.

These traits, however, must be deliberately developed. They will require your undivided attention. These principles must first be converted from neat platitudes into indispensable life habits. Then and only then will they will become gold in your search for treasure. So, read on. Input these principles into your ministry GPS.

It will save you from unnecessary endings.

Preface

PEOPLE SOMETIMES ASK HOW a book came to be written.

In a sense, this one was born out of a groan.

I (Cameron) was lecturing to a group of pastors at a breakfast event sponsored by Fuller Seminary. I had already written two books on pastors' families, and had conducted several related research projects over the years. So when I was asked to speak on ministry stress (as I do regularly) I agreed quite readily.

At some point during the presentation, I made what I thought would be nothing more than a side comment. I mentioned that the last chapter of one of my books had been entitled, "The Care and Feeding of your Pastor," and that I had toyed with the idea of writing an entire book on that subject.

Suddenly and spontaneously, an audible groan went up from several of the pastors. "Do it!" they pleaded. You could hear the urgency in their voices.

Kurt Fredrickson, who directs Fuller's Doctor of Ministry program, was sitting in the audience. A few years before, we had discovered that we shared something unexpected. As teenagers, we had gone to the same high school and the same church at the same time—but didn't know each other, because we were in different classes (for the record, Kurt was a year ahead of me)! Only years later, at Fuller, did we actually meet.

But more than that, we continue to share an abiding concern for the health and well-being of pastors. I knew that if I were going to write another book for and about clergy, I wanted someone of Kurt's pastoral experience on the team, someone who knew what it meant to groan under the demands of congregational ministry. You are now holding that book, the product of our collaboration.

But why, you may ask, do we need another book about pastors? There are many good and helpful volumes out there, many of which are cited here. What makes this one unique?

Part of our hope and vision is that this book will not merely be read by pastors in the privacy of their studies, but by other church members as well—those in leadership, perhaps, or those who for whatever reason want to see ministers thrive. In other words, we want the book to kindle constructive conversations between pastors and congregations, as church members begin to understand what it means to pastor a church.

Thus, we have intentionally written the book with both audiences in mind: pastors and congregations. A third audience, no less important, is pastors-in-training; we have chosen to call this group "seminarians," even though we recognize that the winding paths that lead into and out of seminary don't always have pastoral ministry as their destination. Still, as seminary professors ourselves, Kurt and I believe that many students who are training for the pastorate don't have a clear sense of what it means to minister to real people who have real issues and bring them to church! We hope this book will help fill in some of the gaps.

To keep the material down to earth, each chapter includes a three-part postscript in which we directly make practical suggestions to each of our three audiences in turn. (And yes, it's perfectly permissible to peek at the sections written for someone else—in fact, we're hoping you will!) In addition, at the very end of the book, we've collected a series of personal letters written to you, our readers, by pastors and their family members. Their task was to read the book, reflect on it from their own personal experience, and to share their insights and stories with you. Their contribution is yet one more way to keep our work grounded in the day-to-day reality of ministry.

Part 1 lays the groundwork by surveying the practical and theological context of ministry. Chapter 1 introduces the central tension. Drawing from the language of Hebrews 13:17 (from which we get our title), the actual experience of pastoral ministry can be described as both a joy *and* a burden. The challenge is to respond constructively to the burden, while cultivating a more transcendent joy. Chapter 2 delves into the more challenging side of the tension, reviewing what happens to us physically and psychologically under the conditions of stress and burnout.

There are deeper reasons why pastors experience ministry as both a joy and a burden. Chapter 3 addresses the inescapable tension between the theological and the sociological—between the wondrous truth about the church as declared in Scripture and the far more mundane reality of a particular gathering of Christians in a particular time and place. Chapter 4 deals with yet another related tension: is ministry just a job, or is it a vocation in the best sense of the word—a calling from God? In these two chapters, we want to encourage pastors to see past the messiness of congregational life to the glory of God's church, and to hold on to a sense of divine vocation in the midst of the demands of the job. This is what is needed to go beyond merely coping with burdens, and into renewing the joy of our calling.

Part 2 presents five principles for coping with the different layers of tension described in part 1. Chapter 5 is the pivot point, in which we discuss the meaning of Sabbath—not merely as a spiritual practice, but as an attitude, an orientation to life and ministry. We realize that various traditions understand Sabbath differently, and it is neither our goal to raise nor solve the theological controversies. We're after something different: we want to convince pastors of the necessity of creating sacred space and time in which to be reminded that God is good, faithful, and sovereign. As we will say repeatedly, the ministry belongs first to God. It's God's work before it can be ours; remembering that fact may help us keep things in their proper perspective. And it is difficult to remember or even believe that when we are simply too busy working *for* God to be still and listen *to* God!

Extending from a Sabbath-shaped attitude toward ministry, chapters 6–9 turn to practical matters. Chapter 6 addresses what it means to care properly for these wonderful yet fragile bodies of ours: a decent night's sleep, the right food, and adequate exercise. This may sound like obvious advice, but pastors are notorious for neglecting their physical health! A pattern of ministry that ignores physical self-care is not for that reason more spiritual, and we encourage pastors to model a more holistic understanding of health.

In chapter 7, we discuss what it means to set wise limits that respect the sanctity of every member of the congregation—including the pastor and his or her family. We need social boundaries that help protect against inappropriate intrusions, emotional boundaries that recognize the vulnerabilities we bring with us into the life of the church, and moral boundaries that help us remember which lines never to cross.

Chapter 8 deals with the two sides of healthy congregational relationships: support and conflict. We define a healthy congregation as one in which people care for one another with the love of Christ, a love that also expresses tangibly in support for the pastor. And it is out of this commitment to mutual care that congregations find the resources to deal with the conflicts that inevitably arise.

The ninth and final chapter addresses the very real challenges of being a member of a pastor's family, including church members intruding on the family's time and space, the uprooting of the family when the pastor must move to another church, or the lack of financial security. The spouses and children of pastors face unique demands, and the wise congregation that cares for its pastor must also care for his or her family.

With two authors and three audiences, one of the biggest logistical challenges we faced in writing this book was keeping our pronouns straight! For example, when does the word "we" refer to Kurt and me as authors, and when does it mean all of us, authors and readers together? And together in ministry, or together as Christians in general? We hope the context itself will make these things clear. We have, however, inserted one additional device for the sake of clarity, which you may have already noticed: when one of us is telling a personal story, we'll insert our name in parentheses to identify who's speaking.

As is often the case, books are the work of many more people than just the ones whose names go on the cover. Our thanks to Wayne Cordeiro for writing a generous and encouraging foreword, and to all those whose personal responses are printed at the end of the book. The final product is far deeper and richer for your contributions! Thanks, too, to the other unsung heroes of the writing process, namely, our friends in ministry who read early drafts of the manuscript and gave their insights: Craig Beckett, Chuck Hunt, Anita Liu, Annie McLaren, Danny Martinez, Andy Mattick, Charles Morgan, Candace Shields, and Jeanie Thorndike. Your enthusiasm for the project was an inspiration to us, and gave us the energy we needed to see it through to completion.

The staff at Cascade Books has been a delight to work with, and our respective families have been unfailingly supportive even on the most intensely preoccupied days of writing. Our greatest thanks, however, are reserved for God first and for pastors second. Thanks be to God for the divine grace and patience that allows any of us to be part of his redemptive work in this world. We offer this book to you, Lord, and hope that you will receive it as a token of faithful service. And pastors: thank you for all that you do on the Lord's behalf. What you deal with daily is far more complex and challenging than can be communicated in any book. In gratitude, and with love, we dedicate this volume to you and to your families.

Cameron & Kurt
Pasadena, California, September 2011

PART 1

The Context of Ministry

1

The Joy and Burden of Being a Pastor

Have confidence in your leaders and submit to their authority, because they keep watch over you as those who must give an account. Do this so that their work will be a joy, not a burden, for that would be of no benefit to you.

—Hebrews 13:17

With trembling and joy, the pastor works that fateful space between here and the throne of God. This yoke, while not always as easy as Jesus implies, is often quite joyful. It is a joyful thing to be a pastor, to have one's life drawn toward dealings that are divine; to bear burdens that are, while not always light, at least more significant than those the world tries to lay upon our backs. It is a joy to be expended in some vocation that is greater than one's self.

—William Willimon[1]

THERE ARE DAYS, SOMETIMES seasons, when pastoral ministry is a joy. That's not to say that ministry is easy. Fallible pastors caring for the spiritual vitality of fallible people in a broken world, all groping together to follow Jesus and make a difference in the world—how could that be easy? Pastoral work is frequently messy, but there are moments when those of us who are in ministry are able to see beyond the burdens of the present. Sometimes, we are able to believe that what Jesus said really is *true*: there

---

1. Willimon, *Pastor*, 11.

is more to reality than we often imagine, the kingdom of God bubbling up beneath the things that cause us to toss and turn in our beds. This is the wonderful, mysterious work of God in the midst of the mundane. That is where we find our joy, not in the surface of our circumstances. As Eugene Peterson has said:

> I've loved being a pastor, almost every minute of it. It's a dif-
> ficult life because it's a demanding life. But the rewards are
> enormous—the rewards of being on the front line of seeing the
> gospel worked out in people's lives. I remain convinced that if
> you are called to it, being a pastor is the best life there is.[2]

The apostle Paul also knew such gospel-centered joy. Writing from prison, he smiled just thinking about his beloved brothers and sisters in Philippi. He counted them as his full partners in the cause of the gospel, gladly see-ing this diverse community being formed in the ways of Jesus. He longed for them with deep affection.

A piece of disturbing news, however, had reached Paul. Some dif-ficulty was threatening the unity of the church (Paul, unfortunately for us, does not say what it was). Concerned that they remain firm in the faith, he wrote them a friendly letter to strengthen them in their quest to live by the gospel:

> Therefore if you have any encouragement from being united
> with Christ, if any comfort from his love, if any common shar-
> ing in the Spirit, if any tenderness and compassion, then make
> my joy complete by being like-minded, having the same love,
> being one in spirit and of one mind. (Phil 2:1–2)

"If," Paul said, four times. But what he really meant was "since": he knew their character and had confidence in them. He knew that all the things he said "if" about were already true of the Philippians, evident in the way they related to him, to each other, and to their world. What pastor wouldn't be filled with joy to serve a congregation like that? One where people are like-minded, loving, and united in purpose, where everyone humbly cares as much for others as for themselves (Phil 2:3–4)?

The Philippian church was a good congregation, but certainly imper-fect, as all congregations are. Paul was asking them to hang tough in the face of trouble, letting nothing impinge on their unity. That's what would make the joy he already had in them full and secure.

---

2. Wood, "Best Life," 18.

Make my joy complete! There are two things to take hold of in that short request. On the one hand, Paul's joy is from the Holy Spirit. As Willimon suggests in the quote that opens this chapter, a pastor's joy is not merely situational. Rather, it is intrinsic to the Spirit-filled life (Gal 5:22). Whatever the burdens of ministry, the daily ups and downs, true joy comes from knowing and living into one's calling—the adventure and privilege of participating in the grand work of redemption that God is already doing. This good work can happen in the midst of even the most ordinary and mundane activities.

On the other hand, a pastor's joy is not independent of the spiritual state of the congregation. It matters what the members of the body do, how they live and treat each other. After all, what Paul wanted more than anything else was to see the gospel flourish. That's why he took such joy in his Philippian friends. It's not that their exemplary conduct made his life easier; rather, he rejoiced that the truth of the gospel was on display everywhere in their fellowship and beyond. And he wanted to do whatever he could, even from his remote location, to make sure they didn't lose an ounce of that marvelous, Spirit-filled vitality.

Not all congregations, of course, are created equal! Paul could write glowingly of his deep affection for the community in Philippi, but there were other congregations that sorely tried his patience. Think, for example, about Paul's letter to the Galatians. Classical artists often painted Paul as a man with little hair. If that's how Paul actually looked, the churches in Galatia may well have been the reason.

That letter begins with his regular greeting of grace and peace. Then, abruptly, Paul blasts his hearers with both barrels: "I can't believe your fickleness—how easily you have turned traitor to him who called you by the grace of Christ by embracing a variant message!" (Gal 1:6, *The Message*). Strong words. He is appalled that the Galatians have so easily given up and given in: given up their gospel freedom, and given in to false teaching about the need for circumcision. Indeed, he is so angry that he actually wishes that those preaching circumcision—to put it delicately—would have a disastrous little slip of the knife (5:12). Not surprisingly, Paul hardly mentions joy in the letter, except to wonder where it went (4:15)!

This is why it's important to avoid the occasional temptation to romanticize the early church. We read about the depth of devotion, fellowship, and sharing among these new converts, how they "broke bread in their homes and ate together with glad and sincere hearts, praising God and enjoying the favor of all the people" (Acts 2:42–47). Then we look at our own congregations and wonder wistfully when and how it all went wrong.

If we're looking to rekindle joy in ministry, that kind of nostalgia won't serve us well. Make no mistake: the early church was full of human beings who had not yet reached "the whole measure of the fullness of Christ" (Eph 4:13), and the same is true today. On balance, some early congregations seemed to have it mostly together, as in Philippi. But then there were the believers in Galatia, or Corinth, with their tangled relationships and skewed ways of hijacking the gospel. These are the congregations that try pastors' souls.

Local congregations are always imperfect and broken. Whenever human beings get together, no matter how sincerely they wish to follow the Lord, there will be some messiness. But it is precisely in the midst of the ordinary and the routine that the Lord works, forming a congregation of people who are striving to follow Jesus and to do God's work in the world. Pastors are an important part of this movement, helping to develop congregations, and are themselves shaped in the process as well.

Despite their imperfections, whichever congregation Paul wrote to, he loved them all. His letters could be gentle or harsh, encouraging or in-your-face confronting. But we may be confident that he loved all the people with the love of Christ, however much they exasperated him. He yearned to see Christ formed in them (Gal 4:19). To be sure, some days were better than others. The burdens could be so great that the joy would all but vanish.

But not completely.

John Sanford, writing about burned-out pastors, once said, "It is important to recognize this positive side of the ministering person's life and work, but the happy things in life do not require books to be written about them, so in this book we must deal largely with the unhappy side."[3] Fair enough. Much of this book (especially chapter 2) will deal with the "unhappy side"—the things that make pastoral ministry challenging—with suggestions to pastors, congregations, and seminarians about ways to respond or cope.

But throughout the book, we will also emphasize the other side. We don't just want pastors to survive; we want them to thrive and flourish. And that means more than just learning to cope with difficulty—it means rediscovering, in the midst of difficulty, the joy that drew them into the ministry in the first place. In the midst of the complexities and

3. Sanford, *Ministry Burnout*, 15.

the humdrum ordinariness of day-in and day-out ministry, pastors some-times lose a sense of that calling and its joy. It begins to feel like nothing more than a job, and not a very fun job at that! As Reggie McNeal notes, "it is tough enough to serve a church *with* a call. Without it, the choice constitutes cruel and unusual self-punishment."[4] But when one's true gifts and calling merge in vocational ministry, then even when serving a church is hard, it will be where pastors find their greatest joy.

In chapter 2, we'll deal concretely with the related matters of stress and burnout in the pastorate. These two themes dominate much of what has been written about ministry in recent decades. For now, we will simply set the stage by taking a quick look at the upside and the downside of this "odd and wondrous calling"[5] that is pastoral ministry in its many forms.

Are Pastors Happy in Their Work?

Imagine you're at a party, talking with someone you've just met. What questions do you ask to get the conversation going? Chances are, you'll introduce yourself and ask the other person's name. And most of the time, the next question will be some version of "What do you do for a living?" The answer to that question is central to our identity. And how we feel about our jobs is generally related to how happy we are overall.

In 2007, the National Opinion Research Center (NORC) at the University of Chicago released a report based on nearly 20 years of data collected for the General Social Survey, involving over 27,000 American adults. Among the questions they asked in face-to-face interviews were "How satisfied are you with the work you do?" and "Taken all together, how would you say things are these days—would you say you are very happy, pretty happy, or not too happy?" After breaking out the results by profession, they found one that stood out above all others. People of that profession were not only the most satisfied in their jobs, they were also the happiest in general. Can you name the profession?

And the winner is . . . ? Clergy. Yes, clergy. No doubt many of you reading this book are surprised by that result, and you would be in good company. Jackson Carroll notes that there is a "general perception of cri-sis" regarding the pastorate, so much so that any positive news about the satisfaction and commitment of clergy is met with extreme skepticism;

---

4. McNeal, *Work of Heart*, 99.
5. Daniel and Copenhaver, *This Odd and Wondrous Calling*.

some even accuse the research participants of lying or being in complete denial.[6]

But the data seem relatively clear. Over 87 percent of clergy in the NORC study above said they were "very satisfied" (the highest rating among the options given) with their jobs. By contrast, fewer than half of the group overall gave that answer. And over two thirds of clergy said they were "very happy"—twice the percentage found in the group as a whole.[7] That's probably too large of a gap to be completely explained by mere denial of reality!

Moreover, this is not an isolated finding. In a 2009 online survey, Focus on the Family asked, "How would you rate your general level of fulfillment as a pastor?" Of the over 2,000 pastors responding, 62.4 percent described themselves as "mostly fulfilled," while another 24.7 percent chose "very fulfilled."[8] Other studies have yielded similar results.[9]

Something must be going right. Here's one tongue-in-cheek take on the ministry from Lillian Daniel, a pastor in the United Church of Christ:

> I love being a minister. Even when the ministry is hard, it's more fun than any other job I can imagine. Where else can you preach, teach, meet with a lead abatement specialist, and get arrested for civil disobedience all in the same week? . . . . But mostly I love observing God's presence in the lives of people of faith. Mostly I love the moments when, from the position of paying holy attention to my own community of faith, I notice the power and presence of God.[10]

The joy of ministry is rooted in "paying holy attention" to where the Spirit is blowing through a particular congregation. Does that mean that every satisfied pastor is paying attention in that way? Well, probably not. But it's encouraging to think that behind the job satisfaction statistics we might find the unaccountable grace of God. Not every congregation will be a Philippi, but they're not all a Galatia either.

Having said that, we can also recognize that while feelings of job satisfaction and general happiness are real and important, they don't tell the whole story. Kirk Byron Jones, for example, asks:

6. Carroll, *God's Potters*, 185–186.
7. Smith, "Job Satisfaction."
8. Focus on the Family, "2009 Survey."
9. E.g., Francis et al., "Clergy Work-Related Satisfaction."
10. Daniel, in Daniel and Copenhaver, *Odd and Wondrous Calling*, 2.

I am captivated by God, excited by the gospel, and devoted to the church. Yet, there looms an ominous shadow. If God, gospel, and church are so wondrous, why is it that many involved in ministry today are feeling fatigued and empty?[11]

He's not alone in asking. One study of 1,050 pastors attending conferences in Southern California found that 90 percent of the respondents reported being "frequently fatigued, and worn out on a weekly and even daily basis." Nearly the same percentage had thought of leaving the ministry, and over half said they actually would leave "if they had a better place to go—including secular work."[12]

In the last few decades, more and more books and articles have been published about clergy burning out in the ministry. Perhaps the work is not going as well as hoped, in spite of much prayer, energy, and planning. Conflicts in the congregation inevitably arise, and can be difficult to handle. Frustrations mount, sometimes to the breaking point. And so on. The stories are deeply painful, and many pastors resonate with them.

Moreover, just because ministers say they're happy or satisfied overall doesn't mean that they don't also report a variety of difficulties. Pastors have to deal with everything from family pressures to financial struggles to congregational conflicts run amok. Sometimes it's the discouragement of knowing that no matter what he or she does the pastor can't silence the full gallery of naysayers in the congregation. Here, for example, is a fictitious chain letter that has been circulating on the Internet. It parodies the kind of impossible expectations pastors often experience:

> *The Perfect Pastor.* The results of a computerized survey indicate the perfect minister preaches exactly fifteen minutes. Pastors condemn sins but never upset anyone. They work from 8:00 AM until midnight and also work as the janitor. They make $500 a week, wear good clothes, buy good books, drive a good car, and give about $500 weekly to the poor. They are 28 years old and have preached 30 years. They have a burning desire to work with teenagers and spend all of their time with senior citizens. Perfect pastors smile all the time with a straight face because they have a sense of humor that keeps them seriously dedicated to his work. They make 15 calls daily on congregation families, shut-ins and the hospitalized, and they are always in their office when needed. If your minister does not measure up, simply send this letter to six other churches that are tired of their minister, too. Then

11. Jones, *Rest in the Storm*, xii.
12. Krejcir, "Statistics on Pastors."

bundle up your minister and send him or her to the church on
the top of the list. In one week, you will receive 1,643 ministers
and one of them will be perfect. Have faith in this procedure.
One church broke the chain and got its old minister back in less
than three weeks . . . so don't break the chain.

We suspect this was written by a frustrated pastor! With expectations like
these, it's no wonder that pastors routinely endure the kind of criticism
that leaves them feeling stuck. Speaking from experience, Mark Buchanan
describes the irony:

There are people—more than a handful, I'd say—who find fault
with me. Things I say, or don't say, deeds I do, or don't do, attitudes they detect in me or detect the absence of. Sometimes, I'm
scorned or scolded for personality deficiencies, which—admittedly—I abound in. I am not warm and cuddly like pastor so-
and-so. I am too bloody-minded, or—conversely—an incurable
soft touch. I don't preach a clear vision. I do preach a clear vision, but not a compelling one. I do preach a compelling vision,
but compelling us toward the wrong ends. I talk too much about
money from the pulpit. I don't talk about it enough.[13]

In other words, if you're not fond of criticism, it's a no-win scenario. Go
left, go right, or don't go at all: someone will still be unhappy, and will let
you know about it. These are difficult issues to navigate.

But it's not simply a matter of having to deal with negative demands.
The same responsibility can be a joy in one season—or even in one week!—
and a burden in the next. Preaching is a good example of this. Sometimes
the sermon flows smoothly out of the study and into the pulpit; the pastor
feels in the grip of God's word, preaches with conviction, and the people
respond. When this happens, preaching can be exhilarating. But there are
times when the sermon seems lifeless and stillborn. The pastor tries to
muster the appropriate energy, but feels like he or she is just going through
the motions. This can go on for weeks at a time, even months, and the
reasons are varied. During these seasons, preaching feels like "delivering
a baby on Sunday and finding out Monday that you're pregnant again."[14]

And sometimes pastoral ministry feels like having a low-grade fever:
it's not bad enough to land you in the hospital, but you just feel off, or under the weather. The point is that it's not either-or: pastors are not simply

13. Buchanan, *Spiritual Rhythm*, 79.
14. Ibid., 88. See also Cordeiro, *Leading on Empty*, 34.

happy or unhappy, and the ministry is not simply either a joy or a burden. As with life itself, it's both-and. L. Gregory Jones has put it this way:

> We should not be surprised that people recognize that ordained ministry is a satisfying vocation. But we should be surprised and troubled that this vocation is beset by challenges, obstacles and systematic distortions that make it difficult to experience satisfaction in the daily practice of ministry.[15]

We're not sure about the "surprised" part of that quote; the general impression is often given that ministry is more burden than joy—much more. But we agree wholeheartedly that every Christian should be troubled by the challenges of the pastorate.

We have taken the title of our book from Hebrews 13:17. The writer gives the following advice to all followers of Christ: "Have confidence in your leaders and submit to their authority, because they keep watch over you as those who must give an account. Do this so that their work will be a joy, not a burden, for that would be of no benefit to you." The word translated as "burden" literally means "groaning"—and as we said in the preface, this book was born as a response to the groaning of local pastors. What can pastors and congregations do to make the work of ministry more of a joy and less of a burden?

Yes, there is joy in ministry—real joy, not mere job satisfaction—and when asked, many pastors will tell you that they are doing fine, thank you. But there are also very real burdens that come with the mantle of ministry, and it should be the concern of all believers to address these, for the love of Christ's church and its pastors. We hope that our examination of the challenges will reassure pastors that much of what they struggle with is normal and expectable. And we hope equally that this peek into the lives of pastors will motivate others to want to do something positive to lighten the load.

Ministry Is a Lot of Work!

A large part of the challenge, as we shall see, is that pastors carry a great deal of responsibility, in congregations where there are multiple and often competing expectations of the pastor's role. Many church members really don't know what clergy do with their time. As one church consultant has written, "An embarrassing truth about the work of clergy is that a lot of it

15. Jones, "Take This Job," 35.

looks like loafing. Who else gets paid to drink iced tea with a wise great-grandmother or toast the giddy joy of newlyweds?"[16] Parishioners may only see their pastor on Sunday, in the pulpit, which prompts the common bit of congregational humor that pastors only work one day a week. Eugene Peterson describes his own reaction to that not-so-funny joke:

> Each week I walk home after conducting Sunday worship and get a personalized version of this as my neighbor, puttering in his yard, greets me with the jibe, spoken as if he had just thought it up, "Finished for another week, huh? Sure must be nice."

Outwardly, Peterson responds politely, but inwardly wrestles with the temptation to lash out at his unsuspecting neighbor's ignorance:

> I mentally write out a description of my workweek that I will later take over and present to him, documenting evidence that will reassure him that I am not a parasite on the system, endangering the property values of the neighborhood with my indolence. He will register total shock and fumble out an apology. But after a long shower and some expertly phrased compliments from my wife on the prophetic originality of the morning sermon the sting is out of his barbs and I shelve my defense for another week.[17]

He calms down, gains some perspective, and shelves his defensiveness. But it's not gone, for he knows that sooner or later the joke will come again—if not from his neighbor, from someone else.

Worship services obviously account for a few hours of the pastor's time, but what does he or she do the rest of the week? That question can be nothing more than a matter of curiosity. But when things get tense it can morph into a more nagging consumerist demand: "So just what *are* we paying the pastor for anyway?" It might help if parishioners understood better what pastors actually do.

Pastors have many, many roles to play. The most obvious and public ones are preacher, teacher, and liturgist. Whatever others may think of their preaching, pastors who take seriously the responsibility of proclaiming God's Word from week to week spend long hours reading and studying in preparation for worship services. The congregation may see none of this. Additional hours are spent caring pastorally for the congregation, as in counseling and visitation. There are countless administrative

16. Hotchkiss, "Why Pay the Preacher?"
17. Peterson, *Working the Angles*, 63–64.

responsibilities: managing the budget, overseeing staff, writing for the church newsletter, and making sure someone takes care of that pesky leak in one of the classrooms. And with those many and varied responsibilities come meetings, meetings, and more meetings. Add to this the heartache of walking with people through personal difficulties and social injustice, and the often-frustrated desires to see people grow in their walk with Christ, and to see their congregations grow and make an impact in their communities, is it any wonder that many pastors find ministry so challenging? It is never just a job, but always mysteriously more, involving radical servanthood and even suffering. It is not merely about the spiritual formation of congregations, but of the pastors themselves.

In addition, many professionals, such as lawyers or physicians, are able to specialize in their particular areas of expertise and interest, but pastors are typically generalists: they wear many hats, and some fit better than others. Some pastors love to preach, but feel uneasy in the role of church administrator, chief financial officer, or personnel director. Some would rather counsel one-on-one with parishioners than be in the pulpit. But many pastors must in fact do all these things, regardless of skill or inclination.

The broad variety of roles and skills required is part of what makes the pastorate so challenging. Glenn Palmberg, retired president of the Evangelical Covenant Church, told us in a private conversation that "being president of the Covenant is the second most difficult job I have ever had. The most difficult was being pastor of a local church." Similarly, in his personal diary, Reinhold Niebuhr wrote that being a pastor "requires the knowledge of a social scientist and the insight and imagination of a poet, the executive talents of a business [leader] and the mental discipline of a philosopher."[18] We hasten to note, however, that Niebuhr's point was not to despair over how hard it was to be a pastor, but to marvel at the incredibly multifaceted contribution that could be made by a dedicated pastor.

A national telephone survey of over 800 clergy, conducted in 2001 for the Pulpit & Pew project at Duke University Divinity School, confirmed that the pastorate is indeed a full-time job and more.[19] For full-time Protestant clergy, the average (median) workweek is about 50 hours. Overall, about a third of that time goes to sermon and worship preparation, and a fifth to pastoral care, though men spend proportionately more time on the former and women on the latter. On average, African-American pas-

18. R. Niebuhr, *Leaves*, 173–74. Quoted by Jinkins, *Letters*, 5.

19. See Carroll, *God's Potters*, appendix A.

tors appeared to have the busiest schedules, clocking in at over 70 hours a week.[20]

There are various factors that seem to contribute to longer work-weeks. Urban pastors log more hours overall than do their rural colleagues. Pastors of larger churches spend more time preaching, probably because of multiple services. They also spend more hours in administrative tasks.[21] This may be because as churches grow leadership requirements change, with the result that pastors of large congregations must often function as if they were CEOs of religious organizations.[22] On the other side, many smaller congregations struggle to support a full-time position. Often, the only way to staff such churches is for pastors to work more than one job, or serve multiple congregations.

Pastors are expected to serve at professional levels of competence, but are generally paid less than others with comparable levels of training and education, particularly in small congregations.[23] Thus, the pattern of working two jobs, in order to both sustain a living and to serve the church, is becoming increasingly common among pastors. The Presbyterian Church USA, for example, sees bivocational pastoring as a growing trend.[24] One study suggests that roughly a third of Baptist and Pentecostal clergy are bivocational, together with 45 percent of independent Protestants.[25] Bivocationality is common among Hispanic pastors serving poor congregations, and one study reports that 43 percent of African-American pastors are bivocational.[26]

But it's not just poor congregations that are seeing an increase in bivocational pastors. More churches are realizing the sad reality that they just can't afford a full-time pastor. Some pastors and churches have adopted a bivocational stance as a missional strategy.[27] Not surprisingly, bivocational pastors are more likely than their full-time counterparts to say they are satisfied with their salary and benefit arrangements (presumably because of their *other* job!), but indicate that they feel like second-class citizens

20. McMillan, "What Do Clergy Do All Week?"

21. Carroll, *God's Potters*, 111–14.

22. Galindo, *Hidden Lives*, 89–90.

23. E.g., McMillan and Price, "How Much Should We Pay?"

24. E.g., General Assembly Mission Council (PCUSA), "Tentmaking"; Odom, "Two-Way Street."

25. Carroll, *God's Potters*, 82.

26. Hernandez et al., "Strengthening Hispanic Ministry"; McMillan and Price, "How Much Should We Pay?," 14.

27. Brown, "Sacred Space."

among other pastors and within their denominations.[28] And that's to say nothing of the pressures of working two jobs.

Thus, despite possible appearances to the contrary, pastors are definitely *not* loafing! Ministry can be satisfying work, but there's a lot of it. Pastors are busy doing what the life of the congregation demands. As we will continue to explore throughout this book, this busyness can have important consequences for the pastor's well-being. Like anyone else, pastors need well-rounded lives that allow for other activities, and plenty of much-needed Sabbath rest. And they need congregations that understand and support this.

The Real Challenge

Seen from a worldly perspective, pastoral ministry can be both deeply satisfying and profoundly challenging. Practical steps can be taken to build on the satisfying aspects while coping with the challenges. Yet this is potentially treacherous territory. As Thomas à Kempis wrote, no one "can live in the public eye without risk to [one's] soul."[29] Joy is first and foremost a theological issue, a question of faithful imagination and the ability to peer behind and beneath the surfaces of ministry. Thomas Currie reminds us that the pastorate is usually "unglamorous work," and observes that "there seems to be a lack of wonder or sense of mystery or wellspring of joy that accompanies and sustains Christian ministry today. . . . We have grown busy, but not joyful."[30]

Underneath any discussion about the nurture and care of pastors in a local setting is our strong and profound conviction that God is at work in the church and in the lives of his people. The Spirit of God was at work in the church in Philippi. The same Spirit is still at work today, in every congregation, whether we recognize it or not.

The exact nature of the challenges, of course, will vary from one congregation to the next, or even from one kind of pastoral appointment to another. The leadership challenges of the senior pastor are different from those of the associate, who generally works under the senior's authority. This is sometimes a smooth working relationship, and sometimes not. A solo pastor has different challenges than one who has multiple staff, especially if that solo pastor is also bivocational. Female clergy face different

28. Carroll, *God's Potters*, 175.

29. Thomas, *Imitation*, 39; cited by Jinkins, *Letters*, 13.

30. Currie, *Joy*, 2, 5.

struggles than their male colleagues, for whom gender expectations are seldom a critical issue. And couples in which both husband and wife are ordained face their own unique challenges, and even these may vary depending on whether they serve the same or separate churches.

Add in the different variables of culture, denominational expectations, and congregational characteristics, and the permutations are endless. We can't, of course, deal with all of these possibilities. Depending on your interests as a reader, you may feel that some are getting short shrift. And there are no simple solutions. But there are general principles that seem to hold across a variety of pastoral situations. In the second part of this book we will present five of these principles, which we hope will be helpful to pastors and congregations alike.

For the moment, though, the central question is this: Is it possible to be joyful amidst the challenges? We believe that it is, provided that joy is not equated with the promise of continual smooth sailing or a problem-free ministry. All Christians, including pastors, can cultivate richer soil in which God can plant the gift of joy. For pastors in particular, much of this turns on a matter of perspective, on the meaning given to the experiences of ministry. Jesus once told his followers:

> Come to me, all you who are weary and burdened, and I will give
> you rest. Take my yoke upon you and learn from me, for I am
> gentle and humble in heart, and you will find rest for your souls.
> For my yoke is easy and my burden is light. (Matt 11:28–30)

Reflecting on this saying, Willimon writes, "When is a burden light? It is when we find our burdensome lives caught up, elevated, borne aloft by something greater than our lives."[31] Our hope is that this book will help tired pastors renew that spiritual vision.

To that end, the next three chapters will try to build some perspective. Chapter 2 will explore the themes of stress and burnout, with a particular emphasis on the role of meaning and interpretation. In chapters 3 and 4 we propose that the experience of ministry is framed by two essential tensions: first, the tension between the theological ideal of the church and the reality of any particular congregation; and second, the tension between ministry as a God-given calling and ministry as a job.

That last point, the tension between the job and the vocation, will be a theme that runs throughout the book. We might think of these as the horizontal and vertical axes of ministry respectively. The job aspect of

---

31. Willimon, *Calling*, 119–20.

ministry has to do with human expectations and requirements, as in "Your *job* as pastor is to _____." The expectations might come from the congregation, the denomination, the ministry situation itself, or even the pastor's own self-defined role. But notice how different it would be to say, "Your *vocation* as pastor is to _____." Here we must deal with the transcendent, with God's call upon pastors to use their gifts in the service of the kingdom and a specific local congregation.

And therein lies the rub. The horizontal and the vertical, the job and the vocation, cannot be neatly separated. That is the nature of God-given ministry in a church that exists on earth and is necessarily filled with real people. There is no other kind of church—dream as we might!—and thus there is no other way. But there can be tension between the two aspects. To put it simply, ministry is experienced as more burdensome when the job obscures the vocation, and is experienced as more joyful when one's vocation is discovered and rediscovered amidst the demands of the job.

There are congregations who want their pastors to do a job for them, but have no understanding of the pastor's vocation—nor indeed of their own. Ministry by definition occurs in the nexus of relationship between a pastor and a congregation. Thus, if the congregation does not know or accept its own calling to be the people of God, the pastor's sense of vocational joy will suffer as a consequence.

There are denominations who want pastors to do a job for them, and leave it to the pastors to nurture their own sense of calling. And there are pastors who have yet to really discover their true vocation, lost in sea of good intentions, ideas, techniques, and images. It is often the nature of ministry that many clergy must find their calling while doing their job. Sadly, it is also the case that some may focus on the job for so many years that both the calling and its attendant joy seem ever elusive.

Can pastors perceive the presence of God's church in the midst of the imperfect saints with whom they minister? Can they reach past the frustrations of their earthly careers and renew their sense of vocation, of being called by God? If they can say yes to both of these questions, or at least stammer out the beginning of a yes, they will know more and more the joy of obedience to a surprisingly merciful God.

Postscript

To Pastors:

If the statistics are to be believed, there are a lot of satisfied pastors out there. Are you one of them? Maybe that's too black-and-white a question: there are aspects of the ministry you find satisfying, perhaps deeply so, and others that are a constant source of frustration. In recent years, you may have experienced a steady shifting of the balance toward the latter. We expect that's a major reason why a pastor would pick up a book like this in the first place.

Take a moment to do a mental survey. What is it about your current appointment that burdens you? What do you wish God would change?

Or let's put the question a little differently. Imagine that you had a safe place to pour out your longings and frustrations to your congregation, a context in which you knew that they would *get it*—really get it. What would you say to them? What would you want them to understand about what it means to be a pastor? To be a church? To follow Jesus together?

Now think about the other side. Is there anything about your current ministry that brings you joy? If ministry has become so burdensome that you can't answer that question, try this one instead: what one small thing have you seen that gives you a glimmer of hope that the Holy Spirit may yet be alive and well in the congregation? If you can name that one small thing, then begin paying holy attention: where else in the congregation might God be working?

It's important to be realistic about the challenges of ministry, of working with imperfect people in an imperfect world. We'll name some of those challenges in the next chapter. But it's possible, even necessary, to cling to hope while giving the challenges their due. The two sides are closely related: the better you are able to deal with the burdens, the easier it is to hold on to hope, and yes, even joy. That is our prayer for you, and our goal for this book.

To Congregations:

Think about the verse from Hebrews in the opening epigraph of this chapter. It's an instruction to believers as to how they should relate to those in leadership. You may have questions about your own pastor's qualifications as a leader, and you may be justified in your concerns. But the passage teaches that there is a two-way mutual responsibility. Pastors are directly accountable to God for how they use their pastoral authority. And the congregation is responsible to respect that authority, so that the ministry is a joy and not a burden.

Our hope is that you're reading this book because God has laid it on your heart to begin caring for your pastor in a more tangible way. Maybe your church is going through a pastoral transition, and you're wondering if something could be done better or differently this time around. Or perhaps you've begun to notice your current pastor fraying a bit around the emotional edges. Either way, you're wanting to do your part to safeguard the personal and spiritual vitality of your pastor, for the benefit of all. From the bottom of our hearts, thank you!

One of the reasons we wrote this book was to help church members understand better what it means to be a pastor. Are you aware of all the roles your pastor plays, or how much time is devoted to each? Of these roles, do you know which ones best fit with your pastor's gifts and preferences, the ones that help your pastor remain convinced of his or her call to the ministry? On the other side, do you know which roles feel like a poor fit, the ones that sap your pastor's energy and enthusiasm? We're not saying that the pastor should only have to do the things that come easily or naturally. But the plain fact is that pastors can't do everything that is needed for a congregation to thrive spiritually. God doesn't give all the gifts that are intended for the body of Christ to one person.

So here is the single biggest piece of advice we can give to congregations who want to keep their pastors enthused about the ministry: take seriously—utterly seriously—your own calling to be the church, to be Jesus' representatives here on earth. The most gifted pastor in the world can't make this happen unilaterally, and that's not God's intent. Paul himself would insist that the unity of the believers in Philippi was not the result of his excellent leadership, brilliant preaching, sterling intellect, or remarkable organizational skills; it was a work of the Holy Spirit, empowering people to live in ways worthy of their gospel calling. And what gave him joy was that the people understood this, and stepped up to the plate.

Here's the reality of how many people experience the church: it's a place you go to get your needs met, to have the pastor minister to you in some way, or even just to feel like you did your religious duty for the week. At some level, pastors want their people to be involved, to be active in knowing and exercising their gifts. But if people resist, sooner or later pastors will fall back on trying to do everything single-handedly, as if somehow they could be the whole body of Christ by themselves.

This is not what the church was meant to be, and it will lead to over-worked and discouraged pastors. So as you read through this book, think about how your congregation can empower your pastor to discover, use, and develop his or her God-given gifts, in a way that helps you to discover, use, and develop your own. Doing this will lighten your pastor's burden in ways that will benefit the health of the whole congregation.

To Seminarians:

In seminary classes and ministry seminars, I (Cameron) sometimes ask, "How many of you grew up in a pastor's family?" Usually, only a small percentage of the students raise their hands. Then I begin to speak about the realities of serving a congregation. Many students, it seems, find it easier to imagine the joys as opposed to the burdens. When I tell stories of how congregations can mistreat their pastors, the PKs (preachers'/pastors' kids) in the group nod gravely and knowingly, while some of their class-mates merely gape. "Really?" their facial expressions seem to say. "That kind of stuff happens at *church*?"

Unfortunately, yes.

We repeat: there is much God-given joy in ministry, despite the bur-dens, and there is good reason to believe that the majority of pastors find their work deeply meaningful. But there often seems to be a thin line be-tween pastors who thrive and those who throw in the towel. Our advice to you, while you are still in seminary, is twofold: be intentional about getting the preparation you need, and nurture your sense of vocation.

As we noted earlier, much of your time as a pastor will be devoted to the pulpit and the study. Most seminary curricula prepare you well for these roles, emphasizing the development of your exegetical, theological, homiletic, and liturgical knowledge and skills. But seminaries don't train you to do everything that the pastoral role may require, whether it's writ-ing and balancing a budget, managing staff, or knowing what to say when someone is suicidal, or criticizes you to your face. So stay alert to addi-tional training opportunities. Be in it for the long haul: plan on learning new skills for the rest of your life.

If we could emphasize one specific area of skill development, it would be this: learn good "people skills" like communication and con-flict management (see chapter 8). When pastors get in trouble with their congregations, it's usually not about their theology or their lackluster preaching, even if these are the issues being debated on the surface. Typically, it's much more about mismanaged relationships, particularly when a conflict is brewing.

Can you listen calmly to people who vehemently disagree with you, so that they actually feel heard? Can you manage the relationship between two people who disagree with each other in a meeting? Do you generally know when to be open and transparent, versus when you've said too much? Can you challenge and encourage at the same time?

We'll say more about the emotional dynamics of congregations later. For the moment, ask yourself honestly, "How well do I work with people, especially those who make me frustrated, angry or anxious in some way?" If your answer to that question is "Not very well," then start working on your relationship skills *now*. Trust us: you're going to need them.

Don't get us wrong, though. Even the most skillful of pastors don't necessarily have a compelling sense of vocation. We emphasize skill building here because much of the stress of transitioning into a church is dealing with the job aspects of ministry. The better your skills, the easier the transition, and the less likely you are to lose sight of your vocation. But you can't lose what you don't have. Nurture your sense of calling through prayer and conversation with those who know your gifts. That's what you'll need to hang on to when the job gets tough!

2

Understanding Stress and Burnout

The more hours per week one works, the more likely one is to complain of stress due to congregational challenges, report that work prevents spending time with one's children, say that one's spouse expresses resentment over the time the work of ministry takes, and say that it is difficult to have a private life apart from the clergy role.... The more one is able to take time away from the job, the less the stress.

—JACKSON CARROLL[1]

I would guess that 95 percent of all stress originates with other people.

—ARCHIBALD HART[2]

PASTOR WAYNE CORDEIRO HAS written a deeply honest reflection about his own struggles with the joys and burdens of ministry. Some of you reading this book will recognize parts of your own story in his. Driven by a compelling vision, Cordeiro gave his all to the ministry. He founded a church that grew rapidly, and helped to plant over a hundred more. Out of that ministry came the presidency of a new Bible college and a writing career. By many measures used in business or ministry, his success was staggering, and he loved his work.

1. Carroll, *God's Potters*, 125.
2. Hart, *Adrenaline and Stress*, 105.

But the constantly expanding demands began to take their toll. Family struggles and losses added to the constant pressure, the burden of responsibility. Because he had learned to manage external appearances, no one really knew what he was going through—nor was he ready to admit it to himself. Eventually, however, he was forced to wrestle with the plain fact of his exhaustion and its meaning:

> Ministry became more arduous. My daily tasks seemed unending, and e-mails began to stack up. People I cared deeply about became problems to be avoided, and deliberating about new vision no longer stirred my soul. Although I never doubted my calling and gifting, what began as a joy that filled me now became a load that drained me. But I didn't know where I could trim. People were coming to Christ and lives were being changed. How could this all be wrong?[3]

Then one evening, in California for a speaking engagement, Cordeiro was engulfed by the symptoms of chronic stress. He was out for a jog when the emotional tidal wave hit:

> One minute I was jogging along on the sidewalk, and the next minute I was sitting on the curb, sobbing uncontrollably. I couldn't stop, and I didn't have a clue what was happening to me. Somehow I made it through the speaking engagement that night and limped back home. . . . [M]y situation seemed to go from bad to worse. I began developing physical symptoms: erratic heartbeat, difficulty in breathing, insomnia. . . . For over thirty years I had invested my life in Christian ministry. . . . Along the way, I had segued from one ministry to another, adding more and more responsibilities—without pauses. But now I wasn't sure I could keep going.[4]

"Well, of course," some might say, "obviously he took on too much!" And with the perfect 20/20 clarity of hindsight, it would be hard to disagree.

But that's not a terribly helpful response. After all, who really anticipates this will happen to *them*? If pastors believe they are doing what God has called them to do, and God seems to be blessing the ministry, shouldn't they take on that next responsibility, and the next one after that? Isn't that what it means to be devoted to serving Jesus and the gospel? Doesn't the example of Jesus himself prove that ministry is all about personal sacrifice?

3. Cordeiro, *Leading on Empty*, 22.
4. Ibid., 23.

Well, yes—but not without some judicious qualification. Pastors understand what it means to be called to a life of service, and engage that life willingly. At the same time, however, members of any given congregation are likely to have quite different ideas about what form that service should take. And realistically, however doggedly these ideas might be voiced, they can't all be treated as if they came straight from the mouth of God. Nor must every ministry opportunity should be pursued without question simply because someone insists that it should be—even if that someone is the pastor! It takes wisdom and discernment, individually and corporately, to make good choices.

As we saw in the last chapter, the life of the pastor can be busy, busy, busy. But busyness is not an end in itself. There are so many responsibilities, and only so much time and energy to give. What will the priorities be? How does one choose wisely?

Everyone knows that pastoral ministry can be demanding. The problem is not that ministers and their families are unwilling to make sacrifices for the sake of the church and the gospel. Rather, as William Willimon insists, the real problem is that the good of the pastor's marriage and family life is sometimes sacrificed for the wrong reasons:

> What is immoral is not one's suffering in service to the gospel, but rather one's suffering in service to triviality. What kills pastors is not service to the cause of Christ, for such service carries with it its own invigoration. What is so destructive is being asked to sacrifice marital happiness and family tranquility, for those whose demanding self-centeredness has become an unbearable burden upon the pastor.[5]

Willimon is not simply focusing on those people in any congregation who can make life difficult for the pastor. His larger concern is the way in which many pastors, congregations, and even denominations have lost their sense of mission—and have substituted consumerism instead. Churches become places where people go more to get their personal spiritual needs met than to worship and to serve.[6]

In such a climate, job trumps vocation, and pastors settle into a one-foot-in-front-of-the-other routine. Willimon quotes what was said to him by one denominational official: "It is not that pastors are not working hard, it is, rather, that too much of the work they do is hardly worth doing."[7] It's

5. Willimon, *Calling*, 113.

6. E.g., Roof, *Spiritual Marketplace*.

7. Willimon, *Calling*, 114.

one thing to be merely busy; it's another to be meaningfully engaged in work that really matters. If pastors must be stressed, therefore, then, as much as possible, let it be for good reasons!

The life of ministry, by its very nature, cannot be stress free. To believe otherwise is naïve at best, unbiblical at worst. Nor *should* it be stress free, for without challenge there can be no growth.[8] In ministry, as in life, there will be good days and bad, days of triumph and elation, and days of defeat and drudgery (and in between, days where the hours tick by just trying to figure out what to write in the church newsletter). Pastors rejoice when they see lives transformed by the gospel, and then despair to see the petty bickering that plagues the flock.

We believe that stress in the ministry is inevitable, and that it is better to understand it than to try to eliminate it. To that end, we'll begin with a non-technical explanation of stress and its relationship to health, before reviewing the ways in which pastors have consistently found the ministry to be stressful. We'll also address the issue of burnout and its implications. Although we'll make some practical suggestions in this and subsequent chapters, we don't intend to present a primer on stress management. Others have already done that much better than we could, including some of the people referenced in the footnotes. Our concern is to help congregations and seminarians understand what pastors struggle with behind the scenes, and to help struggling pastors to know they're not crazy. More than that, we hope our discussion of stress will point pastors back to the more fundamental questions of meaning and vocation, which will be addressed in the chapters that follow.

What Is Stress?

The idea of stress is not a new one. In the sixteenth century, scientists were already trying to predict the amount of stress physical objects could bear without breaking. For example, if you visit a hardware store to buy a length of rope, you'll be confronted with a variety of choices. How thick? What material? Twisted or braided? Depending on the combination of these factors, each type of rope will have a "load limit" that tells you how much strain you can put on it before it snaps. That's how an engineer would describe stress.

But when it comes to people, physical metaphors like these can only take us so far. Ropes are inanimate objects. It's possible to talk about load

8. E.g., see Aldwin's notion of "transformational coping" in *Stress*, ch. 13.

limits because, overall, the same type of rope will reliably break under the same conditions of load. As human beings, we're more flexible, more variable. Our bodies are built to react to demands in ways that maintain a complex and shifting balance of a variety of physiological factors. "Stress" is the word we use to describe how our bodies adapt and respond automatically when that balance is disturbed.

Physiologist Robert Sapolsky believes we can learn a lot about stress by imagining ourselves as zebras.[9] (There's a point to this, we promise.) What do zebras worry about on any given day? Other than being chased and eaten by a lion, not much. In order to survive on the savanna, zebras must be able to respond quickly and automatically to emergency situations. They can't stand around thinking, "That shaggy-looking creature over there reminds me of the beast that ate Uncle Harry. Perhaps it would be prudent of me to find somewhere else to hang out for a while." Rather, as soon as the threat is recognized, their bodies must be primed to run for their lives—*now*. When the emergency is over, their bodies calm back down, and they go back to doing whatever zebras do in their spare time.

In this way, human beings are a lot like zebras (though some camera-laden tourists on safari act much less intelligently around lions than zebras do). Most of us are unlikely to meet a lion on the street, but there are other potential life-and-death situations—a mugger with a gun, or a distracted driver barreling toward us unaware. In situations like these we go into emergency mode, classically known as the "fight-or-flight" response. Adrenaline levels shoot up; our hearts start pounding, pumping blood into the muscles we need to escape. Our senses get sharper. All of these reactions are automatic; we don't consciously decide to tense up or raise our blood pressure. But these and a host of other bodily responses help us cope with emergencies. And as with the zebra, when the threat has passed, our bodies return to baseline: our heart rate and breathing slow down to normal, and so on.

Understood this way, the stress response can be seen as a good thing: we're wired to survive. Similarly, it's important to recognize that even positive experiences—like winning the lottery!—can trigger the stress response. Being hyped up on adrenaline can be pleasurable, even addicting.[10]

Here's an example with which many pastors should identify. Sometimes you get into the pulpit and feel like you're on fire. The words flow

9. Sapolsky, *Zebras*.
10. Hart, *Adrenaline and Stress*, ch. 6.

freely and with enthusiasm. You're watching people's faces as you speak; they're nodding in agreement, and some are visibly moved. You sound the final "Amen" and get ready to move to the back of the sanctuary to shake hands and greet the congregation.

There's only one problem: your hands feel like ice! You try to warm them as inconspicuously as possible, but it doesn't always work. Why does this happen?

You're experiencing a stress reaction. The surge of adrenaline you felt during the sermon was exhilarating, but with it come the other symptoms of stress. The fight-or-flight response increases the amount of blood supplied to some parts of the body, but decreases it to others. So while your leg muscles may need more glucose- and oxygen-rich blood in an emergency, your body cuts down the amount flowing to your extremities, to reduce bleeding in case of injury. This restricted flow explains why your hands get cold. In fact, as Christian psychologist Arch Hart suggests, this involuntary response can be used as a simple and reliable way to monitor your stress level:

> Since only the hands get cold under stress—not the face—you can place your hands on your cheeks and "take your temperature." If your hands feel colder than your cheeks, you are likely to be having an adrenaline surge. The greater the difference in temperature between hands and face, the greater the stress reaction.[11]

The nice thing is that you can do this anywhere—though in some settings, you may have to feign surprise to get away with it!

Thus, although stress is usually spoken of as a bad thing, this isn't necessarily the case. It is simply how our bodies respond when the various demands of life knock us a bit off balance. The stress response is a survival mechanism, a way of adapting to the push and pull of life. And the demands that trigger it are not always unpleasant ones, especially if we've learned to enjoy the adrenaline rush.

Then what's the problem? Why are so many people sounding the alarm about the negative impact of stress on our physical and emotional well-being?

Here's where we have to recognize the important ways in which we are quite *different* from zebras. Our striped friends may respond quickly and efficiently to the hungry lion they notice right now. But they spend no time at all wondering if they're going to run into a lion *tomorrow*. For

11. Ibid., 122.

good or ill, human beings have the unique capacity to imagine a future and worry about it. More broadly, the point is that the stress response doesn't need some external environmental threat to trigger it. Internal psychological triggers will do just fine.

Having an actual fight with your spouse, for example, will set off the red alert: your pulse rate and blood pressure will go up, your hands may go cold and clammy, you will become even more sensitive to perceived insults. And tomorrow, next week, or even years from now, merely *remembering* that fight vividly enough can trigger the same reaction. Or your spouse can simply enter the room and, without a word, give you that *look*—you know the one we're talking about—and your alarm systems will go off as if the fight had already begun.

Again, here's an example for pastors. Remember that really difficult board meeting, the one where you returned home to rant and rave to your spouse? Or the conversation where your district supervisor never seemed to listen to anything you were saying? Or the church member who questioned whether you really believed the Bible? Or the neighbors that complained to the city council that your church's building program was going to ruin their property values?

Substitute any conflict you've had in the ministry—one that you found difficult to handle emotionally. Remember the situation in as much detail as possible. Imagine being in it again. What are you feeling now?

The point is that there doesn't have to be an immediate, external threat. The stress response can be triggered psychologically. Though psychological stressors might seem to be "softer" demands than, say, being chased by a lion, their impact should not be underestimated. As physician Richard Swenson has written, "Chronic uncertainty, sustained levels of increased vigilance, or struggling with a mental task are more stressful than chopping wood."[12]

To this point, we've characterized the stress reaction as *automatic*, which makes the most sense when considering true life-and-death situations. When survival is on the line, you have to be able to respond without thinking, and the stress response handles this nicely. It's automatic in the sense that breathing is—you don't have to think about it for it to happen.[13]

But that doesn't mean that what we think is irrelevant—far from it. Imagine again the pastor who has just preached an energetic sermon and

12. Swenson, *Margin*, 46.

13. Both breathing and the stress reaction are functions of the *autonomic* (roughly, what we've been calling "automatic") nervous system.

whose hands are cold due to the adrenaline rush. The pastor thinks, "Oh no, my hands are *freezing* again! I have to shake hands with all these people; what are they going to think when they grab hold of these ice cubes?" Standing in the doorway as the congregation files past, the pastor makes brief eye contact with one of the more opinionated parishioners further back in line. "Here we go," the minister groans silently, "I wonder what he'll find wrong with the sermon *this* week." But the man merely shakes the pastor's hand and mutters, "Nice sermon." And unbidden, a wary thought pops into the pastor's mind: "I wonder what he meant by that?"

Contrast that with the pastor who thinks, "Ah, there go my freezing hands again. Guess I'll just warm them up as best I can." Or, "Here comes Brother Jones; he certainly keeps me on my toes!" Or, "Well, I didn't expect a compliment from Brother Jones this morning! Even if he meant something else by that, I think I'll just enjoy the moment for what it is." Which of these pastors is going to be calmer by the end of the morning?

In other words, beyond the extremes of life-and-death emergencies, there is no simple relationship between how severe a demand is on the outside and how our bodies respond on the inside. Between the two stands the cognitive process of *appraisal*. Stress doesn't depend solely on "what happens" but on how we *interpret* what happens. What we think—how we think—matters. As renowned stress theorist Richard Lazarus has written,

> It is the meaning constructed by a person about what is happening that is crucial to the arousal of stress reactions. . . . The psychological meaning a person constructs about an environmental event is the proximate cause of the stress reaction and the emotions it produces.[14]

Or as Sapolsky puts it, "It's not just the external reality; it's the meaning you attach to it."[15]

The impact of external events is filtered through psychological factors. For example, when pressed by potential stressors, we do better if we have supportive relationships, if we have enough information or forewarning to prepare ourselves, or if we believe that we can still have some control over the outcome.[16] Conversely, if we're socially isolated, taken by surprise, or feeling helpless, we're likely to experience more stress, even in the same situations.

14. Lazarus, *Stress and Emotion*, 55.
15. Sapolsky, *Zebras*, 263.
16. Ibid., ch. 13.

And because of this psychological dimension, it's possible to be stressed out nearly *all the time*. This is the part that's crucial for your health. There's nothing wrong with stress if you can calm down and return to normal when the real crisis is past. But the response is supposed to be a temporary, need-based adjustment, not a chronic state of being. To use an analogy, "Adrenaline arousal can be compared to revving up a car engine, then leaving it to idle at high speed."[17] Imagine what that would do to a car. To stretch the analogy a bit, if the accelerator is floored too long or too often, the braking system will also begin to malfunction, and you'll find it harder and harder to slow down even when you want to.[18] And what starts the engine in the first place is the *meaning* you assign to potential stressors.[19]

Thus, a short-term stress reaction in response to a real external situation isn't a bad thing, particularly if you have to run for your life! Chronic stress, however, can wreak havoc with health in a number of ways. Ask people to name a stress-related ailment and they'll probably think of ulcers, and rightly so.[20] But chronic stress has also been linked in complicated ways to clinical depression, heart disease, a compromised immune system, and other problems.

The mechanisms for each differ, and are not completely understood. The general principle, however, seems to be as follows. Without our being aware of it, our bodies expend a great deal of energy on growth, maintenance, repair, and other positive projects. But in a perceived emergency situation, the stress response hijacks bodily resources or slaps a cease-and-desist injunction on functions that aren't immediately crucial for survival. In other words, Sapolsky's zebra needs every ounce of energy it can get to outrace a hungry lion. It doesn't need to be expending its energy digesting lunch—not when doing so increases the likelihood that the zebra will *be* lunch.

17. Hart, *Adrenaline and Stress*, 27.

18. Sapolsky, *Zebras*, 48. This refers to the interplay between the sympathetic and parasympathetic nervous systems. The former gives us the emergency response; the latter calms us back down. Chronic activation of the sympathetic system also means constant suppression of the parasympathetic.

19. Sternberg, *Balance Within*, 121. "Perception" is not only conscious, but includes experiences and associations stored in implicit memory.

20. The evidence suggests that ulcers are not directly caused by stress but by a bacterial infection. Stress may then increase the risk of ulcers forming or interfere with the body's ability to cope. Sapolsky, *Zebras*, ch. 5.

The picture is actually much more complex, but overall, when there's no let up in stress it can interfere with bodily processes in ways that damage our health or make us more vulnerable to the challenges that come our way. And because psychological stressors abound in the ministry, everyone who cares about the health of pastors and of the local congregation should stay alert to what they can do to keep chronic stress at bay.

What Makes Ministry Stressful?

As we saw in chapter 1, to say that ministry is stressful seems obvious to many, so much so that any news to the contrary may be greeted with skepticism or scorn. But not all pastors, of course, experience the same degree of stress. There are many variables involved. The pastor's individual makeup is one; the character of the congregation is another. Situational factors vary tremendously between congregations, and even within the same congregation over time.

Many pastors will say they love the ministry and mean it, even admitting the difficulties. Others, however, may have what one pastor calls a "head-in-the-sand mentality," denying that there are any problems whatsoever in their congregations.[21] And many church members really don't know what pastors go through, thereby contributing unintentionally to ministry-related stress.

Thus, at the risk of restating the obvious, in this section we will briefly review and illustrate some of the most commonly cited stressors of the job. The anecdotal and research literature on the subject is extensive, and we don't pretend to cover it all. Instead, to keep things simple, we present three broad categories of stressors: role expectations, intrusions of ministry into a pastor's private and family life, and isolation and loneliness that leaves many pastors without adequate social support.[22]

Role Expectations

As we suggested in chapter 1, pastors have many roles to play: preacher, teacher, liturgist, counselor, evangelist, spiritual director, administrator, business manager, scholar, community activist—and all-around really nice person, someone easy to talk to. Granted, not every congregation will

---

21. Stone, *Ministry Killers*, 62.

22. See the concept of the "triple threat" in Lee and Balswick, *Glass House*, 79–82.

expect all of these things equally, but the pastor will be expected to play multiple roles, and play them well.

Consider, for example, a small and resource-poor immigrant congregation. The pastor may be considered the in-house expert on everything. Even if the pastor doesn't really have all the answers, he or she is more likely to have better access to the answers. The minister may be the default bilingual go-between whenever anxious church members must deal with social institutions, from public schools to the immigration bureau. And community-minded clergy may consider all of this part of their commitment to serve. Add to this the expectations that pastors have of themselves, or the ones handed to them by denominational officials through the appointment process, and you have a very complicated situation indeed.

This is the problem of *role overload*, a concept that comes from the study of organizations.[23] There are just too many expectations for one person to meet. Pastors may have gifts in one area, but not in another. They love preaching, but can't balance a budget; they're good one on one, but more awkward leading groups. Needless to say, seminaries don't prepare students for every role they will encounter in the ministry. Thus pastors often find themselves spending much of their time in roles they don't enjoy and for which they weren't adequately trained, looking for grace and patience while they learn on the job.

And with so many roles to play, odds are that pastors will also experience *role conflict*. For example, the most public role is that of preacher, and the quality of the pastor's preaching is one of the key reasons that people are drawn to a particular congregation. But people have very different ideas about what makes for an excellent sermon. Was it delivered with fire and passion, or with calm reason? Personally moving, or intellectually challenging—with just the right amount of Greek thrown in? Biblically grounded (using the right translation, please!), or topically relevant? And perhaps most critical of all: too short, or too long?

Thus, different members of the congregation may have different expectations of how the pastor should fulfill a single role. Similarly, two roles may conflict with each other, making it difficult to do justice to either. The pastor may be counseling Fred in private, and then be confused about how best to relate to Fred in the context of a church committee. Or the congregation may expect the pastor to be an exemplary spouse and parent,

---

23. E.g., Katz and Kahn, *Organizations*. They use the simpler term "overload"; later researchers add "role."

while also expecting the pastor to be at church every night, and busy every weekend!

There is also the problem of *role ambiguity*, in which pastors don't have the clear information they need in order to know if they're making progress or even pointed in the right direction. Pastors frequently work without clear job descriptions, meaning that new responsibilities can be added at any time, increasing the possibility of overload.

And then there's the perennial problem of defining "success" in ministry. Is it important that the gospel is preached faithfully every Sunday? That the congregation reaches out to the community? That people's lives are being transformed so that they demonstrate the character of Christ? Of course. But these things can be too intangible to define. It's easier to measure success by the size of one's building or budget, by the number of programs and people.

We've talked to pastors who are dejected, who feel like failures, because they're playing the numbers game and losing. In fact, we confess to being a bit ambivalent about having opened this chapter with Wayne Cordeiro's story. We hoped that readers would identify with the story and realize the dangers of ignoring the effects of stress. At the same time, we wondered how many pastors would tune the story out, thinking, "I could never be that successful."

The game of upward comparison is a hazardous one. Parishioners may not say "We think our church is a failure because it's too small" out loud—but the expectation of numerical growth may linger quietly, communicated in ambiguous ways to the pastor. So pastors work harder, measuring themselves against a fuzzy, moving target. This is an invitation to stress.

Intrusions on the Pastor's Private Life

A second category of ministry stressors has to do with the ways in which the responsibilities of being a pastor seep over into the home. (This type of stressor is so common that we will devote an entire chapter to it later.) One common expression of this is the "on-call syndrome," where pastors feel they must be available to parishioners 24/7, for any and every need. Few pastors would balk at taking a phone call from a church member if there were an important need or crisis. The question, however, is what counts as "important."

One pastor, for example, told us of being roused out of deep sleep by a phone call at 3 a.m. "Hello, pastor," said the parishioner, "I hope I didn't wake you up." Some might be tempted to reply, "No, of course not, I've been praying all night!" This pastor, however, gave a more acceptable response: "Don't worry about it. What's up?" There was a pause on the other end of the line, and the sleepy pastor marshaled what reserves of compassion he could, ready to hear a story of pain and crisis. What the caller said, however, was, "Well, my wife and I are going shopping for a new car tomorrow, and wondered if you could come along to bless the purchase." The pastor sighed to himself and responded politely, but thought, "For *this* you woke us up in the middle of the night?"

Again, pastors understand that ministry involves sacrifice, and that includes dealing with intrusions and interruptions into their private lives and routines when need arises. But is every interruption equally valid? Are there limits to acceptable intrusions? If the pastor is on a much-needed vacation and the church is burning down, by all means, call! But if the toilet backs up and no one knows where the plunger is, is that a good enough reason?

Some intrusions are benign. Many pastors are used to being local celebrities, being recognized and greeted in public by people they may not know. It can be enjoyable and affirming to be out to dinner with the family and have a member of the church stop by the table to say hello. But if that person uses the occasion to engage in a ten-minute rant about the church building program, is that OK?

Ministers' spouses have reported being followed in the grocery store by curious church members who wanted to see what they bought. Parsonage families have returned home to find parishioners going through their cabinets and closets, looking for evidence that the pastor really did need the raise that was requested. A pastor's daughter recalls the time when a member of the church came to the front door of the parsonage, demanding that her brother get his feet off the coffee table, which belonged to the church. "Mind you," she explained further, "you can't really see through the living room window from the street." Implication: they were being spied on! Admittedly, these are extreme cases. But many pastors have similar stories to tell.

Thankfully, there are many congregations who are respectful of a pastor's family life and are therefore reluctant to intrude. Ironically, however, this can lead to a different kind of intrusive logic. An unmarried youth pastor was being asked to spend virtually every evening and every weekend in youth activities, and the parents couldn't understand why he resisted the heavy demand. Although it wasn't said explicitly, through side comments and snide remarks the youth pastor got the message: "You're not married; you don't have a life. So why *can't* you give all your time to our kids?"

Isolation and Loneliness

A third common difficulty is the pastor's lack of supportive peer relationships. Everyone needs friends, people with whom one can relax and be oneself, and safely discuss matters of personal importance. But many pastors find it difficult to establish such friendships. Loneliness, in fact, is one of the most common reasons given for leaving the ministry.[24]

Part of the problem is due to role overload and a busy schedule, which make it difficult to find time to socialize. And while many people are able to banter with their colleagues on coffee breaks and around the water cooler, much of a pastor's work is done in near seclusion.

In our opinion, however, the biggest barrier to pastoral friendships comes from the *idealization* of the pastor's role. Deep friendships usually require some sense of mutuality. To borrow a line from the theme song of the popular 1980s television sitcom *Cheers*, "You wanna go where people know, people are all the same." But where is that place for pastors?

The fact is that pastors are often treated as a different species of humanity. People become ill at ease in conversations, as if the pastor would somehow see into the deepest recesses of their souls and call them out for some private sin. London and Wiseman call this the "walk-on-water syndrome":

> Most of us have a story about a friendly stranger in the next seat on a plane who stops talking when he learns his fellow traveler is a pastor. Most of us have been served by a waitress who puts a spiritual spin on the conversation when she learns her customer is a preacher. At other times, conversations shut down completely when a pastor walks up and someone warns, "Clean up your act; the pastor is here."[25]

And if people can't be themselves around pastors, the reverse is also true: pastors can't be themselves around others. They're expected to be different:

---

24. Hoge and Wenger, *Pastors in Transition*, 29, 237.
25. London and Wiseman, *Pastors at Greater Risk*, 37.

more spiritual, more patient, more loving, exemplary spouses and parents, never losing their temper except in holy indignation.

We're not saying that pastors shouldn't be spiritual models to the flock. The question is about how that modeling happens. It's all well and good for a congregation to expect to see the fruit of the Spirit in their pastor. But that expectation won't play out positively unless they too are seeking the same fruit in their own lives. Nor can pastors be good spiritual models without a deep sense of humility and the need of God's grace. Where these things are lacking, pastors and congregations get into an unhelpful alliance. Instead of being spiritual leaders, pastors become spiritual proxies: the pastor's reputation becomes a substitute for the congregation's own spiritual growth.

Some pastors want to be friends with church members, but are gun-shy from previous negative experiences. In an unhealthy congregation, if the pastor becomes too chummy with one person, others become jealous and the rumor mill gets going. Some pastors have gladly unburdened themselves with someone from the congregation that they thought they could trust, only to be publicly humiliated when that person gossiped about what was said in confidence. The lasting pain of that betrayal can result in a lifelong vow of isolation: "I will never let myself be friends with someone from the church again."

So where do pastors go to find safe and supportive friendships? To other pastors? Sometimes this works, though it can require both courage and vulnerability. There can be an underlying climate of competition among pastors, especially those within the same denomination or district. They feel the need to put up a front with their fellow clergy, and worry what stories might leak out if they were to be completely honest with each other. Who wants to be the first to admit being unable to pray, or having real doubts about God's goodness? Or more prosaically, who wants to be the first one to voice his or her resentment toward the district superintendent? Pastors can have supportive relationships with each other, but usually not without a delicate probing of trust, which takes the kind of time, energy, and commitment that many pastors lack.

This portrait of the stressors of ministry may make the pastorate sound like nothing but doom and gloom! That's not our intent. As suggested in the last chapter, we believe that the majority of pastors enjoy being in ministry—at least most days—and hope to stay in it. But the stressors are real, and to an extent even predictable. As we'll see below, pastors who must endure more pressure related to their many roles, and do so with less social support, are more likely to burn out.

What Is Burnout?

Stress, as we've seen, is a normal and necessary part of life. Everyone experiences it, though some more than others. Burnout is a stress-related syndrome experienced at the far end of the continuum, particularly by people in the helping professions.

The concept of burnout became popular in the United States in the 1970s. At first, it was scorned by academics as little more than another pop psychology fad. Since then, however, a significant amount of research has established the construct's legitimacy.[26] Christina Maslach, the premier psychologist in the field, published her first book on the subject in 1982, occasionally citing ministers as examples.[27] That year also saw the publication of John Sanford's *Ministry Burnout*, and the concept has been a staple of the pastoral literature ever since.[28]

There seems to be broad agreement that burnout is common among pastors. In general, "burnout" is shorthand for the emotional collapse or breakdown that sometimes comes as the result of chronic stress. If stress refers mostly to the physiological response of our bodies to demands, then burnout emphasizes the eventual emotional result of being constantly under pressure. In much of the psychological literature, burnout more particularly means *job* burnout, "a gradual process of loss in which the mismatch between the needs of the person and the demands of the job grows ever greater."[29]

It's important to remember this idea of a mismatch when thinking about burnout so that we don't end up blaming the victim. True, there is evidence that some people are more prone to stress and burnout than others, such as those who have less self-esteem to begin with.[30] But job burnout emphasizes the environmental conditions, the climate of the workplace, instead of the person. If pastors are getting burned out, much of it has to do with the conditions of ministry themselves, conditions that

26. Maslach et al., "Job Burnout."

27. Maslach, *Burnout*.

28. Sanford, *Ministry Burnout*. See also Cordeiro, *Leading on Empty*; Jackson's *Mad Church Disease*; Lehr, *Clergy Burnout*; Stone, *Ministry Killers*; Willimon, *Clergy and Laity Burnout*.

29. Maslach and Leiter, *Truth about Burnout*, 24.

30. Maslach et al., "Job Burnout," 410.

are found across many congregations. Thus, anyone who really wants to help must be willing to take an honest look at how congregations treat their pastors. And pastors, for their part, must constantly remind themselves that the job is not identical to their calling.

Maslach and her colleagues describe different kinds of mismatches between the person and workplace-related demands that are more likely to provoke burnout.[31] One, of course, has to do with the *workload*. Does the workplace simply ask too much of people? Or does it require people to do things for which they lack skill or interest? As we've already seen, both of these conditions are often true of pastors because of their multiple role expectations.

A second type of mismatch has to do with *control*. Here the issue is whether the person has the resources and authority actually to get the job done: "It is distressing for people to feel responsible for producing results to which they are deeply committed while lacking the capacity to deliver on that mandate."[32] This is often true of pastors as well, who must juggle their own ministry goals with those of the congregation and judicatory. This is enough of a challenge in itself, even if you assume that the goals are mutually compatible, the resources needed to accomplish them are readily available, and everyone is willing to work together! That situation, however, is far too rare, and pastors can be left profoundly frustrated by the obstacles that keep them from moving vision to reality.

Still a third mismatch is between the work done and the *reward* received for it. Obviously, salary is an issue here. But reward can entail something as simple as appreciation. Many pastors feel that their work on behalf of the congregation is taken for granted. Charles Stone observes that if you ask pastors "what the people in your church could do differently to make your ministry in your church more joyful for you," the number one answer is for church members to participate more. Tellingly, however, if you ask pastors "what people in your church have done for you that has personally encouraged and affirmed you," the number one answer is acts of appreciation, including notes and phone calls that say a simple and heartfelt "thank you." As Stone writes, "small acts of kindness make the greatest deposits into the pastor's heart."[33]

31. Maslach and Leiter, *Truth about Burnout*, ch. 3; Maslach et al., "Job Burnout," 414–15.

32. Maslach et al., "Job Burnout," 414.

33. Stone, *Ministry Killers*, 100.

A fourth area of mismatch concerns the breakdown of *community*, where there is "greater conflict among people, less mutual support and respect, and a growing sense of isolation."[34] As we've already seen, many pastors already feel socially isolated by virtue of their leadership role. Beyond this, however, some congregations (and even pastoral staffs) are racked by division and conflict; for every Philippi, there's a Corinth. In such situations, it's doubly difficult for pastors to find the social support they need, let alone the sense of unity that should characterize a healthy congregation.

This is closely related to a fifth type of mismatch, which is a conflict of *values*. Sometimes this refers to the struggles employees face when asked to do something they believe to be unethical. More generally, though, the problem has to do with the disparity between what organizations say they value and how they actually do business. For the church, the question is—literally—do we practice what we preach? Do our policies and behaviors reflect what we say we believe, what we say is important? The more pastors care about the living embodiment of the gospel, the more painful this discrepancy can be.

A final type of mismatch has to do with issues of *fairness*. This usually refers to inequities in how employees are treated with respect to pay, promotions, and the like. This may be particularly relevant to female clergy. Women pastors seem to experience the same ministry stressors as do their male colleagues. But in addition they often carry the burden of gender stereotypes that undermine their credibility as leaders. Moreover, while all pastors struggle to some extent with the balance between work and family responsibilities, this balancing act can be more problematic for the woman who is expected to lead a church *and* run a household.[35] One might also speculate on how the problem of fairness (and control!) might apply to the sometimes stormy relationship between senior and associate pastors.

When some combination of these mismatches characterize a congregation, pastors will be more likely to burn out over time. It's more than having a bad day. As psychologist Beverly Potter has written, "Burnout is a kind of job depression, a malaise of the spirit. It is not a matter of ability to perform—the victim is physically able to work, but interest is gone, enjoyment is empty, life is drudgery."[36] This job depression is characterized

---

34. Maslach and Leiter, *Truth about Burnout*, 49.

35. E.g., Frame and Shehan, "Care for the Caregiver"; Zikmund et al., *Clergy Women*.

36. Potter, *Overcoming Burnout*, 186.

by three major symptoms: exhaustion, depersonalization or cynicism, and feelings of ineffectiveness.[37]

The first and most widely recognized symptom of burnout is *emotional exhaustion*. When people use the word "burnout" in a general sense, they're usually referring to exhaustion, the part of burnout most closely related to chronic activation of the stress response and the health problems that go with it. On the emotional side, previously meaningful and joyful work becomes oppressive and burdensome. Maslach describes it this way:

> A pattern of emotional overload and subsequent emotional exhaustion is at the heart of the burnout syndrome. A person gets overly involved emotionally, overextends him- or herself, and feels overwhelmed by the emotional demands imposed by other people. . . . People feel drained and used up. They lack enough energy to face another day. Their emotional resources are depleted, and there is no source of replenishment.[38]

Emotional exhaustion is common to people in the helping professions, who often give and give and give without caring adequately for their own personal needs—and this includes many pastors.

As we've already seen, pastors have multiple responsibilities and roles, some of which fit better than others. In a study of nearly 900 Protestant pastors in Hong Kong, the three role stressors of overload, ambiguity, and conflict all contributed to emotional exhaustion. Not surprisingly, role overload had the strongest relationship to exhaustion. In addition, pastors who were exhausted and dissatisfied with their jobs because of these role stressors were also more likely to be seriously thinking about leaving the ministry.[39]

The second characteristic of the burnout syndrome is *depersonalization*. Exhausted and overwhelmed by the demands of others, burned-out helpers often become cynical. They distance themselves emotionally from the people they serve, beginning to see them as objects, "actively ignoring the qualities that make them unique and engaging people."[40] For frustrated pastors, this can take the form of falling into an adversarial way

---

37. Maslach's terms have changed over time, but the underlying basic concepts remain the same.

38. Maslach, *Burnout*, 3.

39. Ngo et al., "Work Role Stressors." The study of 877 Hong Kong clergy used the emotional exhaustion subscale of the Maslach Burnout Inventory, the standard measure of burnout.

40. Maslach et al., "Job Burnout," 403.

of thinking. Congregations in conflict are already prone to an us-vs.-them mentality; burned out pastors may begin to reflect this mood, grumpily thinking of the entire congregation as "them."[41]

The third characteristic is *ineffectiveness*. Pastors can be dealt a double blow here. On the one hand, having too many responsibilities without adequate resources guarantees that some goals simply won't be accomplished. On the other hand, as we've seen, there is the intrinsic problem of tangibly defining "success" in ministry. This ambiguity can be an ongoing source of tension between pastors and the denominational officials to whom they are responsible.

But from the standpoint of burnout, the problem is how pastors evaluate themselves and their fitness for ministry. Burned out pastors fixate on what they haven't accomplished, and tend to blame failures upon themselves. Their discouragement turns into a feeling of personal inadequacy, and they may begin seriously questioning their call.

How big of a problem are we talking about? Stories of burnout are becoming increasingly commonplace, and some believe the problem has reached epidemic proportions. It's impossible to know for certain, of course, how widespread burnout is among pastors. But what we're suggesting through the above review is that, given the pervasive conditions of ministry described, the necessary pieces of burnout may already be present in many pastor-congregation relationships.

Some research evidence is beginning to shed a little light on the subject. One study reported that 11 percent of the more than 700 Dutch Reformed pastors who participated said they suffered frequently from the first dimension of burnout, emotional exhaustion. This is consistent with the rates of burnout in other helping professions. For these pastors, experiences of depersonalization and ineffectiveness were far less common than exhaustion. One might guess that the values of ministry and servanthood would work strongly against depersonalization (or make it harder for pastors to admit their cynicism!). Still, the researchers found that out of the many variables examined, the strongest relationships were between work pressure, exhaustion, and depersonalization. That means the greater the pressure, the greater the exhaustion, and the more exhausted the pastor, the more likely he or she was to be cynical about the ministry.[42]

---

41. Hulme, *Stress in Ministry*, 6.

42. Evers and Tomic, "Burnout among Dutch Reformed Pastors." The study was collected in the Netherlands and used the Dutch version of the Maslach Burnout Inventory.

Other evidence can be found in what is arguably the largest and best-designed study of pastors who have left the ministry. The researchers write:

> [W]e encountered numerous ministers who told us they left because of strain, weariness, burnout, and frustration. . . . These persons usually felt blocked in some way, either by external conditions . . . or by personal inadequacy. Therefore they were frustrated and saw no solution to their malaise except to leave parish ministry. They expressed feelings of hopelessness and isolation, stating that other people did not help them or even want them in the ministry. Many felt lonely and unsupported.[43]

By now, these themes should sound familiar. What were the reasons for these feelings of discouragement and burnout?

> [T]hey felt more stress due to challenges from the congregation; they felt more lonely and isolated; they felt more bored and constrained in their positions; and they felt more doubts about their abilities as parish ministers. The complaints of these ministers were not directed at denominational officials. . . . They saw their problems as within their churches—or within themselves.[44]

Overall, 12 percent of the nearly 1,000 pastors studied—from five denominations—fell into the category of those who left the ministry for reasons of burnout.[45] That may not seem like a high number. But remember: this was a study only of pastors who had already dropped out of ministry. We can't know from that number what percentage of active pastors may already be in the early to late stages of burnout: it may be lower, or it may be considerably higher. We believe there is ample reason for concern, and that more research is needed.

Where Do We Go from Here?

The relationship of a pastor to a congregation is not just a matter of sociology and psychology, but of the gracious and sustaining presence of God through the Holy Spirit. Because of this, ministry is not just a job in the secular sense of the word.

43. Hoge and Wenger, *Pastors in Transition*, 115–16.
44. Ibid., 116.
45. The denominations were: Presbyterian Church USA, Assemblies of God, United Methodist, Lutheran Church—Missouri Synod, and Evangelical Lutheran Church in America.

At the same time, however, pastors experience much of ministry *as* a job, and a demanding one at that. Michael Jinkins reminds us that while "[p]astors and congregations are *God's* people . . . we never stop being *people*."[46] The incarnation of Jesus beckons us to remember that gospel treasure comes in earthen vessels, and not by an accident of fate. This side of Jesus' return, we must of necessity recognize and deal with the ways brokenness shows itself among the people of God, including the things that cause unnecessary stress and burnout.

As we have said, meaning plays a crucial role. Willimon, for example, prefers the terms "blackout" or "brownout" to "burnout." By this he means a crisis of perspective, "the gradual dissipation of meaning in ministry, a blurring of vision, the inability to keep the theological rationale for ministry that is necessary to enliven our imagination."[47] More specifically, for pastors to remain aware of being "baptized, upheld, called, and held accountable to God in Jesus Christ" is their "most powerful resource for surviving and thriving in ministry."[48]

Pastors do try to hold on to the vision of God's church, even when dealing with the most recalcitrant of congregations. Pastors try to hold on to their sense of vocation, of being called by God, even when feeling shackled by more mundane considerations of the job. Both of these tensions are symptomatic of living in the time when God's reign has begun on earth but is not yet complete. And that is why faithfully holding tight to the certainty of God's active interest in *this* congregation and *these* people, despite the difficulties, is the most important thing a pastor can do. Glimpsing the church in the congregation, rediscovering one's calling in the midst of what is otherwise merely a career: these subjects will occupy us in the next two chapters.

Postscript

To Pastors:

We're sure no one needs to tell *you* that ministry can be stressful! That's not a negative judgment upon ministry—whether we're talking about ministry in general, or *your* ministry in particular. It's just a practical recognition of

46. Jinkins, *Letters*, 8.

47. Willimon, *Pastor*, 325–26.

48. Willimon, *Clergy and Laity Burnout*, 87.

reality. Distance runners, for example, may speak in glowing terms of the exhilaration of running. But they don't deny the very real demands that running puts on their bodies; in fact, they prepare for those demands in advance. In terms of stress, the same could be said of running the race of vocational ministry.

We're guessing, then, that you're not asking *if* ministry is stressful, nor *how* it is stressful. Your question is what to do about it. That's what the rest of the book is about, beginning with the larger questions of meaning. We'll make several practical suggestions, and we hope these will be helpful to you.

For the moment, we will simply say this: pay attention to what your body and emotions are telling you. Do you find yourself regularly getting exhausted? Feeling like you don't want to get out of bed in the morning? Dreading that next meeting? Wondering whether you should find another career? Do you get sick more than you used to, or have more trouble shaking off whatever sickness comes your way?

All of these may be signs of stress, and should be taken seriously. Talk to your doctor. Talk to someone safe who knows you well—ideally, someone other than your spouse or children. It's not that discussing these things with your spouse is bad. But remember that if you're stressed out, then he or she is probably already catching some of the fallout, directly or indirectly. In the long run, it's counterproductive to expect spouses to carry both their load and yours. Therefore, if you want to talk about the stressful aspects of ministry to your spouse, be prepared to also discuss honestly how it is stressful for *them* too. Be ready to listen, and to act on what you hear.

We know some pastors who are really skilled at denial. "There's nothing wrong. I can push through this. Let me just get through this building campaign, and everything will be fine." And sometimes that works. But after the building campaign comes something else to take its place, then something else, ad infinitum.

You don't have to be in full-blown burnout mode to take preventive steps *now*. And if you suspect that you *are* burning out, there's a road back. It's not an easy one, and it will probably require some outside help or accountability. But it can be done. So hold on—we'll give you some signposts for the journey.

To Congregations:

Is what we've said about stress and burnout in the ministry new to you? Our guess is that if you're not a pastor yourself but are reading this book, you've already seen some of the signs in your current pastor. Or maybe you're in the process of searching for a new pastor, and are thinking about the one that just left.

Let us first say how much we appreciate the fact that you're reading this! It suggests that you already realize, at some level, that the relationship between a pastor and a congregation is a *partnership*. You don't hire a pastor to be a vendor of religious services, to be judged solely by some measure of professional competence. And you know that you're not simply a religious consumer. You bring your own gifts to the social and spiritual mix that is congregational life. And that means that you have a responsibility for what you bring and how you bring it.

Willimon has written that "congregations get the clergy they deserve—that is, a complaining, demanding, uncaring congregation is usually rewarded by a defensive, complaining pastor."[49] That is certainly true, but we don't want to give the impression that there are good congregations and bad congregations, and that bad congregations are entirely to blame for a pastor's woes. Every congregation is a hodgepodge of people with different stories, personalities, and goals.

Maybe you know that you personally wouldn't call your pastor at three in the morning unless it was a *real* emergency! But you can't assume that everyone else in the congregation thinks or feels the same way. And if things like these *are* happening, don't expect your pastor to bring it up in casual conversation. There may be much more going on behind the scenes than you know.

What can you do? If your immediate concern is with the stress level of your current pastor, you need to create a safe context for honest conversation. And we do mean *safe*. Don't take for granted that because we're all brothers and sisters in Christ we automatically know how to deal with sensitive information and hurt feelings. If it means getting someone from the outside to act as a neutral consultant, do it. Some denominations even have resources of this kind to help smooth the process.

As you read this book, we hope that you'll come up with a number of ideas that best fit your particular situation. Read back over this chapter. Ask yourself if the workplace characteristics described are in any way true

49. Ibid., 78–79.

of your congregation, then prayerfully decide what to do. Here are a few suggestions:

- First, consider working with your pastor to create a committee whose responsibility is to make sure that the pastor and other key leaders are properly cared for. Some pastors are not terribly good at taking care of their own needs, and may need a little help from a congregation that cares!

- Second, take the time to express real appreciation. For example, don't just say, "Nice sermon, pastor." Instead, write a card or an email that says how the sermon impacted you, how the Holy Spirit spoke to you through it. Pastors don't just want to hear that they've done a good job (though that's nice when they can get it!)—they want to know that what they're doing is making the kind of difference that truly serves God.

- Third, invite the pastor (and his or her family, if there is one) to dinner. Don't feel like you have to discuss the Bible or church matters the whole time. Instead, do what you would do with people you wanted to get to know as Christian friends. Some pastors would love a chance to have fun, to laugh and play. And by the way, the pastor doesn't have to be the one to pray a blessing over the meal. *You* do it, and try not to think about whether the pastor is scrutinizing your prayer!

- Fourth, remember that congregations do not communicate their expectations with a single voice, and that too many expectations, or unclear or conflicting ones, create stress. Don't make your pastor serve several masters who don't agree with each other—that's a recipe for burnout. Make job expectations clear and consistent, with the pastor accountable to some group that is empowered to represent the whole.

- Finally, when you want to give your pastor unofficial personal feedback, try to make observations without tying them to expectations. You'll know you've succeeded in doing this if the pastor appears to make no changes based on your advice, and you don't feel the need to grumble or complain, whether in public or private. Help others to do the same. That's one concrete way to honor your pastor's authority and judgment!

To Seminarians:

Chances are you're in seminary because you've sensed some kind of call from God to the ministry. For some of you, the call is quite clear and unambiguous; others of you are uncertain and still exploring. And having read what we've said about stress and burnout in the pastorate, you may be having second thoughts!

Some pastors leave the ministry because of disappointed expectations. Seminary tends to fill your head with lofty ideals, and you may graduate with holy zeal for all the spiritual reforms you're going to institute as soon as you land your first pastorate. But then reality hits. It may take months or years to find a workable appointment. Or you find yourself ministering in ways and in places you never anticipated, working with people who don't always appreciate your new ideas. Ministry seems more stressful and less fulfilling than you had supposed. And you wonder if you (or God!) somehow made a mistake.

It doesn't happen to everyone. But some version of that scenario is probably more common than we would like to admit. So we're glad you're reading this *now*!

Far be it from us, as seminary faculty, to poke too many holes in those lofty ideals. But stay open to the idea that a calling to serve God and the gospel does *not* necessarily mean vocational ministry as a pastor (more on this in chapter 4). And even if you do decide that this is what God wants you to do, be realistic about what it means to serve a congregation of people who are as imperfect as you are (more on that in chapter 3). That means that you should start developing good habits now; don't wait until you're actually serving a congregation to learn the skills you need. Learn how to monitor your own stress levels, to pay attention to your body and emotions. We'll make further suggestions in the chapters to come.

3

Congregations: The Real and the Ideal

Our ministries can help transform the Church and help the Church transform
the world. But we must be sure that it is the Church that we are talking about:
the Church in all its thus and so-ness, in all its contradictions and compromises,
in its circus of superficiality and moments of splendor.

—RICHARD JOHN NEUHAUS[1]

There is far more to the church than meets the eye.

—EUGENE PETERSON[2]

FOR TWENTY-FOUR YEARS I was the pastor of a local congregation (here
and throughout the rest of the chapter, all of the first-person references
are from Kurt). I was living out of a sense of call that had been on my life
since I was a teenager. Fresh-faced and loving God, I was eager to serve the
church, captivated by the idea of working with God's people and making a
difference in the world. But sometimes, usually in the middle of a contentious meeting, I would be struck by the discrepancy between my dream
and the reality of congregational life. It happened often.

I once attended a conference that pictured new ways of doing church.
Returning home to my congregation, refreshed and on fire, I was ready to
adopt new methods that would change our part of the world. But my new

1. Neuhaus, *Freedom for Ministry*, 9.
2. Peterson, *Practicing Resurrection*, 114.

48

ideas were met with resistance and skepticism. I was crushed. Was I the only one in our congregation who wanted to move forward?

The church I served was located in a part of town zoned for horses and other animals. I was getting ready for worship one Sunday morning, five minutes before the start of the service, when a member of the congregation came running up to me and said, "Pastor, there's a sheep (a real sheep!) in the parking lot. What are you going to do?" And I thought to myself, "I'm the pastor of this church, and I have to take care of a stray sheep?" It wasn't the kind of shepherding I had in mind.

✳ This is life in a real congregation. The Word became flesh—a union of the divine and human. The church is also flesh, created by the Spirit of God among real people—people with bodies and histories and personalities. Budget fights, worship wars, frayed nerves, and skewed agendas—*this* is church, the real church, the church that pastors serve.

Lillian Daniel writes about the meeting she attended that was supposed to be a discussion of how to minister, beyond just serving meals, to overcome the systemic issues of homelessness in their community. But the conversation soon deteriorated into a debate about "chili mac"—the macaroni-and-cheese/canned-chili casserole they had been serving at the shelter. Can we get the chili cheaper? Big cans or little? Do we buy grated cheese, or grate the cheese ourselves? The argument went on for nearly an hour, and Daniel began to wonder if this was to be the only fruit of her three years of graduate training. And then, a moment of grace that transformed the meeting. Someone said thoughtfully, "I'd hate to be homeless on a cold night like this." Pastors understand both sides, the frustration and the glimpses of hope: "Christ crucified and resurrected prepares us to find majesty in the ordinary, mystery in the concrete, love in the midst of feuding, a ministry of tending to the details in the midst of grated cheese."[3]

Spend any time around a local congregation, and you quickly realize that it is a unique and wonderful and complex and troubling place. Congregations are full of people who want to do good and serve the Lord and care for each other. These same people, however, can sometimes get sidetracked. And there are some whose antics keep pastors awake at night, praying in perplexity, "Lord, is *this* what you called me to do?" The so-called invisible and universal church is an ideal that we only find in its embodied form: congregations of sometimes broken, sometimes beautiful saints.

3. Daniel, in Daniel and Copenhaver, *Odd and Wondrous Calling*, 7.

The Local Congregation: Mysterious and Messy

The church is made up of real people in real contexts. The gospel meets the reality of the fractured and fractious world God loves in the local congregation, which is "composed of equal parts mystery and mess."[4] The church is the bride of Christ, chosen from before time to be his holy people engaged in mission in the world—that is deep mystery. But the fact that it is fallible people who are chosen and loved and joined together—that's the messy part!

On the one hand, congregations can seem quite earthbound. To the social scientist, the church is a human institution, subject to common and measurable forces. On the other hand, the theologian uses grand phrases to describe the church, noble aspirations into which a congregation should live. Both points of view are true, and we see the tension in ourselves every day. Avery Dulles notes:

> To the Christian believer, the church is not a purely human thing; it is not simply of this creation or of this world; rather, it is the work of God who is present and operative in the Church through the Holy Spirit, in whom Christ continues his saving presence. Sociologically, the Church is a fact of observation, accessible to persons who do not have faith. Theologically, the Church is the mystery of grace, not knowable independently of faith.[5]

This tension between the ideal church and the real congregation, between the magnificent and the mundane, has always been the story of the church. While we understand the church to be universal and global, existing for over two millennia, the church we know on the ground is the local congregation.

Pastors understand this tension acutely, aching to see God move in people's lives, wanting to impact their communities for good. Pastors are full of hope, but sometimes very frustrated. Whether it's stray sheep or chili mac, they are routinely confronted with the everydayness of their work. Lofty concepts about the church get sidelined in the press of the urgent challenges and tasks of the day.

The church is seeing some troubling times. Scandals, misplaced priorities, and contentious debates cast a negative shadow as people switch

---

4. The phrase is attributed to Eugene Peterson and cited by Yancey, *Church: Why Bother?*, 45.

5. Dulles, *Models of the Church*, 114.

from one church or one denomination to another seemingly at whim. The practice is common enough to prompt a wry bit of humor that's been making the rounds. Here's one version:

> Did you hear about the guy stranded alone for thirty years on a little island? He finally waved down a ship, and when the first mate came ashore in a lifeboat, he saw three huts at the edge of the jungle. "What are those huts?" he asked. "Well," the castaway replied, pointing to the first hut, "That one is where I live, and," pointing to the third, "that's where I go to church."
>
> "What about the middle hut?" the first mate asked.
>
> "Oh," the man said, "that's where I used to go to church."[6]

This, unfortunately, is the reality of congregational life.

Many are choosing not to associate with traditional local congregations at all. For some, this means abandoning the institutional church in favor of a more personal but vaguely defined "spirituality." Some say they're leaving the church to save their faith. People are willing to admire or even love Jesus—it's just that they have a hard time with his followers. As David Kinnaman has argued, many young people understand the fundamentals of the gospel message, and even know some Christians personally. But what keeps them outside the church is the perception that Christians are hypocrites who define themselves primarily by what they oppose.[7]

Overall, local congregations struggle to be relevant in a changing world without selling out. Followers of Jesus want to live out a faith that is generous, but also full of conviction. Church leaders seek ways to serve others but don't want to get caught up in a consumer mindset that's all about meeting individual needs. None of this is easy.

And congregations are subject to anxiety and interpersonal distress.[8] Gather people together in any type of grouping—Little League, PTA, Rotary—and there will be disruptions and disagreements. The same is true of the church. A congregation is made up of people who are sometimes broken and in pain. They carry real life issues with them, some tragic, some petty, but all with the potential for trouble. Believers are the beloved of Jesus, but don't always behave in lovable ways. We joke about how much we love the church—except for its people. But it doesn't seem so funny when we realize the joke is about us.

6. Kinnaman and Ells, *Leaders That Last*, 43.

7. Kinnaman and Lyons, *Unchristian*.

8. E.g., Steinke, *How Your Church Family Works*.

The stories of Jesus' disciples are a good reminder: even those who walked daily with their Lord could be clueless and small-minded. In chapters 8–10 of the Gospel of Mark, Jesus tries three times to tell his disciples that he is going to suffer and die. The first time, Peter argues with him and has to be sternly reprimanded (8:31–33). The second time, the disciples avoid the topic and choose instead to argue among themselves about which of them was the greatest (9:30–34). The third time, Jesus repeats his prediction in grisly detail: he will be handed over, sentenced to death, mocked, spat upon, flogged, and killed, before rising again from the dead (10:33–34). The disciples' response? James and John ask Jesus for special places of honor, provoking the resentment of the other disciples (10:35–41).

If even Jesus had to deal with this, should we be surprised by the disappointing things that happen in the congregations where we worship and minister? Some pastors begin to despair over the messiness of their congregations. We heard of one pastor who quit his church hoping to find a group of people who would be 100 percent committed to living out their discipleship. Good luck with that! For as Eugene Peterson writes,

> Anybody who has spent any time at all in the company of Christians knows that none of us whom Paul calls saints is a saint in any conventional sense. . . . Adultery and addictions, gossip and gluttony, arrogance and propaganda, sexual abuse and self-righteousness are as likely to occur—even flourish—in congregations of Christians as in any school or college, any bank or army, any government or business. . . . And there is no use looking around for a congregation that is any better. It has always been this way. As far as we can anticipate, it always will be.[9]

We have feet of clay, and we know it. We cannot transcend that earthiness on our own. Hope comes only when we realize that the power for transformation comes from God.

All of this is the consequence of God's choice to take on human flesh, and to further incarnate the gospel through the church. God's strength is perfected in human weakness (2 Cor 12:9); God's plan is for his power and glory to shine through the mundane and everyday. As the apostle Paul reminds us, "But we have this treasure in jars of clay to show that this all-surpassing power is from God and not from us" (2 Cor 4:7). The miracle of the church—and it *is* a miracle—comes almost incognito in the fragile and

9. Peterson, *Practicing Resurrection*, 80.

unremarkable form of ordinary clay. As theologian Richard John Neuhaus puts it, the rank-and-file members of North American churches

> are the ones who do the unheroic, routine things like show-
> ing up on Sundays, paying the bills, harassing their pastors,
> saying their prayers, hoping for heaven, and, more often than
> not, trying to be decent to those both more and less fortunate
> than themselves. And in the midst of muddling through, there
> is occasional ecstasy, occasional heroism, the occasional act of
> self-surrendering love. It is all very human, and any serious con-
> versation about Church and ministry must begin at that very
> human level.[10]

The congregation *is* the church, despite the appearances. It is God's choice to convey the riches of gospel treasure through ordinary and sometimes cracked pots. We are not permitted to second-guess him on this. But if we are to see the congregation as God does, we may need to have our vision renewed.

The Invisible Made Visible

The Bible employs a variety of rich and inspiring images of the church: the people of God, the body of Christ, the temple of the Spirit.[11] These are vivid ways of describing the church of the past two thousand years, located in every part of the world, made up of a mosaic of peoples and nations, expressed in countless ways across many traditions. This is the church pastors are called to serve with enthusiasm, even while remaining mindful that the ordinariness of congregational life can cloud the grander vision. It takes faithful imagination to know that the invisible reality of God's church is also the reality of the visible, local congregation: your congregation.

The people of your congregation are the people of God. That is the reality, however things may seem. God is a sending, missionary God, and the church participates in God's mission as a chosen people, called out to bless the world in Jesus' name. The author of 1 Peter writes,

> But you are a chosen people, a royal priesthood, a holy nation,
> God's special possession, that you may declare the praises of
> him who called you out of darkness into his wonderful light.

10. Neuhaus, *Freedom for Ministry*, 6.

11. E.g., Bloesch, *The Church*; Kung, *The Church*; Moltmann, *Church in the Power of the Spirit*; Newbigin, *Household of God*; Watson, *I Believe in the Church*.

> Once you were not a people, but now you are the people of God;
> once you had not received mercy, but now you have received
> mercy. (2:9–10)

The author is writing to scattered and persecuted Christians, a church visible only to the imagination, a church in search of an identity. He gives them one by ushering them into the age-old story of God's chosen people. He deliberately echoes the covenant language God used on Mount Sinai:

> Now if you obey me fully and keep my covenant, then out of
> all nations you will be my treasured possession. Although the
> whole earth is mine, you will be for me a kingdom of priests and
> a holy nation. (Exod 19:5–6)

1 Peter tells these Gentile Christians—tells us—that they used to be on the outside of the story, but no more. A motley and diverse crew of individuals, strewn across the known world, is now collectively the chosen and cherished people of God. But being a called and chosen people is not an excuse to sit back and revel in one's good fortune. There is work to be done, priestly work. The church is called to a life of holiness and service.[12]

In tangible ways, therefore, the church engages in service, in the neighborhood and around the globe, extending the work of God in the world. Consider: what if the Lord returned in an instant and all the Christians in your town were gone? Would anyone in your neighborhood notice? If they did, would they be happy or sad? In short, would anyone miss the Christians if they left?

I had a crisis of ministry in the midst of my work in a local congregation. Our church was doing good work. But I found myself becoming more and more isolated from the broader community and less effective in ministry. I sensed that if our congregation was suddenly raptured from earth, very few people in our community would know that our church was gone. We did a great job of taking care of each other, but we were not engaged in our world. Something had to change. My role began to shift towards being a more *missional* pastor.

In our American culture, fewer people are engaged in the life of a church. Christianity's influence is waning, and the texture of pastoral ministry must also change. Kennon Callahan writes, "The day of the professional minister is over. The day of the missionary pastor has come. . . .

---

12. Newbigin, *Church in a Pluralist Society*, 83.

The day of the churched culture is over. The day of the mission field has come."[13]

As a pastor, I could no longer remain in my office, surrounded by the walls of the church. Writing sermons and discipling and caring for people in the congregation were still important tasks, but engaging only in those tasks left me isolated from the wider community. So I got more involved in community concerns. I joined Rotary. I became a police chaplain.

Our church made a deliberate effort to be people who extended the good news of Jesus into our city. Located in the suburbs, we began to realize that we had become ingrown and isolated. We needed to be a church that people in our community would miss. We planted a Hispanic congregation that began sharing the church facilities—which meant having to learn how to be with each other and work side by side in our city. We were active together in ministries to serve the homeless and to prevent homelessness. Our suburban congregation, where problems often hide behind closed doors or backyard fences, was forced to face the realities of mental illness, addiction, and poverty. Needless to say, being the people of God pushes us outside our comfort zone. But such is the church's priestly calling.

The people of your congregation are also the body of Christ, a people knit together by God. Again, that is the reality even when what we see gives us reason to doubt. The church is not a club where members come and go for their own personal benefit. It is not a mere assembly of persons; it is a people formed and gathered together in Christ.

The apostle Paul writes, "So in Christ we, though many, form one body, and each member belongs to all the others" (Rom 12:5). There is a fundamental shift in identity. The Christian life is not about individuals and their separate projects, for that is to think more highly of ourselves than we ought (Rom 12:3). Rather, believers are bound together and committed to each other as the body of Christ, according to God's design and purpose (1 Cor 12:18). And one tangible expression of that reality is that the members of the body care for each other, support each other, and encourage each other.

This isn't just pie-in-the-sky theory. When someone is broken and in pain, the church responds in compassion, offering solace and aid. When someone is having trouble following Jesus well, the church comes alongside to counsel. When someone is sick, the church rallies and prays.

13. Callahan, *Effective Church Leadership*, 3, 13.

A few years ago, my family went through a significant medical crisis. In the midst of that crisis, when I was angry and in despair, the congregation gathered around my family. They loved us and prayed for us and supported us. I thank God for the privilege, as a pastor, of experiencing the church at its best, a fallible congregation being the body of Christ. We are family, and we do not let go of each other.

You've seen this, haven't you, even in the most troubled of congregations? Even when conflict threatens to divide the church, somehow people still reach out in time of need. It's the reality of Christ's body, the unifying and sanctifying work of the Holy Spirit, peeking out from amidst the brokenness. It's nothing less than the miraculous presence of God in the midst of the mundane. Don't miss it when it happens; don't take it for granted.

And finally, the people of your congregation are the temple of the Holy Spirit. That is the reality to which the apostle Paul points:

> you are . . . fellow citizens with God's people and also members of his household, built on the foundation of the apostles and prophets, with Christ Jesus himself as the chief cornerstone. In him the whole building is joined together and rises to become a holy temple in the Lord. And in him you too are being built together to become a dwelling in which God lives by his Spirit. (Eph 2:19–22)

Again, Paul draws Gentile believers into the ongoing story of God's covenant people. The wall dividing Jews from Gentiles has been broken down through the cross, making the two into one people (Eph 2:11–18). And there's more: by making peace between Jews and Gentiles, God has started a massive building project. It begins with Jesus as the cornerstone, the reference point that keeps the building true. Against the cornerstone is laid the foundation of the apostles and prophets. But the crowning image is of the temple that rises upon that foundation—God's church, a very dwelling place for his Spirit (e.g., 1 Cor 3:10–17).

Is that the vision we have in mind when we look at our congregations? That those who were formerly far away from each other have been brought together, joined together, into a place where the Holy Spirit takes up active residence? There is, of course, the sociological reality to deal with: it's not as if Gentile and Jewish believers found it easy to live and worship side by side, whatever Paul might say. Cultural and ethnic tension can be felt in the book of Acts, Paul's letters, and indeed the whole history of the church right up to the present, including our own congregations.

But what motivates us to pursue peace, if we don't know that peace has already been won through the cross?

The church, and not merely its individual members, is the temple of the Holy Spirit, a place where God is present even when we are too distracted or disappointed to notice. It is the indwelling presence of the Spirit that makes us the people of God and the body of Christ (cf. 2 Cor 6:16). It is the Spirit that gives us the faithful imagination to see through the ordinary to the extraordinary, to believe the truth about the church. The Spirit births, enlivens, and empowers the church, distributing the gifts needed for her mission and ministry. In ordinary places among ordinary people, God shows up and amazing things happen: lives are transformed, people are reconciled, communities change.

As a pastor, I have sometimes used a phrase that sends people who know me running (literally!): "I have a plan for your life." It's my way of telling people that I see a place where their gifts and passions might intersect a need in the church or the community. But not everyone is ready to believe that they have gifts to contribute, or feel ready to contribute the ones they have. I once used the dreaded phrase to ask a woman to lead our drama ministry. To my delight, instead of running away, she took on the job with both passion and excitement. It enriched our church and our worship. Even more, I saw this woman's faith deepen. So it is with the church. When people are gifted by the Spirit, when others recognize and empower those gifts, when those gifts are used in faithful service to honor Christ, it can bring great joy to the congregation.

This is the church we serve: the people of God, the body of Christ, the temple of the Holy Spirit. This is grand theological language, rooted in a grand vision. The work of the church is grounded in nondescript neighborhoods and ordinary congregations. But it is always bigger than what we do, and more than we usually imagine.

Here Is Where the Lord Works

Congregations are the reality of God's church in time and space, the church that we warmly embrace one day and argue with the next. The local congregation is where the Lord works. And it is by faith that we must believe the Lord is working, even when we can't make out what he's doing. Speaking into the sometimes rancorous debates about worship, Neuhaus redirects our attention to what really matters: "*The* Christian mystery is the presence of Christ among his people, the reality of the Kingdom's presence because the King is present where two or three are gathered in his name."[14] God is present, and it's our job to pay attention.

Paul writes in Galatians 3:28, "There is neither Jew nor Gentile, neither slave nor free, nor is there male and female, for you are all one in Christ Jesus." The gospel breaks down dividing walls, whether based on ethnic, economic, or gender differences. This is the reality of the church, the Holy Spirit's work in congregations.

Consider again the believers in Philippi. Paul had a deep affection for these people. Who were the members of that congregation? There was Lydia, a convert to Judaism who owned her own business and was therefore a woman of means. She gladly received the gospel and was baptized with her entire household (Acts 16:11–15).

There was also an unnamed man who worked as a jailer. He had been responsible for guarding Paul and Silas after they had been illegally arrested and flogged for exorcising a spirit from a slave girl. At midnight, God shook the darkened prison to its foundations, waking the sleeping jailer. The cell doors flew open, and the chains binding all the prisoners came loose. Thinking the prisoners had escaped, the jailer moved to kill himself. But Paul quickly intervened, assuring him that no one had left. Confronted simultaneously by the frightening power of God and the mercy that spared his life, the man fell to his knees and believed. And as with Lydia, his whole household was baptized (Acts 16:16–34).

Later, in prison again, Paul wrote to his friends in Philippi, remembering fondly their partnership with him and each other in the cause of the gospel. He encouraged them to continue their unity in the Spirit, "being confident of this, that he who began a good work in you will carry it on to completion until the day of Christ Jesus" (Phil 1:6). We imagine that he was thinking of Lydia and the jailer as he wrote those words, and others who were as different as could be, yet still one in Christ. Who knows. He may even have been thinking about Euodia and Syntyche, who apparently had a conflict to work out between them. But Paul the pastor didn't think of the two women as problems to be solved; they too were his partners in the gospel (Phil 4:2–3). Neither social nor interpersonal differences dampened Paul's conviction that God was at work in this congregation, in and amongst ordinary people in a concrete place.

Eugene Peterson sees the church as "the appointed gathering of named people in particular places who practice a life of resurrection in

---

14. Neuhaus, *Freedom for Ministry*, 137 (emphasis in original).

a world in which death gets the biggest headlines."[15] That describes the congregations in Philippi and elsewhere around the world, including the congregations of which we are now members. This is the church of Jesus Christ—mysterious and messy, transcendent and ordinary. God breaks into the lives of local congregations, which are full of people with hopes and hurts, fears and foibles. The Lord meets us in all these places as we practice and proclaim a life of resurrection.

We can love the church without having to be naïve about it. We are quite aware of the gap between a high theology of the church and the sociological realities of congregations. If we love the church, we must hold on to the hope that the Lord is continuing to lead our congregations toward maturity (Eph 4:15). By faith, we must help the church, in all its fallible local expressions, to become what it truly is in Christ. After all, we may not look much like saints, but the Bible declares that this is in fact what we are.

Pastors are often just putting one foot ahead of the next, trying to keep up with endless appointments and demands. It's easy to get caught up in the routines of church life and not be able to see much beyond them. But there is something grander happening in our congregations. God's new creation is breaking into our world. God is transforming people and congregations and societies. It usually doesn't happen loudly, with fanfare, but in the ordinary things that are so easy to take for granted:

> Every act of love, gratitude, and kindness; every work of art
> or music inspired by the love of God and delight in the beauty
> of his creation; every minute spent teaching a severely handi-
> capped child to read or to walk; every act of care and nurture,
> of comfort and support, for one's fellow human beings and for
> that matter one's fellow nonhuman creatures; and of course ev-
> ery prayer, all Spirit-led teaching, every deed that spreads the
> gospel, builds up the church, embraces and embodies holiness
> rather than corruption; and makes the name of Jesus honored
> in the world—all this will find its way, through the resurrect-
> ing power of God, into the new creation that God will one day
> make. This is the logic of the mission of God.[16]

Can we learn to see anew the marvelous work of God in the midst of these ordinary things, the things that we might find on any given day in any congregation?

15. Peterson, *Practicing Resurrection*, 12.
16. Wright, *Surprised by Hope*, 208.

As I write these words, a new youth minister is sitting in a coffee shop with students before school, getting to know them. This simple act is gospel work, the mission of God. In weekend worship, I look around at the congregation that I once served. I watch them, knowing their stories, understanding their honest desire to be disciples of Jesus. Our history together has had its ups and downs. But I know that God is at work here, extending his mission of love. Taking a church group to Appalachia or Mexico or Albania is part of what God is doing to set the world right. Sermon preparation, Bible studies, counseling sessions, mission trips, car washes, congregational meetings—all of this can be gospel work that changes the world, that changes lives.

This is the work that happens through a local congregation with its feet on the ground. As Lesslie Newbigin asks,

> How is it possible that the gospel should be credible, that people should come to believe that the power which has the last word in human affairs is represented by a man hanging on a cross? I am suggesting that the only answer . . . is a congregation of men and women who believe it and live by it.[17]

It is communities of earthbound but heaven-focused saints, gathered in local congregations, who make the gospel real. It is ordinary people who struggle to live by the gospel that change the world. Earthy local congregations are a gift from God to the world. It's a strange gift indeed. But there is none better, save Jesus himself.

Postscript

To Pastors:

You are engaged in the wonder and the challenges of church life on a daily basis. You know firsthand where the real and the ideal collide. You know both the joy of serving the church and the pain congregations can inflict. And sometimes, in the midst of your work, you wonder if you're simply crazy. You get worn out leading the congregation, and frustrated when you don't see progress. Steps that you think will bring much-needed change are sometimes met with looks of skepticism and even pity. Pastoring a congregation is hard. It hurts and it's lonely.

In this chapter we have tried to lift up a vision of the church that embraces your congregation. Little to nothing of what we've said will be

---

17. Newbigin, *Church in a Pluralist Society*, 227.

new to you. But the vision easily gets trampled by the day-to-day routines of the church. And we believe that the first thing many frustrated pastors need is a renewal of their vision, and hence their sense of vocation.

So take time to ponder again the wonder of God's choice to embody the church in here-and-now, flesh-and-blood congregations. Thomas Currie has put it well:

> A strange place, one might think, to seek or to find the beauty of God, that is, in the gathered fellowship of a not self-evidently beautiful collection of sinners. Yet where else would the God who elects to be glorious in the crucified and risen Lord be confessed and known, except as the head of such a questionable body with such dubious charms? Here is a strange glory indeed, one that is . . . almost irresponsibly fleshly, a glory that sings of the Lord who refuses to be without his own *glorious* people— not, to be sure, his perfect or flawless or even faithful people, but glorious in that they belong to this Lord who chooses to be glorious among them and in that way glorious in all the world.[18]

This congregation, glorious? Yes. Not in obvious ways perhaps. But the joy of ministry begins here, with the faithful ability to recognize and celebrate, even if fleetingly, the incarnate glory of God in the imperfect saints we serve.

Ponder again your congregation's mission. Prayerfully ask yourself, why does *this* congregation exist at this time and this place? Be willing to admit that even pastors get tunnel vision, zeroing in on those aspects of the ministry that they value most. What are you missing? Where is God working in your congregation, in ordinary and unheralded ways? Discuss these questions with other church leaders. Pray that God would give you the eyes to see and the ears to hear, and give thanks for whatever he shows you.

As we will say in the coming chapters, pastors can't do this work alone. It is simply too much to shoulder. It's easy to get so wrapped up in ministry that you don't take care of your inner life, or even your physical health. Make sure to spend regular time alone with God, praying for vision, praying for your congregation. Seek out and develop strong relationships with trustworthy people with whom you can be brutally honest. Often this will be another pastor. Be companions on the journey. Help each other to keep your love for the church alive and growing, dream together about what the church might become, and pray for each other's ministry.

---

18. Currie, *Joy*, 46 (emphasis in original).

To Congregations:

Being a pastor is a wonderful calling, but it isn't easy! We hope that this chapter has given you new insights, not only into the nature of pastoral work, but into this miraculous and messy thing called "the church." God works through local congregations to do amazing things in and through ordinary people. It happened in ancient Philippi, and it is still happening today, in congregations just like yours.

Your pastor isn't the only one with hopes for what the congregation can be and do. If you are in leadership, you may have your own vision of how your congregation's mission should be embodied. But it's extremely important that there be like-mindedness among the leadership so that people aren't trying to row the boat in opposite directions! That only leads to wasted effort and frustrated pastors.

God's work is always bigger than any of our ministry plans or projects. In the eternal scheme of things, the success of his redemptive efforts ultimately doesn't stand or fall on what we do; we are merely privileged to get in on the action. That gives us the perspective we need. The primary question we must ask ourselves is always, what is *God* doing? Where is his Spirit already moving in our midst, in ways that might have escaped our notice?

That question can't be answered all at once, and any decent answer is likely to be multifaceted and evolving. The conversation itself can be revealing. Work at keeping the lines of communication with your pastor open and honest, with everyone attentive to what God may be saying to the *congregation*, and not merely to individuals.

To Seminarians:

What has been your experience of congregations thus far? We've had many and varied conversations with new seminary students about this. Some come to seminary full of enthusiasm, buoyed by the love and support of their home churches. Others, often those who grew up in pastors' families, bring a mixed bag of emotions, ranging from bemusement to bitterness.

Which category seems to fit you better? Either way, as you prepare for vocational ministry, you need to do so with your eyes wide open. If you're more in the first category, don't let these first few chapters scare you off. Be alert to the messiness of working with real people. If you're more in the second category, you may be so aware of the messy part that the miraculous is harder to see. Keeping your eyes open means something different, as Frederick Buechner has expressed:

> It is our business, as we journey, to keep our heart open to the bright-winged presence of the Holy Ghost within us and the Kingdom of God among us until little by little compassionate love begins to change from a moral exercise . . . into a joyous, spontaneous, self-forgetting response to the most real aspect of all reality, which is that the world is holy because God made it and so is every one of us as well.[19]

Churches will always have challenges—expect that. But you don't have to shy away from ministry in the local church. Yes, it is hazardous, hard, front-line work. But it is also full of rewards, especially when you trust God to show you how he is working even in the most difficult of congregations.

As a seminarian, you are in a wonderful season of preparation. Don't let your studies remain theoretical. Always seek to connect what you learn in academic settings with ministry on the ground. Use your studies to refine your ministry practices and perspectives. Gather friends together to dream and think outside the box. What breaks your heart? What breaks the heart of God? Are you hearing a fresh word from the Lord?

And above all, be sure to attend to your walk with the Lord. You don't minister out of your education; you minister out of your life. Develop good practices now that form and strengthen your spiritual life.

19. Buechner, *Longing for Home*, 120–21.

4

Being a Pastor: The Calling and the Job

The great ethical danger for clergy is not that we might "burn out," . . . not that we might lose the energy required to do ministry. Our danger is that we might "black out," that is lose consciousness of why we are here and who we are called to be for Christ and his church. . . . Periodic refurbishment of our vision is needed.

–WILLIAM WILLIMON[1]

Who me? A pastor?

Many of you reading this book have heard the testimonies, or have given the testimony yourself: "I used to have nothing to do with God, even ran as fast as I could in the other direction. But God never gave up on me. He pursued me; he drew me to him. And although I never would have imagined it, he even called me to be a pastor! I couldn't get away from that call, even though I resisted it for a long time. Now, every once in a while, I'll meet up with people who knew me from the old days. I'll tell them I'm a pastor. And they'll look at me with a blank expression, and say something like, '*You*? You've got to be kidding.'"

The apostle Paul could probably relate. He had formerly bent his entire being to eradicating the pesky sectarian movement that had grown up

---

1. Willimon, *Calling and Character*, 21.

around the crucified Jesus. But then, on the Damascus road, he actually met Jesus—or better, Jesus met *him*, stopping him in his tracks and striking him blind. The call was straight to the point: "I am Jesus, whom you are persecuting. Now get up and go into the city, and you will be told what you must do" (Acts 9:5–6). It doesn't get much clearer than that!

Sometimes the call to ministry, like Paul's, is unambiguous, even miraculous. Margaret McGhee, for example, grew up as the daughter of an African-American Baptist preacher, and later married a minister. She knew that God was calling her into the ministry, but resisted it, repeating to herself all the arguments why she couldn't possibly have that kind of call. She tried to bargain with God, but couldn't shake the visions she knew God was sending her. She tells her story this way:

> I knew God had a call on my life, but I had not accepted it. I was going to do it my way. . . . But . . . I still had visions and dreams. The Lord was trying to set this thing in order and in place. . . . I was in prayer, and all of a sudden what we would call the Glory filled the room, just an awesome presence of God. I remember my doorbell ringing. . . . My friend Renee came in. . . . She said I immediately began to speak in tongues and then give the interpretation. . . . God told me when I would start the church. . . . The date and the time. He told me what to expect and why he had called me. He told me that the church shall be called New Horizon. And he healed my body of all my infirmities. At that time, I was a diabetic on 87 units of insulin a day. I have not had any insulin since then. I've been healed of diabetes.[2]

For some of us, if we're honest, her story (or Paul's, for that matter!) is a little frightening. This isn't the kind of God who simply sits around waiting for us to comfortably decide on our own what we want to do with our lives. This is a God who breaks in, who pursues and intervenes, sometimes dramatically.

Does God really work this way? Simply put, yes. Many of you reading this book have similar stories. But does he *always* work this way to get someone's attention? No. Not everyone has a "Damascus road experience," not even in the Bible. For some, the call comes quietly, over a period of time. The experience is less of a miraculous interruption, and more of an inner confirmation. Eugene Peterson, for example, had not intended to become a pastor, but a seminary professor. Newly married and unable to make ends meet on what he was being paid to teach biblical languages,

2. Constantine, *Travelers on the Journey*, 27–28.

he temporarily accepted an associate pastor position to supplement his income. It was only gradually, over the next three years, that their respective vocations took shape: he would be a pastor, and she, a pastor's wife.[3] The calling, in other words, was revealed during the pastorate, not before.

We're familiar with both kinds of stories in the lives of our seminary students. There are those who come to seminary because they are absolutely certain of their call; many have stories of God's undeniable and powerful intervention. And there are those who sense something like a call, but hesitate to give it that name. They've heard no clear voice. They have only a vague sense of disquiet, a prompting, and nothing more. They come to seminary to explore. Some test the water, while others jump in with both feet! And eventually, they may grow more confirmed in their call through the experience of ministry itself and the responses of others.

People often ask pastors how they chose to be in ministry, and some expect stories like those of Paul, or Samuel (1 Sam 3), or Isaiah (Isa 6:1–8). But the language of "choice" needs to be revised. To be sure, there *are* choices and decisions to make: Do I really pursue this? Do I need to go to seminary? If so, which one? But at some level, to say that one "chooses" to go into the ministry may be misleading. As Thomas Long has put it, "as a matter of fact, we did not choose it at all. It chose us. We were chosen for it."[4] The sense of having been chosen may be subtle, or it may be obvious. Either way, it is central to what it means to say that one has been called by God to the pastorate.

This is important, because what keeps pastors going through the ups and downs of ministry is a sense of vision. It would be one thing if there were nothing but ups, with no downs. But as we've insisted in previous chapters, that's not how it works. The expectations can be daunting, as illustrated in this cynical but often accurate job description:

> *Wanted*: Person to fill position that involves important but undervalued work; exact job description unclear. Long hours; must work weekends and holidays. Low pay. Master's degree required; doctorate preferred. Must be accomplished at multitasking, including running an organization without clear authority to do so. The successful candidate will be skilled as a public speaker, manager, politician, and therapist, and will

---

3. Peterson, *The Pastor*, ch. 2. Ironically, his wife Jan had felt the call to be a pastor's wife before they met, and gave it up to marry him.

4. Long, "Of This Gospel," 39.

devote significant time each week to pastoral visits. The position reports to multiple bosses.[5]

Nor are pastors the only ones who must struggle with the burden of unrealistic expectations. We don't know enough about the men married to female pastors yet (though see chapter 9), but many books document how the wives of male pastors must also contend with the complicated and conflicting expectations of others. They often struggle with stereotypes of the perfect pastor's wife, such as the godly woman who also plays the piano, sings, and has "a signature, oft-requested food dish."[6] Here's another job description that could go alongside the one above:

> Applicant's wife must be both stunning and plain, smartly attired, but conservative in appearance, gracious and able to get along with everyone, even women. Must be willing to work in the church kitchen, teach Sunday School, babysit, . . . wait table, never listen to gossip, never become discouraged . . . yet be fully aware of all church problems so she might "pray more intelligently."[7]

Though somewhat exaggerated, these are tongue-in-cheek representations of the real frustrations faced day in and day out by pastors and their families. We will return to the issues of boundaries and family life in later chapters.

Who would want to serve in such a role? In spite of the craziness of the task, many men and women do. They are eager to serve the church as pastors, and want to do it well. They serve as senior pastors, solo pastors, as staff ministers, as clergy couples. They serve full-time, and increasingly part-time in a bivocational capacity.[8] These are not positions to enter into lightly. Nevertheless, many gladly enter into pastoral ministry, eyes wide open. Why? Not for fame or fortune. Rather, it's because the task of serving a church is the greatest of joys for those who are called to it.

Being a pastor is both a rewarding vocation—a *calling* in the best sense of the word—*and* a hard job. The work of the pastor is varied and demanding. No two days are the same; each can be an adventure. Pastors walk with people through the best of times and the worst of times, the

5. Jones and Armstrong, *Resurrecting Excellence*, 26.

6. McKay, *Cute Shoes*, 48.

7. Dobson, *More than the Pastor's Wife*, 22, quoting from Nordland, *Unprivate Life*, 12, with the final comment added by a personal friend.

8. Bonhoeffer spoke radically and prophetically about pastors moving into bivocational ministry in order to fulfill a missional vocation. See Bonhoeffer, *Letters*, 282.

celebrations and sorrows. They proclaim good news and urge people into lives of discipleship. And through it all, they must be driven by a vision of congregations and worlds transformed if they are to make it through the inevitable seasons of discouragement. Willimon puts it this way:

> There are many times in the pastoral ministry when we see no visible results of our efforts, have no sense that people are getting better because of our work among them, have little proof of our effectiveness. . . . In those moments, our only hope is to cling to our vocation, to adhere to the sense that God has called us . . . that God has a plan and purpose for how our meager efforts fit into God's larger scheme of things.[9]

Pastors need to be "big picture" people, and need congregations who are learning to be the same: who are striving to be the church that Jesus has called them to be. Here is a job description more appropriate to that vision:

> *Wanted*: Persons for a vocation that leads God's people in bearing witness to God's new creation revealed in Jesus Christ by the power of the Holy Spirit. Work schedule is shaped by relationships, focusing on what is important in people's lives, and depends on regular rhythms of work, rest, and play. Compensation is shaped by a mutual discernment of what is necessary in order for the persons (and, where appropriate, their families) to have an appropriately well-lived life. The vocation involves cultivating holy dispositions, preaching and teaching, nurturing rigorous study, and shaping practices of faithful living in church and world. Lifelong education and formation is expected in order to enable others also to grow throughout their lives. The successful candidate will collaborate with others towards the same ends. The vocation reports to God.[10]

This is the church that God continually calls into being, in the mutual relationship of pastors and congregations alike. This is the kind of ministry people sign up for, the reason that men and women become pastors in the first place.

And this is the vision that grabbed my heart when I (Kurt) was seventeen. In college and seminary, all my paid and volunteer jobs pointed toward that goal. I was blessed with great mentors who allowed me to shadow them, dispelling any naively romanticized notions I had about the

9. Willimon, *Calling and Character*, 22.

10. Jones and Armstrong, *Resurrecting Excellence*, 27

work. I knew early on that being a pastor involved long hours, poor pay, and difficult struggles with people. The work would never be done, and would often be criticized. And *still*, I couldn't imagine doing anything else! I was blessed to serve the same congregation for twenty-four years. To this day, even after having resigned the pastorate to serve pastors in a seminary setting, I can't think of a better or more fulfilling life.

The perpetual danger is that the busyness and frustrations of ministry can begin to obscure a pastor's sense of calling, and the joy that goes with it. They lose the sense that, as Buechner has put it, "the place God calls you to is the place where your deep gladness and the world's deep hunger meet."[11] Can the vision be retrieved or cultivated? In this chapter, we'll explore what it means to be called to the pastorate.

The Three Faces of Pastoral Ministry

The role of pastor has sometimes been defined in grand terms. Here's one example: "the pastor is a member of the Body of Christ who is called by God and the church and is set apart by ordination representatively to proclaim the Word, administer the sacraments, and to guide and nurture the Christian community toward full response to God's self-disclosure."[12] That is, to say the least, a theological mouthful!

But grand definitions like this need to be broken down to get at the heart of pastoring a church. There are, of course, the tasks and functions of the pastorate, including the proclamation of the gospel and presiding over the sacraments. But to be a pastor is to be much more than a functionary, and the definition hints at these other aspects. There is a great deal that can be said about what it means to be "called by God and the church," not to mention what it means to be set apart by ordination.

It would take volumes to do these topics justice. Our more modest goal in this section will be to look at the role of the pastor as it has been classically viewed from three overlapping vantage points: call, profession, and office. These three perspectives in turn highlight different aspects of the work of a pastor, namely, his or her gifting, competence, and authority. Our hope is to rekindle a sense of wonder among both pastors and congregations.

---

11. Buechner, *Wishful Thinking*, 95.
12. Oden, *Pastoral Theology*, 50

The Call to Be a Pastor

Lest we forget, *all* believers, by virtue of baptism, have been called to serve and bless the world through the church. Not every Christian will be an ordained minister, but all are gifted in some way to minister to others in the name of Jesus. Not every Christian will be a career missionary, but all are called into a relationship with God, which includes taking their place in God's kingdom mission. This is true of every follower of Christ.

While all believers are called to and gifted for ministry, Scripture suggests that there is a special calling on the pastor (e.g., Eph 4:11). Some pastors report a sense of being gripped—or even tackled!—by God in a way that upends one's plans and priorities. Reggie McNeal says, "This kind of call orders life around it. Personal ambitions and goals become subservient to it. The called live for a larger world than just themselves and their families."[13] When God touches lives in this way, those who are called may say that there's nothing else they can do but serve the church in a pastoral role.

Beyond the call to discipleship, which applies to all believers, there is a call to ministry, which according to H. Richard Niebuhr involves three elements. First, there is an inner or *secret* call. This is "that inner persuasion or experience where a person feels himself [or herself] directly summoned or invited by God to take up the work of the ministry."[14] Many pastors can remember a moment or a process in which the invitation became clear: a dawning, a realization that serving in the church was the best and the most important task for their life. It's the press of the Holy Spirit, working from the inside out.

As we've seen, the apostle Paul received a straightforward and unambiguous call on the Damascus road, and later knew himself to have been set apart by God since his very birth (Gal 1:15). The prophet Jeremiah also had a clear commission (cf. Jer 1) and described God's word as a fire burning to get out (Jer 20:9). Today, many pastors begin with a sense of a desire kindled in their hearts, a burden to serve the church. They begin to examine themselves, wondering if they're up for the task. They may seek the counsel of others, asking friends and mentors, "What do you think? Should I do this?"

13. McNeal, *Work of Heart*, 98.
14. H. R. Niebuhr, *Purpose of the Church*, 64.

How others answer the question may depend on the evidence of an outward, or *providential* call.[15] Those who are called into ministry are equipped with appropriate abilities and competencies that are useful for ministry to and through the church. These do not, of course, come to a person completely developed. They are honed and refined over a lifetime. But those who are called to pastoral ministry frequently sense that they are somehow gifted for the work. And as they exercise these gifts, others may recognize and respond to their demonstrated aptitude. Some pastors will say that they first became aware of their calling when someone asked, "Have you ever thought about becoming a pastor?"

With time and experience, a person may become more and more clear that the pastoral vocation is a fitting direction. They get excited about the prospect of serving in the church, and look for ways to do so: part-time or full-time, with a paycheck or as a volunteer. Others affirm their giftedness. The thought of seminary or Bible college often enters the picture.

I (Kurt) dove into ministry opportunities, volunteering at my church and working at a Christian summer camp. I loved it. When I was doing ministry, I felt alive and fulfilled; when I was doing other types of work, I was frustrated with longing. I sought out mentors, seasoned pastors who guided me and chided me, offering much-needed advice along the way.

All of this leads, third, to what Niebuhr referred to as an *ecclesiastical* call, a more formal invitation "by some community or institution of the Church to engage in the work of the ministry."[16] This ecclesiastical call is usually preceded by specific theological training, and by an internship in a church setting. Pastoral candidates are examined by others to determine if they are fit for ministry. Then, through a ceremonial process such as the laying on of hands, a body of believers, through ordination, licensure, or commissioning, sends them out into ministry.

This is typical of the journey of a pastoral call. Let it be said that we affirm the priesthood of all believers, and that the task of ministry belongs to the whole church. Yet we do not wish to minimize the marvelous call to pastoral ministry. As Neuhaus has written, "Those who have been touched by the burning coal from the altar, and whose touch has been ratified by the call of the Church, must not pretend that nothing special has happened to them."[17]

---

15. Ibid., 64.

16. Ibid.

17. Neuhaus, *Freedom for Ministry*, 219.

My (Kurt's) ordination to Word and Sacrament by the Evangelical Covenant was a very significant process. After an intense time of examination, the Covenant said I was competent for ministry. At the denomination's annual meeting, hands were laid on me and I became an ordained minister. I wasn't given new ministry gifts at that moment. There was no voice from heaven, and I didn't feel different. I had already been ministering for years. But it wasn't about me as an individual; it was an act of the church to endorse one of its own, to publicly confirm and celebrate my call. One of my friends, unfortunately, said while I was in the ordination process, "I don't need to go through all that work. For $25 I can get ordained online." Sadly, he missed the spiritual significance of the day.

Here we must insert a cautionary note. The same process of ordination and ecclesiastical call that sets people apart for ministry can also usher them into a ministerial guild that suppresses or demeans the ministry of lay people in the church. Power and social significance come with the pastoral role. Individual pastors are tempted to abuse that power, and the guild itself can become self-serving and self-protecting. The temptations must always be recognized and our sinful responses held in check.

This is because the call to pastoral ministry comes from God. It is not a static thing that can be possessed. We have to be careful with our language. To say that one "has" a call isn't quite right; better to say that one "is called," to emphasize the continual summons into a particular relationship of faithfulness to the One who calls. Ministry begins as a gifting by God and from God. It is God who calls people; it is God who gifts people. True ministry is not a mere human doing, but is empowered by the Holy Spirit (1 Thess 1:4–5). Willimon reminds us:

> Ministry is therefore something that God does through the church before it is anything we do. Our significance, as leaders, is responsive. We are here, in leadership of God's people, because we have responded to a summons, because we were sought, called, sent, commissioned by one greater than ourselves that our lives might be expended in work more significant than ourselves.[18]

Are we preaching to the choir? Perhaps. If you're reading this as a pastor, it's not as if you don't already know these things! But we can forget. We get busy; we get frustrated. And along the way, we begin to believe that the ministry is *our* work, that it stands or falls on our effort, that it gives us our own personal sense of dignity or significance. Against this, we must

18. Willimon, *Calling and Character*, 16.

remind ourselves continuously that it is the Lord who gifts people in the church for vocational ministry. Those who hear the call simply submit and respond in humility.

The Pastorate as Profession

Thus, the pastor is called into the ministry by God. From another angle of vision, the pastor is also entering a profession. Professionals such as physicians, lawyers, teachers, and ministers are people who have received specialized formal education, are credentialed by some public standard, and abide by a code of conduct. As professionals, pastors should engage in lifelong theological education and training for the practice of ministry. Pastors are expected to be competent, "capable of leading wisely and of providing particular services to the community."[19] Certainly, no congregation wants an incompetent pastor!

The perspective of the pastor-as-professional has become more prominent in recent decades, with the corresponding focus on knowledge, skills, and tangible measures of success. It has not always been so. In the earliest days of the church, the pastor was predominantly an apostle, engaged in the task of extending the gospel. [20] As the church became more intertwined with culture (especially after the Roman emperor Constantine's official endorsement of Christianity as the state religion), the role of pastor shifted to that of priest and chaplain. During the Reformation, the role shifted again, to emphasize the importance of teaching the Word. And in more recent times, the role of clergy shifted again from pedagogue to professional.

This professional characterization of the clergy continues today. By extension, churches are often seen primarily as businesses, or organizational machines, particularly as they grow beyond the face-to-face relationships of smaller congregations. Good businesses are to be run well and efficiently, and pastors are sometimes encouraged to learn new insights from the *Harvard Business Review*. The pastor becomes less of an apostle, priest, or teacher, and more of a CEO.

This is not necessarily a bad thing. Churches are, after all, institutions. They are not only that, but they are *at least* that, and we need not run from that description. Organizational structures are important to the ongoing work of a congregation, and it is better to be intentional about

19. Jones and Armstrong, *Resurrecting Excellence*, 84.
20. Guder, *Missional Church*, 190ff.

them. Pastors must guide and guard their congregations with discernment, through their leadership and administration. At the same time, they must also resist the ever-present temptation to believe too much in their own power and control—that is, in congregations where they actually *have* some power and control!

The problem comes when pastors and congregations begin to judge the "success" of the ministry in ways more appropriate to the corporate world than God's kingdom. Many pastors fall into the numbers game when they get together, in a not-so-subtle game of one-upmanship. Pastors of small congregations often feel like second-class citizens, believing (sometimes against their better judgment!) that if they were *really* doing their job well, the church would be growing. Members of the congregation may think the same thing, and communicate their dissatisfaction in direct and indirect ways. This can lead to gnawing self-doubts and a downward spiral of discouragement for the beleaguered pastor. Obviously, in a job that requires initiative and self-motivation, this can be a serious problem!

There is certainly a professional aspect to the work of a pastor, who should be both learned and competent. There is no excuse, for example, for coming to the pulpit ill prepared. The vast majority of pastors want to serve well, and desire the knowledge and skills needed for effective ministry.

But a pastor is more than what the world would characterize as a professional, at least by modern definitions. We need to get back to the more original sense of a professional as one who professes, because this is the core of the pastorate. As Willimon has put it, "We have degraded 'professionals' by making them primarily people who *know* something that the rest of us do not, rather than being people who the rest of us *are* not."[21]

All of this is to say that the perception of the pastorate as a profession must never be allowed to overshadow its nature as a calling from God:

> Ministry is not merely a profession, not only because one cannot pay pastors to do many of the things they routinely do, but also because ministry is a vocation. Ministers are more than those who are credentialed and validated by the approval of their fellow members of their profession. Ministers must be called.[22]

Pastors, therefore, are those who do not merely look to increase their professional competence, as useful as this may be. As big-picture people, they intentionally reflect on their ministry and ask, "Where is the presence and

21. Willimon, *Calling and Character*, 32 (emphasis added).
22. Ibid., 33.

power of God being manifested in this congregation's life, in my life, and in my pastoral leadership?"[23]

Thus, while being a professional is an important aspect of pastoral work, we must guard against what Os Guinness has called the "Protestant distortion," where the meaning of "vocation" is reduced to little more than what most people mean by "job."[24] A denominational official, for example, once pressured the ministers under his supervision to wear neckties, since that's what professionals should do! And it's true that some members of the congregation will look askance at the male minister who doesn't wear a tie, or the female minister who doesn't dress formally enough. (Then again, there are church subcultures in which people will be put off if the pastor dresses *too* formally.) It can be prudent—especially for a new pastor!—to avoid flagrant violations of a congregation's unofficial dress code. But all such considerations are secondary to the heart of the calling.

Pastors can get so caught up in the profession that the ministry becomes a mere job or career. As a job, the ministry demands much; it takes its toll and saps the spirit. Exhausted or disillusioned pastors lose their passion; the vitality drains out of their witness and leadership. They find themselves simply going through the motions of worship, preaching, and the tasks of ministry. They become aloof and isolated. When profession routinely supersedes vocation in the pastor's imagination, the life of ministry can become hollow and empty.[25]

The Office of the Pastor

The pastorate is a calling from God, albeit one with professional aspects. From a third perspective, seeing pastoral ministry as an office highlights the pastor's authority as a representative of Jesus Christ in and for a community.[26] Pastors, particularly those with a sense of their own inadequacy, may recoil from this sense of office and authority. Personally, I (Kurt) prefer to be called by my first name. But some people can't do it, no matter how much I encourage them. To them, I am and must be "Pastor." I represent something greater. This is a key aspect of the pastor's work that must be recognized, to avoid its misuse wherever possible.

23. Jones and Armstrong, *Resurrecting Excellence*, 6.
24. Guinness, *Call*, ch. 5.
25. Jones and Armstrong, *Resurrecting Excellence*, 95.
26. Ibid., 86.

At a deeper level, like it or not, it is the pastor's role to represent God, and some people are apt to equate what pastors say and do with the divine. As Ray Anderson reminds us, "Whether we realize it or not, every act of ministry reveals something of God. By act of ministry I mean a sermon preached, a lesson taught, a marriage performed, counsel offered, any other word or act that people might construe as carrying God's blessing, warning, or judgment."[27] This is a sacred trust, requiring diligence and thoughtfulness on the part of conscientious pastors.

As mentioned in the previous chapter, I (Kurt) serve as a volunteer police chaplain in my town. One Sunday after church, I was called to the hospital because the child of one of the officers had nearly drowned. The child survived, but with severe brain damage. Months later, I was walking the halls of the police station and ran into the officer. He stopped me and asked a question: "Where was God when my child was at the bottom of the pool?" Whatever I said, right or wrong, became the word of God at that moment to him and to his family. Pastors, how can we bear the weight of that responsibility, unless we know we are called to it?

Again, we believe in the priesthood of all believers. And pastors should be working hard to empower people in their congregations to use their gifts in all types of ministry. Still, many in our culture "send for the priest," so to speak, in times of trouble. While I (Kurt) was serving as a youth pastor, a friend of mine fell off a roof and was badly hurt. He was rushed to the hospital, and the church gathered around him. I offered comfort and prayers, as did others. But when the senior pastor walked into the room, there was a shared sense that the *real* prayer powerhouse had arrived!

This is not, unfortunately, an unusual scenario. How many hospitalized church members have complained of being ignored by "the church," not because their brothers and sisters haven't come to pray with them, but because the *senior pastor* hasn't visited? In some cases, not even the associate will do. This is not, of course, the proper response; theologically, it is simply wrong. And pastors can work to change this response over time. But meanwhile, they must take seriously the fact that they are the representatives of God to their congregations.

The pastor-as-office perspective reminds us that the work of the pastor is always greater than any human being. The pastoral office bears witness to Jesus and to the inbreaking of God's kingdom. As representatives of Jesus Christ, pastors strive towards holiness. Though all followers of

27. Anderson, *Soul of Ministry*, 7.

Christ are to imitate him, the pastor is to be an exemplary person, "adorn-ing . . . the gospel with a holy life."[28] All of this is true, despite the fact that pastors have their own struggles in trying the best they can to follow the ways of Christ. Pastors do not come to the role having been fully formed in the faith. Rather, they are shaped over time, through obedience to God's call, in the midst of day-to-day interactions with ordinary congregations. As Eugene Peterson has put it,

> The congregation is the pastor's place for developing vocational holiness. It goes without saying that it is the place of ministry: we preach the word and administer the sacraments, we give pastoral care and administer community life, we teach and we give spiritual direction. But it is also the place in which we de-velop virtue, learn to love, advance in hope—become what we preach.[29]

This is both the incredible responsibility and the wondrous promise of be-ing a pastor: to preach out of who you are, with your eyes focused on Jesus, in order to become what you preach and start the circle anew.

A Shepherd's Life of Service

All of this, finally, adds up to a life of service. Losing that sense of service distorts the call and the ministry. As Jesus demonstrated in John 13, a towel and a basin should be the symbols of a pastor's work. Pastors are not a privileged or elite class; they serve God by serving the church.

And ministry belongs to the entire church, not just to pastors, who may be perceived as the "paid professionals." True, some are ordained and thus are set aside in a public sense, but this means being designated to the task of equipping others to follow Jesus and to minister for his name's sake. The apostle Paul reminds us:

> So Christ himself gave the apostles, the prophets, the evange-lists, the pastors and teachers, to equip his people for works of service, so that the body of Christ may be built up until we all reach unity in the faith and in the knowledge of the Son of God and become mature, attaining to the whole measure of the full-ness of Christ. (Eph 4:11–13)

---

28. Neuhaus, *Freedom for Ministry*, 210.
29. Peterson, *Unpredictable Plant*, 21.

Pastors equip the flock for their own works of service. The whole body is to be built up, to become mature, to grow into the fullness of Christ. Considering that Paul also says that Jesus was the embodiment of the fullness of God (Col 1:19), this is an astonishing statement indeed!

Paul speaks of laboring to see Christ formed in the followers of Jesus (Gal 4:19). But it is a labor of love; Paul writes to his pastoral charges with the affection of a father (e.g., 1 Thess 2:7–12). Thus, like parents, in grief and joy pastors serve (*diakonia*) with all of their being. That is the primary work of clergy, and what makes the job so demanding.

Pastors are shepherds. The image of shepherd is found throughout Scripture, both in the Old Testament (e.g., Ps 23; Isa 40:11; Ezek 34) as well as in the ministry of Jesus (e.g., Matt 15:24; Luke 12:32). The New Testament specifically uses this metaphor to describe leaders in the church (e.g., John 21:16; Acts 20:28ff.; Eph 4:11; Jude 12; Heb 13:20; 1 Pet 2:25). Shepherds nurture and lead; they guide and protect. As Thomas Oden says, the vocation of a pastor is

> to know the parish territory, its dangers, its green meadows, its steep precipices, its seasons and its possibilities. The pastor leads the flock to spring water and safe vegetables. The flock recognizes their own good through the shepherd's voice. They do not see it in their interest to follow strangers. They know their own shepherd will not mislead them. The shepherd is able to anticipate their needs in advance and is willing to deal with each one individually.[30]

Sounds ideal, doesn't it? We're sure that many pastors and congregations alike could read Oden's description and sigh, "If only." Pastors of large churches might also balk at that description, for it seems to imply the kind of intimate personal relationship that would be impossible in a congregation of hundreds. Realistically speaking, not all shepherding can be done by the senior pastor! But we shouldn't allow practical limitations or unfortunate experiences to rob us of a rich biblical vision.

Here's the bottom line. We may think of sheep as being cute and cuddly, but the reality is that shepherding is hard, unglamorous work. Pastors, like shepherds, sacrificially give themselves away. What sustains them in this life of service?

---

30. Oden, *Pastoral Theology*, 52

Perhaps we should shift the metaphor slightly. As some would say, pastors are not simply shepherds, but "undershepherds" in apprenticeship to the risen Christ, the Chief Shepherd.[31] The First Epistle of Peter reads,

> To the elders among you, I appeal as a fellow elder and a witness of Christ's sufferings who also will share in the glory to be revealed: Be shepherds of God's flock that is under your care, watching over them—not because you must, but because you are willing, as God wants you to be; not pursuing dishonest gain, but eager to serve; not lording it over those entrusted to you, but being examples to the flock. And when the Chief Shepherd appears, you will receive the crown of glory that will never fade away. (1 Pet 5:1–4)

Shepherds watch carefully over their sheep. As 1 Peter says, they should do so willingly, even eagerly. But neither Peter, nor Paul, nor Jesus himself romanticizes the work. How can it be done eagerly, knowing the cost?

It can't—not consistently—unless the pastor clings with both hands to the hope of sharing Christ's glory. First Peter appeals to Christian leaders as one who has witnessed firsthand both the suffering of Jesus and his resurrection to new life. When the author writes to persecuted Christians, he doesn't dwell on the present, but on the future. Hang in there, he says, because for the faithful, the best is yet to come (e.g., 1 Pet 1:3–9). Be faithful undershepherds, and do so gladly, knowing that when the Chief Shepherd returns you will share in his glory.

If you're a discouraged pastor, that may sound like cold comfort. But that is the comfort we are given. Yes, in the coming chapters, we will make recommendations about things that we hope will smooth some of the rough spots in ministry. But on your better days, you already know the truth: the more you care about the things of God, the more clearly you see the sin of this world, the more you wrestle with the brokenness even of the church . . . the more you will suffer. And in the face of that truth, you cling to the faith that God has neither abandoned you nor given up on his church. His plan will be accomplished. You have the promise of glory. Without that, neither our recommendations in this book nor anyone else's will amount to much. With it—well, let's find that out together.

Thus, pastoral work is a calling, a profession, and an office, a sacred vocation that emerges out of a person's life.[32] Recognizing the giftedness of a call, fortified by education and skills for competent ministry, enveloped

---

31. Ibid., 51.
32. E.g., Palmer, *Let Your Life Speak*.

in God's kingdom mission, pastors engage in the work of the church. It truly is an odd and wondrous calling.

But before a pastor is a pastor, he or she is first and most simply a child of God.

Every so often, pastors or members of their congregations forget that pastors are people. They are called by God, yes—but so are all believers called to participate in ministry. They teach, but are always learning. They seek to live exemplary lives, as examples to the flock, but they are indwelt by one and the same Holy Spirit who should animate every Christian.

This is not to say that pastors are, as the saying goes, "just human."[33] When people make mistakes, they're apt to say, "Well, you know, I'm only human." It's a way of recognizing that all human beings are fallible, that no one is perfect, at least this side of heaven. And that's certainly a good thing to remember in the face of all the expectations that are put on pastors.

But sometimes "I'm just human" is a way of shrugging our shoulders at sin. It's true that no believer is perfect, not even pastors. But Jesus calls all of his followers to *be* perfect (Matt 5:48), or as James says, to be "mature and complete, not lacking anything" (James 1:4). We can understand, with compassion, why humans fail. But we cannot stop there, as if failure was all there is. We're not "just human." We're fallible people who are nevertheless called to perfection, and to be living testimonies to what God has meant human life to be.

So pastors are people—real people, with all their faults and idiosyncrasies. There are days in which the work seems impossible, the gifts inadequate. But their calling is to live in a way that demonstrates what is possible through the power of God and the indwelling of the Holy Spirit. And they spend a lifetime calling others to do the same. The work they do is first of all God's, before it can be theirs. Their vocation is not to slave away in isolation at an impossible job, but to participate in the work that God is already doing, a glorious work of redemption and restoration that sometimes involves deep suffering.

But also deep joy. To hold on to that calling, the pastor must first receive the embrace of the Lord. It is only from that place of humility, weakness, and submission that the pastor is able to do the work of the ministry, willingly, eagerly. It is in that place that pastors truly hear the words of Jesus: "Fear not" and "Follow me."

And they follow, most of the time, fearlessly.

---

33. Willimon, *Calling and Character*, 45.

Postscript

To Pastors:

Our hope is that, in reading this chapter, you have a renewed sense of the wonder of your pastoral vocation, your calling. We firmly believe that pastoral ministry is much too difficult a row to hoe without it. As Willimon suggests in the quote that opens this chapter, "blacking out" may be the real precursor to "burning out." We need to constantly renew the vision that led us to ministry in the first place.

Can you think back to that time when you knew you were called to ministry and couldn't imagine living your life any other way? You may have faced many discouraging episodes since then. But do you still have that sense of calling? What's changed?

What experiences have you had that help to reaffirm that call? For example, where do you see your ministry going well? What is it about shepherding that is most fulfilling to you? How can you strengthen that area of your ministry so that you can deepen your appreciation of how God has gifted you?

Beware the tendency to get so wrapped up in the busyness of ministry as a job that you neglect the essentials. In the next chapter, we will address the importance of cultivating a heart attitude of Sabbath rest. We don't need to tell you how important it is to immerse yourself regularly in the disciplines of prayer and the Word, and to pursue a life of integrity and holiness.

But we urge that, as you do so, you ask God to keep you mindful of the big picture. Your vocation may be expressed in the job, but can't be reduced to it. Let's face it: there are many things about ministry that you probably don't enjoy, because they don't represent the gifts that God has given you. It comes with the territory. But don't get stuck there. If you're getting lost in the demands of the job, ask God to renew your vocation, your sense of being called into a relationship with him. It's out of that relationship that you serve.

And while you're at it, ask God to reassure you that it is not your responsibility to save the world, nor is it to fix every problem in your congregation. The work of ministry is hard, but it's God's work first. It's not about you; it's about God and his plan of redemption, in which you have the privilege of participating. Ask him to help you remember that your calling is to partner with him, not to do everything yourself. And if possible, find others who will help you maintain that perspective, who can help you do what you want your congregation to do, namely, to cultivate the kind of faithful imagination that can see beyond the pressures of the present to the purposes of God. As Lillian Daniel has written,

> Sometimes it takes holy imagination just to remember a call, to imagine one, not in the sense that the call is an illusion created by us, but when we imagine, we see what we do not know; we see the possibilities God has for us.[34]

So what is *God* doing, in and through your congregation? It takes a Spirit-filled and prayerful imagination to perceive the movement of God when you're frustrated!

To Congregations:

You may not recognize it, but your pastors have been on a fantastic pilgrimage that has led them to your congregation. And you yourselves are on a pilgrimage. The life of a congregation is a mutual partnership between pastor and people, shepherd and flock. All are called to ministry.

As we've said above, the pastor has a special calling. But that calling is to empower and equip others to discover and pursue *their* calling. Members of a congregation, for example, will often be burdened with a vision for new and much needed ministries, and promptly bring their ideas to the pastor. But then they may expect that it's the *pastor's* job to do something about it. And each person who does so may be unaware of how many *other* people in the congregation have done the same thing.

Have you heard anyone in your church grouse, "What are we paying the pastor for?" That's a warning sign that the professionalized view of the pastor as hired gun has too strong a grip on the congregation. You may have legitimate concerns about your pastor's professional competence, and these are important. But that conversation must always take place in the context of a mutual relationship in which pastor and congregation are seeking God's will together, asking what God wants to do through your church for the community and the world.

Do you want your pastor to thrive? Then do two things. First, be the kind of people who want to be used by God in the service of his kingdom. Don't just suggest new ministries; learn to be ministers. Don't expect your pastor to do it all; seek your pastor's help in discovering what God is calling you to do yourself.

34. Daniel, in Daniel and Copenhaver, *Odd and Wondrous Calling*, 7.

Second, consider what you can do to confirm his or her call. You don't have to think that everything your pastor does is terrific. Like other Christians, they have gifts in some areas and may need development in others. But it's vitally important to not take your pastor's gifts for granted.

This, for example, is the deeper reason why we suggested in an earlier chapter sending your pastor notes of appreciation. It's not just a technique for reducing your pastor's stress; they need to know that their efforts are not in vain. They need confirmation of their call. So consider: what can you do to be that kind of encourager? If you're not sure, you might even ask the pastor.

To Seminarians:

Some of you came to seminary to explore or confirm your call, and were excited to be in a place where you anticipated being spiritually formed. To learn from Bible scholars, theologians, experienced ministers—what could be better than that? For many of you, seminary has been a place of deepening and growth, a blessing in every sense of the word.

But let's face it. For others, seminary has been a disturbing and destabilizing experience. You've been exposed to points of view that you never knew existed, and you are still trying to make sense of them. You've sat in classes that spent more time breaking down old beliefs than building up new ones, all in the name of scholarship. And you may be getting ready to graduate with the uncomfortable feeling that you're really not sure any more what you believe about things that used to seem secure.

Part of this is because seminary education itself has been profoundly affected by the model of pastor-as-professional. Seminary develops your critical skills. But there is always the danger that you will learn to dissect God more than to love him with all your heart, soul, mind, and strength. There is no question that you need to develop your knowledge and skills as a pastor-in-training—everything from how to exegete texts in their original languages, to how to preach with passion and clarity, to how to sit with people in their distress, to how to manage a church budget. But you must personally bring an extra dimension to your studies, something that is not always cultivated in the professionally oriented classroom: the dimension of imagination.

What we mean by that is that it's not enough to stuff your head full of knowledge, pass your exams, and graduate. In and through your coursework, as well as outside of it, you must constantly develop the imagination to perceive what God is doing and to know your part in it. It's one thing to enter the scholarly debates about who authored which book of the Bible; it's another to look through those authors' eyes as they struggle to tell the story of God's redemptive work in the world. The former, of course, informs the latter. But without the latter, the former will be useless to you as a pastor.

Toward that end, we urge you to use your seminary experience as a vehicle to constantly reflect on your call. What is the vision that first drew you to the possibility of the pastorate? To seminary? Don't take the call for granted; don't be passive in confirming it. Some of the books cited in the notes may help you in this area.[35]

As you learn professional knowledge and skills, you should always be open to recognizing where you may need additional training beyond what your seminary education can give you. At the same time, however, you must fight the temptation to believe that one more book, one more class, or one more seminar is by itself going to make you competent for ministry or take away the anxiety about your adequacy. What can you do to keep up your guard against this kind of careerism?

Finally, as you prepare to step into the pastoral office, you need to accept that you will be expected to be an exemplary and holy person. This is not something that can be put off until someone challenges your integrity. So what practices are you incorporating into your life now to mature as a believer into the fullness of Christ?

35. Cf. also Johnson, *Hearing God's Call.*

PART 2

The Principles

5

Cultivate a Sabbath Heart

God gave us the gift of Sabbath—not just as a day, but as an orientation, a way of seeing and knowing.... It is both time on a calendar, and a disposition of the heart.

—MARK BUCHANAN[1]

Sabbath, rather than being the opposite of work, becomes the very thing that characterizes our work. For from rest and godly reflection comes genuinely humane work. When we are reflecting God appropriately, therefore, all our work will be seasoned with Sabbath.

—DARRELL COSDEN[2]

The Crowds

Like first-century celebrity hounds, the crowds had a knack for sniffing out where Jesus could be found. As Jesus' reputation spread, more and more people attached themselves to him. There were the true seekers among them, but also the merely curious and those who were looking mainly to see what he could do for them. Some were a little of each.

1. Buchanan, *Rest*, 2–3.
2. Cosden, *Earthly Work*, 110.

Reading through the Gospel of Matthew, you can imagine the crowds swelling as the story proceeds. Jesus called his first disciples and embarked on a preaching tour of Galilee. News of his healing prowess spread like fire, and people streamed to him from miles around.

At one point, Jesus looked around him, saw the crowd, and sat down to teach them what we know as the Sermon on the Mount. When he finished, the crowds were astonished at the personal authority with which he taught. That only cemented his reputation. When he came down from the mountainside, the multitudes continued to trail after him.

Matthew then tells of one healing miracle after another. Jesus dared to touch a leper and pronounce him clean. He healed the servant of a Roman military officer, without even being in the neighborhood, just by speaking the words. He healed Peter's mother-in-law with nothing but a touch. And more and more people were brought to Jesus, to be healed of their diseases, to be freed of their demons. Jesus worked on into the night. Such was the people's pain, and the corresponding compassion of God.

If we're honest with ourselves, the example of Jesus' compassion can be intimidating. The way Matthew describes it, Jesus gives and gives, and the crowds never let up. Is there a limit? The people and their problems press Jesus from every side. Will he go on healing whoever comes to him with whatever infirmity or illness, no matter how long it takes?

Here is Matthew's answer: "When Jesus saw the crowd around him, he gave orders to cross to the other side of the lake" (Matt 8:18).

As far as we know, the crowds hadn't thinned out. People didn't get tired of hanging around and go home. They didn't discuss with each other how they should at least have let Jesus and his disciples have a coffee break. Rather, they came to Jesus with their need, and waited for him to do something about it.

And what he did, at least this time, was to turn to his disciples and say, "Get in the boat—we're leaving."

It's not the response we might have expected.

Matthew doesn't give the reason for Jesus' behavior, but we can make an educated guess. Jesus obeyed an alternating rhythm of public ministry and solitude, work and rest. It was his habit to seek time to be alone with God and pray (e.g., Matt 14:23; Mark 1:35; Luke 5:16; 6:12). Mark, in fact, describes a situation similar to the one we've seen in Matthew, and with a similar response:

> Then, because so many people were coming and going that they
> did not even have a chance to eat, [Jesus] said to [his disciples],

"Come with me by yourselves to a quiet place and get some rest."
So they went away by themselves in a boat to a solitary place.
(Mark 6:31–32)

In other words, Jesus got into a boat and left behind the demands of the crowds, taking the disciples with him. They went in search of solitude and rest.

The irony, in Mark's account, is that when the boat landed, Jesus found that the crowds had run on ahead to meet them. There were 5,000 men and untold women and children. He looked upon their lostness and took pity on them, feeding their souls with his teaching, and their bodies with a miraculous multiplication of five small loaves and two fish.

But the point remains: though Jesus' compassion was boundless, he still took time to renew himself spiritually. And this is not simply a matter of "taking a well-deserved break from his useful but exhausting ministry. He is honoring a deep spiritual need for a time dedicated not to accomplishment and growth, but to quiescence and rest."[3] If Jesus himself did this, can any of us afford to do less?

All Christians share the calling to embody the self-sacrificial caring of Christ. The particular challenge for pastors is that this calling is a very public one; that's the meaning of their ordination. But not all pastors are equally adept at maintaining their spiritual equilibrium.

Mark Buchanan, for example, tells of a pastor who had been retired from the ministry for three years after having served for nearly half a century. The man had the unfortunate habit of taking the demands of his congregation into himself, creating a constant pressure that deadened his spirit. The pastor openly admitted,

> I guess I never learned how to let things go. I carried the church's problems always, everywhere. I got so bottled up with it. Then I'd go on vacation and fall to pieces. It was like lapsing into a coma, or trying to break a drug addiction. I got sick. I wasn't able to sleep, or I couldn't wake up. I got angry and depressed. I withdrew. Coming back, I was almost paralyzed. I begged God to let me go, let me do anything but this. Only I had no motivation for anything. I'm still getting over that.[4]

By now, you probably recognize the signs of chronic stress and burnout, the emotional and spiritual damage that can be wrought by a ministry

3. Muller, *Sabbath*, 58.
4. Buchanan, *Rest*, 18.

that ignores the alternating rhythm of spiritual engagement and spiritual retreat.

There is a time to work, and a time to rest. There is a time to be with others, and a time to be alone with God. At one level, this might translate to the simplistic advice that pastors need to take a break from ministry now and then. True enough. At a deeper level, however, the issue is not merely the quantity of time, but its quality: not just *how much* but *how*. For the quality of our rest will ultimately be reflected in how we work; the way we spend time with God will show up in the way we respond to others.

What we will suggest in this chapter is that all Christians need the spiritual freedom that comes as a gracious gift through the discipline of Sabbath-keeping. Yes, we know—the very idea may raise some hackles. It may sound like we're subverting a gospel of grace by sneaking religious works through the back door. We assure you that this is exactly the opposite of our intent!

Or perhaps our putting "freedom" and "discipline" in the same sentence may seem odd. Some of you may have grown up in traditions that had rules about Sabbath-keeping, and they were oppressive and stifling. It was the one day of the week when every kid in the neighborhood other than you had fun.

But it doesn't have to be that way: Sabbath can and should be about enjoying a regular opportunity to experience the liberating goodness of God. We believe this is particularly true for pastors who have found ministry burdensome while trying to preach a message of grace. For some pastors, Sunday is *never* a day of rest—and they may struggle to find any semblance of Sabbath on the other six days. When this is the case, both the pastor's spirit and the ministry will eventually suffer. Sabbath is a gift to weary pastors, one that needs to be treasured and protected.

One of my (Kurt) seminary professors was brutally honest and transparent in the classroom one day. He was reaching retirement age and had just been diagnosed with cancer. He said to us, "I spent my life giving myself to the church, promising my family that when I retired I would devote myself to them. Now I am about to retire and my life is being cut short. Invest your life in what is most important each and every day." Why should any pastor have to live with that kind of regret? Practicing Sabbath is an act of resistance, saying no to all the pressures and demands of church work that wither the soul. And as we hope to show in later chapters, wise decision-making in ministry and the Christian life comes from a heart formed by the Sabbath.

Taking Sabbath More Seriously

From the beginning, a Sabbath rhythm was woven into the very fabric of creation. In six days, the Bible tells us, God created the heavens and the earth. It's a simple enough statement; but our imaginations can only play around the edges of such a truth. In *The Chronicles of Narnia*, C. S. Lewis gives us the marvelous image of the great lion Aslan singing creation into existence, as one of the children listens:

> In the darkness something was happening at last. A voice had begun to sing. . . . Its lower notes were deep enough to be the voice of the earth herself. There were no words. There was hardly even a tune. But it was, beyond comparison, the most beautiful noise he had ever heard. It was so beautiful he could hardly bear it. . . . Then two wonders happened at the same moment. One was that the voice was suddenly joined by other voices; more voices than you could possibly count. They were in harmony with it, but far higher up the scale: cold, tingling, silvery voices. The second wonder was that the blackness overhead, all at once, was blazing with stars. . . . One moment there had been nothing but darkness; next moment a thousand, thousand points of light leaped out. . . . If you had seen and heard it...you would have felt quite certain that it was the stars themselves which were singing, and that it was the First Voice, the deep one, which had made them appear and made them sing.[5]

Six glorious days of creation. And then, a seventh day to complete the rhythm:

> By the seventh day God had finished the work he had been doing; so on the seventh day he rested from all his work. Then God blessed the seventh day and made it holy, because on it he rested from all the work of creating he had done. (Gen 2:2–3)

Abraham Heschel observes that we would expect God, having created the heavens and the earth, to sanctify a *place*. But no: "it seems as if to the Bible, it is *holiness in time*, the Sabbath, which comes first."[6]

It is this holiness, ordained by God from creation itself, that bids us to respect the Sabbath. The longest of the Ten Commandments reminds us of this:

---

5. Lewis, *Magician's Nephew*, 106–7.
6. Heschel, *Sabbath*, 9.

> Remember the Sabbath day by keeping it holy. Six days you shall labor and do all your work, but the seventh day is a Sabbath to the Lord your God. On it you shall not do any work, neither you, nor your son or daughter, nor your male or female servant, nor your animals, nor any foreigner residing in your towns. For in six days the Lord made the heavens and the earth, the sea, and all that is in them, but he rested on the seventh day. Therefore the Lord blessed the Sabbath day and made it holy. (Exod 20:8–11)

We are not commanded to *make* the Sabbath holy—it already is. We are only commanded to keep that fact in mind as we follow God's lead by setting apart a day to enter his rest.

As those who preach a gospel of grace, Christians sometimes have an ambivalent relationship to commandments. It's not that we think the prohibitions against murder, idolatry, and adultery are bad ideas. Nor do we balk at the idea of honoring our parents (though some would have a harder time with this than others!). But the Sabbath commandment—which for many has come to mean, "Thou shalt go to church on Sundays"—feels a little too much like a religion of works. We know church is important, and we go as often as we can—let's just not get legalistic about it, OK?

It's worth remembering that God gave the Sabbath to his people *before* he gave them the law. You know the story. The Israelites had experienced a stunning escape from the Egyptian army, one that left no doubt in anyone's mind that they would all have been dead were it not for the mighty intervention of God. Once the shock had worn off, they danced and sang praises to the Lord.

But in the very next scene of the Exodus drama, the people started complaining that there was no water to drink. So God provided water. Then there was nothing to eat, and they began having delusional daydreams about how much they missed the all-you-can-eat Egyptian buffet they had left behind. So God provided food: quail, and a mysterious bread from heaven that they nicknamed "manna" (which was apparently Hebrew for "We don't know what it is but we'd better call it something").

The instructions that came with the manna were simple: every day, gather what you need for your family. Don't keep any leftovers; it will spoil. There's just one exception: on the sixth day, gather a double portion, because there won't be any manna to gather on the seventh day. You can keep what's left overnight this time, and it won't spoil. God commanded that the seventh day be "a day of sabbath rest, a holy sabbath to the Lord" (Exod 16:23).

Of course, not everyone followed the package directions. The people seemed to hedge their bets, uncertain of whether God could be trusted to provide for their daily needs. Some kept manna overnight and awoke to a maggoty mess; some went out to gather on the seventh day and found nothing. In response to their disobedience, God didn't strike them with lightning or cause the ground to swallow them whole. Instead, he merely said, "How long will you refuse to keep my commands and my instructions? Bear in mind that the Lord has given you the Sabbath; that is why on the sixth day he gives you bread for two days" (Exod 16:28–29).

Isn't this the voice of grace rather than law? Yes, God had given them a strict command. But it is the command to rest, and he has provided everything they need for that day. As Wayne Muller reminds us, "The God who made the Sabbath is not a cranky schoolmaster."[7] It's not a test of how well we follow rules, but an invitation to rest from our labors, in the confidence of God's provision.

Pastors have a hard time believing this, too often living in a mad dash to satisfy their own sense of inadequacy or stave off the critic who doesn't think the pastor works hard enough. I (Kurt) often described my pastoral ministry as commanding a motorboat. Full throttle, I would speed toward a determined goal—and swimmers and ducks had better stay out of my way! In exhaustion, however, I learned that sailing is a far better way. Sailing means attending to wind and waves and currents. Sailing can be exhilarating, but there are also times of calm. As a motorboat pastor I was in control. Learning to be a sailboat pastor meant I had to learn to rest, to relax, and to trust the Lord. This is Sabbath work.

A similar note is struck by the other version of the Sabbath commandment, found in the book of Deuteronomy. The second is nearly identical to the first, but the reason given for our obedience has changed. If the Exodus version of the Sabbath commandment goes back to creation, the Deuteronomic version goes back to the Exodus event itself:

> Observe the Sabbath day by keeping it holy, as the Lord your God has commanded you. . . . Remember that you were slaves in Egypt and that the Lord your God brought you out of there with a mighty hand and an outstretched arm. Therefore the Lord your God has commanded you to observe the Sabbath day. (Deut 5:12, 15)

7. Muller, *Sabbath*, 31.

In America, we are used to thinking of freedom as freedom from coercion, from others telling us what to do. But here, God seems to be saying, "Obey my commandment, *because* I have set you free."

That ironic tension can be seen behind Jesus' approach to the Sabbath. Six times in the Gospels he clashed with Jewish leaders over the Sabbath. In the Gospel of Mark, two of these confrontations are narrated in sequence (Mark 2:23—3:6). In the first, the Pharisees had their watchful eye on the upstart Jesus and his disciples, and caught them picking grain as they walked through the fields.

When challenged for allowing his disciples to work on the Sabbath, Jesus didn't deny the charge. Instead, he cited legal precedent in King David, and even said of himself, "the Son of Man is Lord even of the Sabbath" (Mark 2:28). Clearly, these are both messianic claims. It motivated the Pharisees to watch Jesus even more closely, looking for an excuse to accuse him of vandalizing the Jewish faith.

Thus follows the second story, in which Jesus dared to heal a man's diseased hand on the Sabbath. Instead of ducking the issue, Jesus openly confronted those gathered in the synagogue: "Which is lawful on the Sabbath: to do good or to do evil, to save life or to kill?" (Mark 3:4). No answer. He then commanded the man to stretch his hand out, and it was spontaneously healed—giving no solid grounds for his opponents to make an accusation. But it didn't matter. To them, he was a dangerous subversive, and they went out to plot his undoing.

Jesus said, "The Sabbath was made for people, not people for the Sabbath" (Mark 2:27, TNIV). Participation in God's Sabbath rest was meant to be a sign of God's unique covenant with his people, the last thing God made sure to get straight with Moses before sending him down Mt. Sinai with the stone tablets (Exod 31:12–18). But by Jesus' day, Sabbath observance appears to have taken on a defensive and legalistic tone. Jesus, far from throwing the Sabbath over, reinvigorates its true meaning and purpose: the Sabbath was for healing and restoration, an Exodus sign of liberation from bondage.

It can be for our liberation as well.

We take the Sabbath seriously, but not as a religious work demanded of us by God to earn his favor. We do it because he has commanded us to abide by the rhythm built into creation's foundation, a day set aside as holy by God, a day of both rest and freedom. Dorothy Bass, reflecting on the Sabbath commandment in Deuteronomy, has put it well:

> Slaves cannot skip a day of work, but free people can. . . . To keep sabbath is to exercise one's freedom, to declare oneself to be neither a tool to be employed—an *employee*—nor a beast to be burdened. To keep sabbath is also to remember one's freedom and to recall the One from whom that freedom came, the One from whom it still comes.[8]

Bass reminds us that Sabbath is about freedom. And though it may be difficult for us to stay alert to the many ways in which we are enslaved, she emphasizes one in particular: our captivity to understandings of work that crush and dehumanize us.

Pastors are used to a life of overwork. As one pastor put it, "The meter is always running." In one candid interview, a pastor described his week. Sunday morning, the pastor arrived at church at 6:30 in the morning and preached three services. Immediately after the last service, he left to counsel a severely distressed couple until 2:30. In the afternoon, he received a phone call from a suicidal man who didn't identify himself and had to be tracked down, resulting in phone calls until after midnight. Monday was supposed to be his day off, but he received a call to minister to a parishioner couple whose baby had been rushed to the hospital. The baby died that evening, and the pastor stayed with the couple through the night. The memorial service was on Thursday—his day to prepare the Sunday sermon. And if people find it difficult to get on his schedule in the office, they'll look for him at the coffee shop. He summarized:

> The end result is emotional exhaustion. I now literally leave town to get some quiet time. . . . I won't have a day and an evening off together for at least another month. . . . I need some off-duty time. I need an emotional sabbath.[9]

This isn't a matter of selfishness. He cares about people, and will drop whatever he's doing when a real need arises. But he wishes that people would be a little more thoughtful about distinguishing the urgent from the things that can wait. It's a matter of survival.

Congregations are subject to the madness of endless activities just as pastors are. We fill up the church calendar with activities day after day, week after week. Not only is this frantic pace unhealthy for people, the over-enriched calendar pulls families in many different directions and apart from each other. Sabbath as resistance screams out, *Enough! Stop,*

8. Bass, *Receiving the Day*, 48 (emphasis in original). Note: while we have followed the convention of capitalizing the word "Sabbath," some authors do not.

9. Quoted in Ulstein, *Pastors Off the Record*, 18–19.

rest. Church leaders must set the tone. If we are to find freedom by taking the Sabbath more seriously, it will require a change of heart and mind that allows us to take ourselves *less* seriously.

Taking Ourselves Less Seriously

Back in chapter 1, we mentioned that the first question people usually ask when they meet someone, after finding out their name, is what they do for a living. By the answer to that question, we silently arrange ourselves according to status: rich versus poor, educated versus uneducated, prestigious career versus dead-end job. Our work is not just important to our identity; it can be the cornerstone of our self-worth.

All this says something about our societal values: "we often emphasize the side of production, activity, and work and then complain about burnout and stress."[10] Being busy is a sign of personal importance. "I know you're really busy, but . . ." is a standard preface to an apologetic request. "I've been really busy" is the all-purpose excuse that everyone's supposed to accept, even if grudgingly.

We know we need rest. If we refuse to recognize it, sooner or later our bodies will force the truth on us. But what are we supposed to do in the face of a culture that insinuates that the only legitimate rest is one that is "well deserved," and only well deserved when one has worked to the point of exhaustion? There will probably be those in any congregation who believe that a pastor who rests is not going about the Lord's work with due diligence. And there are pastors whose anxious busyness suggests they believe it themselves.

It is here that Sabbath-keeping, whatever its form, can be a subversive activity, an opportunity to "act out the reality that ultimately our worth comes from being loved by God, not from what we do."[11] As Heschel has written, the Sabbath

> is a day in which we abandon our plebeian pursuits and reclaim our authentic state, in which we may partake of a blessedness in which we are what we are, regardless of whether we are learned or not, of whether our career is a success or failure; . . . whether we accomplish or fall short of reaching our goals.[12]

10. Postema, *Catch Your Breath*, 30.
11. Baab, *Sabbath Keeping*, 95.
12. Heschel, *Sabbath*, 30.

Sabbath declares our Exodus freedom from demeaning definitions of our worth. We let go of the need to produce or succeed, get ahead or get the grade, and instead relax into the providence of a loving Father.

To do this requires a shift in our understanding of work itself, and the rhythm of Sabbath can help us learn it. The traditional Jewish celebration of Sabbath begins at sundown on Friday and ends at sundown on Saturday. It is welcomed as an honored guest, with prayer and the lighting of candles. The practice reflects a Hebraic understanding of day. Genesis 1:5 reads: "And it was evening and it was morning, first day"—and the refrain is repeated throughout the six days of creation.[13] For the Jews, the "day" does not begin in the morning, but in the evening. After all, darkness came first; day did not exist until God created light.

Eugene Peterson calls this the "two-beat rhythm" of evening first and then morning.[14] This rhythm reverses the mindset in which the day begins when we get out of bed and start working, and ends in the evening when the day's efforts are done. This is not a minor matter, for it up-ends how we understand the relationship of our work to God's:

> Day is the basic unit of God's creative work; evening is the beginning of that day. It is the onset of God speaking light, stars, earth, vegetation, animals, man, woman into being. But it is also the time when we quit our activity and go to sleep. Then I wake up, rested, jump out of bed full of energy, grab a cup of coffee, and rush out the door to get things started. The first thing I discover (a great blow to the ego) is that everything was started hours ago. All the important things got underway while I was fast asleep.[15]

The work God gives us to do is important, but never ultimate. We have neither the power nor the responsibility to keep the world spinning on its axis. Our work has value because it aligns with God's creative and redemptive design; but it is always his work first, before it can be ours, and then only by grace. This is the two-beat rhythm to which we must attune ourselves: "Evening: God begins, without our help, his creative day. Morning: God calls us to enjoy and share and develop the work he initiated."[16]

This is what it means to begin cultivating a Sabbath heart. The Sabbath must not be simply a day off, as if the only thing that mattered was to

---

13. Translation by Alter, *Genesis*, 3.
14. Peterson, *Working the Angles*, 69.
15. Ibid., 67–68.
16. Ibid., 68.

stop working for twenty-four hours. We might be able to get some much-needed physical and emotional rest that way, and that would be a good thing. But it would leave our understanding of work, and our relationship to it, untouched. Our attitude would still be that our six working days are the days that matter, and the Sabbath would play the subordinate role of restoring the energy we need for the *next* six days. Peterson would consider this a "secularized" and "utilitarian" approach to Sabbath, out of step with its true rhythm.[17] Heschel would agree:

> [T]he Sabbath as a day of rest, as a day of abstaining from toil, is not for the purpose of recovering one's lost strength and becoming fit for the forthcoming labor. The Sabbath is a day for the sake of life. Man is not a beast of burden, and the Sabbath is not for the purpose of enhancing the efficiency of his work.[18]

Just as evening precedes morning, God's work precedes ours. Sabbath affords us the opportunity to get our priorities the right way around. It's a sign that shows we know that we can't save the world—that's God's job, and we participate by his gracious invitation. As Walter Brueggemann has written, "The Sabbath . . . announces that the world is safely in God's hands. The world will not disintegrate if we stop our efforts."[19] There is great freedom in that truth.

This points, however, to a particular occupational hazard for pastors. As we have seen in previous chapters, pastors can be subject to a bewildering variety of role expectations. Some are implicit, others explicit. Some come from the congregation, others are self-imposed. A cartoon once portrayed a pastor bent over double from the weight of carrying the church building on his back, as a parishioner asked, "Excuse me, pastor, are you busy?"

The weight of these expectations tempts some pastors to take themselves very seriously indeed. Peterson believes that pastors are especially prone to "the sin of reversing the rhythms":

> Instead of grace/work we make it work/grace. Instead of working in a world in which God calls everything into being with his word and redeems his people with an outstretched arm, we rearrange it as a world in which we preach the mighty word of God and as an afterthought ask him to bless our speaking; a world in which we stretch out our mighty arms to help the oppressed and

17. Ibid., 66.
18. Heschel, *Sabbath*, 14.
19. Brueggemann, *Genesis*, 35.

open our hands to assist the needy and desperately petition God to take care of those we miss.[20]

When this happens, pastors begin to believe that their work is too important to take a Sabbath. The unconscious belief seems to be, "God's work must be done—and how will that happen if I rest?"

Pastors need the Sabbath to maintain or restore a right order to their work. William Willimon has put it this way: "It is crucial for pastors to carve out some means of Sabbath as a witness that God, not pastors, preserves the church."[21] There are two phrases we want to emphasize in that pithy quote. First, "as a witness." To whom? Pastors themselves, for one. But also congregations, who sometimes put more stock in the pastor's job responsibilities than the ministry of the Holy Spirit.

Second, the phrase "carve out" implies a deliberate act, a staunch commitment to making Sabbath-keeping a priority even when the schedule seems impossible. Pastors don't punch a clock; in some ways, their work is never done. Teachers (and seminary professors!) understand this: there is always the pressure to use every hour of every day constructively, preparing for the next lesson, and the next, and the next. But one teacher, taking a stand against the guilt-driven urge to fill every moment with schoolwork, has left us this gleaming pearl of wisdom: "Show me a person who can't get their work done in six days, and I'll show you a person who can't get their work done in seven."[22]

Those are the words of a heart being formed by the Sabbath.

Real Rest

Have you ever had the kind of vacation where you came home more tired than when you left? Most of us have probably done it. We say that we're looking forward to getting away from the daily grind. But then we bring the same frenetic attitude and lifestyle of clock-watching and to-do lists with us. It's like a contest to see who can visit the most points of interest. There's more of hurrying than of resting, and when we finally return home, we're no more ready to go back to work than when we left. We tell people who ask that we need another vacation to recover from the first one. And we say it not just with regret, but with a touch of pride. It was a

20. Peterson, *Working the Angles*, 71.

21. Willimon, *Calling*, 143.

22. Quoted in Bass, *Receiving the Day*, 60.

"good" vacation in the manner of a "good" day at work—successful, maybe even *productive*. Want to see the pictures?

This might be fun or exciting. But it's not real rest.

We are invited to enter into God's rest, the repose that he has graciously built into creation itself. Rabbinic tradition has it that while God created the heavens and the earth in six days, there was also something God created on the seventh: *menuha*, which suggests a still, tranquil peacefulness.[23] The Sabbath is not merely a day to run away from work, but a day to run to God: to lay aside our anxious striving, acknowledge our dependence on him, and there find peace.

Ministry can be a burden, but the burden is not meant to overwhelm. Imagine Jesus saying this to overstressed pastors:

> Are you tired? Worn out? Burned out on religion? Come to me. Get away with me and you'll recover your life. I'll show you how to take a real rest. Walk with me and work with me—watch how I do it. Learn the unforced rhythms of grace. I won't lay anything heavy or ill-fitting on you. Keep company with me and you'll learn to live freely and lightly. (Matt 11:28–30, *The Message*)

What we are suggesting is that one of the ways we "learn the unforced rhythms of grace" is by keeping Sabbath. This is not the heavy yoke of legalism, but an invitation to attach ourselves to a Master who will teach us how to live with a lighter, Sabbath-filled heart.

Let us give you fair warning, though. Busyness isn't merely something that others force on us. If no one else did it, many of us would probably do it to ourselves. We can come to rely on sheer busyness to give us a sense of meaning and worth, or to avoid things or people we'd rather not face, including our own neediness:

> This is one of our fears of quiet; if we stop and listen, we will hear this emptiness. . . . If we are terrified of what we will find in rest, we will refuse to look up from our work, refuse to stop moving.[24]

Depending on how much you've come to invest in your own busyness, or how addicted you have become to your own adrenaline, you may find it difficult to rest. You may feel fidgety or anxious, guilty or just plain lost. It may take a while—a long while—to develop new habits and new ways of thinking. Give it time, stay with it, and get help and counsel if you need it.

23. Heschel, *Sabbath*, 22–23.
24. Muller, *Sabbath*, 50.

The older we've become, the more my wife and I (Cameron) have changed our way of thinking about vacation. Our kids are grown, so we don't do family vacations much anymore. It's just the two of us, and neither of us feels compelled to run around and see all the sights. Vacation is for relaxing, for slowing down, even if it means just sitting in a hotel room to read a book.

On one of our recent vacations, we found an inexpensive but nice motel overlooking a marina. We dumped our luggage on the bed and stepped out on the balcony. The weather was sunny, but a cool breeze wafted over us from the water. With a deep sigh, I pulled up a chair and flopped down to stare at the boats that were lazily drifting past.

And then, suddenly, I was overwhelmed with emotion, as if being in this place had unleashed something I didn't know was there. I had no words, only the sense of being released, or at least paroled. It was not until that moment that I realized how stressed I had been, the moment when I felt an invisible burden being slowly lifted from my shoulders.

We no longer wait for vacations, which are too short and too few to do the job. Sunday is our Sabbath, in keeping with the tradition of honoring the resurrection. On Sunday mornings, I am either teaching a Bible class or preaching. But the afternoon and evening is set aside—kept holy!—for Sabbath rest. We prepare for it in advance on Saturday by making sure we're ready for Monday. We protect it by adamantly resisting the temptation to get busy and do something needful.

On the Sabbath I might journal, conversing with God as my thoughts meander back over the week. I keep a stack of books at the ready. Not books that I need for sermon or lecture preparation, but books I want to read for my own personal and spiritual edification, books that don't have any immediate payoff in terms of professional productivity. Christian books, of course, but also Tolstoy, Dostoevsky, Dickens. My wife and I have recently read Dickens's *A Tale of Two Cities* and George Eliot's *Silas Marner* to each other.

We talk, play games, or watch old black-and-white movie classics. Sometimes, I just sit and stare, or lean back in the recliner and take a nap. It still surprises me to realize how much I had been running on adrenaline during the week, and hence how exhausted I can feel on Sundays, when I actually allow myself the luxury of a nap! Then I might wake up and do a crossword puzzle (preferably of the "cryptic" kind). And at the end of the day, we take Communion together, and thank God for the gift of the body and blood of Jesus, and of his rest.

Your Sabbath may look very different. Take a walk to clear your mind, to meditate, or just to enjoy God's creation. Have a picnic with people you love. Play with your children; teach them to treasure having a day of rest. Read a psalm out loud, and put some feeling into it. Sing. Laugh. Cry. But do it all in God's presence, and with holy abandon.

At the beginning, it can be useful to make a list of possible Sabbath activities—not as obligations, but as a hedge against all the other things that will beg for your attention when there's no plan in place. Lynne Baab suggests three questions to use as a filter when making up your list: "Does it promote rest and relaxation? Does it bring delight and enjoyment? Does it give you a sense of holiness and sanctity?"[25] This is a good place to start.

Different ways of honoring the Sabbath, though, may be appropriate to different seasons of life.[26] There are seasons of light, where Sabbath may be marked by a sense of celebration and the sheer joy of life itself. In darker times, a deeper kind of solitude may be needed, a time to cry out to God, lower our brittle defenses, and allow him to thoroughly search our hearts. It can be both a frightening and a humbling experience, but one that will yield its own fruit.

Pastors in particular may need the quiet and the distance to notice "what God has been and is doing" and to hear his voice.[27] We really believe that pastors who never experience Sabbath rest will find it difficult to hold on to their vocation amidst the demands of the job. And without that firm sense of calling, the joy of ministry becomes elusive or even non-existent.

Congregations are prone to relying too much on the pastor to hold the ministry together. For their part, many pastors are all too willing to collude, taking themselves and their work far more seriously than they do the need for Sabbath rest. If this sounds like you, then use Sabbath time to revitalize your sense of vocation. Let God show you where the invisible church is peeking out at you through the cracks of your visible congregation. Practice gratitude for these glimpses of grace, even when (or especially when!) there seems to be little for which to be thankful.[28]

And remember that Sabbath is not a legalistic observance, something we do because we think God's going to be unhappy with us if we don't. What if a real need comes up? Didn't Jesus do good on the Sabbath?

---

25. Baab, *Sabbath Keeping*, 84.

26. Buchanan, *Spiritual Rhythm*.

27. Peterson, *Working the Angles*, 73.

28. For preliminary evidence that a grateful disposition is related to better adjustment for pastors, see Lee, "Dispositional Resiliency."

Absolutely—and we should be open to doing the same. But here's the question: are we doing good out of a sense of freedom or compulsion? With joy or resentment? With the sure knowledge that God is the one who saves the world, or with the anxious suspicion that things will fall apart if we don't hold them together?

Relax. Let go of all religious performance anxiety about the day. You're not being graded on faithfulness or technique. Instead, open your heart to receive a day of freedom and rest. It's a gift from God, a much-needed miracle of grace delivered directly to your door.

Postscript

To Pastors:

When, if ever, do you take a Sabbath? If this is not your regular habit, even one real Sabbath day may convince you of the need. In one of the Doctor of Ministry courses that I (Kurt) teach at Fuller, we require students to take a four-hour silent retreat—getting away from the busyness of ministry and simply being alone with the Lord. Many students have never done this before, and find the experience restorative. They often say, "This will become part of my life routine." Pastors need to make Sabbath practices a part of their lives daily, weekly and annually.

Jewish families celebrate on Saturday, while most Christian families have traditionally observed the Sabbath on Sunday. But Sunday may feel like a workday to you, especially if you have to prepare both morning and evening services. If necessary, find some other day of the week. Many pastors use Monday as their Sabbath; it allows for some recovery time after Sunday, and is hopefully far enough from the following Sunday to escape immediate deadlines. But some other day may work better for you, or may need to be carved out of your schedule.

Resist the temptation to short-change the Sabbath by cramming in an hour or two here and there. It's true that once you've established a Sabbath rhythm, you'll be better able to grab Sabbath-like moments throughout the week, where you can re-enter a more restful state even in the midst of difficulties. But we sincerely doubt that those moments can be had without establishing the habit of the day first, without having a heart that is being shaped by that weekly habit.

You're going to need some help to make this work. We believe that Sabbath is a gift to your whole congregation, not just you, and the gift is best enjoyed together. If you believe that as well, then teach your congregation about the spiritual importance of Sabbath freedom and rest; show them the beauty of the gift. Then ask them to help you model it.

Don't think or talk about it as merely a "day off" from ministry responsibilities. In a practical sense, it may be that, and a day off can be a good thing. But that language puts the matter in the wrong meaning framework, turning a conversation about spiritual discipline into an employer-employee negotiation. Instead, come to that conversation with the conviction that this is something you need to help each other discover and practice.

And perhaps most importantly, honoring a regular Sabbath day, or even taking a longer sabbatical, can be an important sign of what you really believe about the church and your vocation as a pastor. As Willimon has written,

> We are free to let go of the church, free to take regular sabbatical, because we rest in the conviction that Christ is really present in the church, that Christ will preserve the church and that the gates of hell, or even our day off, will not defeat the church.[29]

Do you really believe that? Does your congregation? Is there a shared myth that the church will fall down if you personally don't hold it up?

If so, then honoring the Sabbath may be the first step toward true freedom, for you and your congregation both. We'll say more in the coming chapters about how a Sabbath-shaped way of thinking might apply to other areas of your life and ministry as well.

Learning a rhythm of restfulness is one side of the Sabbath coin. The other purpose of getting out of the normal routine of ministry is to grow and be stretched in new ways. We believe that every pastor should be on a path of lifelong learning. The world keeps changing, and you will need new tools to stay vibrant and fresh. At the risk of sounding self-serving, that's why there are Doctor of Ministry programs! But there are other ways to stay on a growing edge. The best of lifelong learning opportunities will stimulate new thinking and stir the pot in surprising ways. So go to conferences, talk to and learn from other pastors, and make the time to read—a lot. Read theology, of course, but also the best of novels and non-fiction. It will deepen the wells from which you draw.

---

29. Willimon, *Calling*, 144. Again, despite the language Willimon uses, we don't recommend thinking of the Sabbath as a "day off." The reality, of course, is that without help, this is how your congregation might think of it.

To Congregations:

Sabbath rest is not just for pastors or religious professionals. It's for every believer. We realize that, for some of you, the idea of setting aside a weekly day of rest sounds impossible, like committing financial suicide. We won't pretend to have the answers to all of that.

But you still might agree that this is part of what enslaves us as a society. At every level of wealth, money is a graceless and demanding task-master, though those with more of it may be slower to notice. As a church, we need to take a stand against a culture of overwork. We need to live in ways that give the lie to the idea that our value as human beings—or even as Christians!—comes from what we produce.

Sabbath is one way to do this. And if your congregation is going to take this seriously, you need your pastor to be a good model of Sabbath rest.

Help your pastor keep the Sabbath holy. Think carefully about how to set boundaries that will allow your pastor a day of freedom to rest, pray, and play. This isn't just time off for good behavior. It's a necessary spiritual discipline: necessary to your pastor's spiritual health and, both directly and indirectly, to the congregation's as well.

Some pastors find it difficult to let go of responsibility, even for a day. What he or she needs to be assured of is that you, as a congregation, really can take care of yourselves and the church. Or better, that you know how to lean upon God and his Spirit, instead of on the pastor. What can you do to build that confidence?

Consider, too, whether your pastor needs a sabbatical. Many pastors need extended time away, to renew their relationship with God, to learn new skills, to refresh their vision and their enthusiasm. A recent survey of Presbyterian clergy, for example, found that while a minority of the pastors responding had ever taken a sabbatical, the majority of those who had were funded by their congregations. Most of these pastors also reported improvements to their emotional, spiritual, and physical health, as well as to the performance of their ministerial duties.[30]

Similarly, give your pastor time away for learning and ministry development. Conferences and other forms of continuing education will

---

30. Research Services, PCUSA, "Findings." Of the 725 pastors responding, only 22 percent had ever taken a sabbatical. The vast majority of pastors who took sabbaticals reported them to be "helpful" or "very helpful" to their emotional health (91 percent), as well as their spiritual (89 percent), and physical health (77 percent). In addition, 79 percent said their sabbatical led to "improvement in their ministerial duties."

not only stretch your pastor's thinking, it will provide much needed time away from the pressures of day-to-day ministry. Your pastor will come back refreshed and energized. Don't think of professional development as a bonus; make room in the budget. It's vital to the health of your pastor and to your congregation.

Overall, be attentive to signs of burnout (chapter 2). Pushing worn-out pastors to continue to perform does no one any good. Even if your pastor is not burning out, make sabbatical leave part of your regular plan. To do this, you'll need to make sure that you have a strong team of con-gregational leaders who, with the pastor, share a common vision and com-municate and work well together.

To Seminarians:

We know: graduate school isn't the most conducive environment for developing a Sabbath heart. Your professors expect a lot of you, some-times more than you think you can give. You expect a lot of yourself. The environment is often competitive. Some students feel forced to desperate measures just to keep up. Saying that you need to honor a Sabbath day may sound like just one more requirement to squeeze into a crowded schedule. After all, don't you need Sunday to catch up on all that assigned reading?

But here's the thing: spiritual formation won't wait until later. You're being formed now, perhaps even *de*formed, by a graduate subculture of endless busyness. We've spoken with so many seminary students over the years who entered their studies full of hope and enthusiasm. They were looking forward to learning from some of the best biblical scholars, theo-logians, and ministry experts on the planet. Many managed to hang on to that early eagerness throughout their seminary careers.

And many didn't. The critical academic mindset and just plain busy-ness made theological study an end in itself rather than a means to God, who got pushed further and further to the margins.

We suspect that the difference lies in personal habits of spiritual dis-cipline, habits that simply cannot be taken for granted. It doesn't work to wait for the busyness to pass, to wait until after you get your diploma to settle up with God—especially if you're going to be thrust into full-time ministry. If anything, when that happens, you'll need the habit of a Sab-bath rhythm even more.

Whatever it takes, think carefully and creatively about your weekly schedule, and your personal and spiritual goals. Sabbath is a gift to you from God—take it. Make the time to cherish it. Develop the discipline now, so that it becomes your natural rhythm, then let that be part of your conversation when you are interviewed for a ministry position. In that way, you will carry in your person the vision of freedom you would wish for the all the members of the congregations you serve.

Once you're out of school, you might relish the thought of no books, papers, or lectures for a while! We understand. Just remember that learning doesn't end once you get your degree. Indeed, full-time ministry is apt to make you keenly aware of all the things you didn't learn in seminary! So be a lifelong learner. Look for relevant conferences and workshops to attend. Ask around to find out what other pastors have found helpful. Get in the habit of reading good books that will stretch your thinking and bring some holy disturbance into your life. Spend time with other thoughtful people, whether pastors or lay people, to discuss current books—theology, non-fiction, novels. This will help stir your ministry imagination and keep it fresh.

6

Take Care of the Body God Gave You

A minister of the gospel must understand the serious necessity of caring for oneself in a manner that promotes health and longevity. . . . Most clergy are caretakers of others . . . but rarely are they good caretakers of self.

—GARY KINNAMAN AND ALFRED ELLS[1]

We need to restore the value and sacred respect we have lost for our bodies.

—ALFRED HELLER[2]

AS WE WRITE THIS, the Christmas shopping season is upon us, and people's thoughts turn toward the holidays. Ask around in any congregation, and you'll find a wide assortment of family traditions associated with Christmas. Is there a big celebration with lots of relatives, or a quiet day with only the immediate family? Is the celebration on Christmas Eve or Christmas Day? If the family has a Christmas tree, is it real or artificial? If it must be a real tree, what kind? Break one or more of these traditions in a family, and someone is likely to say, "It just didn't feel like Christmas."

Congregations have their traditions too. Is there a Christmas Eve service? A pageant or children's program featuring pint-sized shepherds and wise men? Does the church reach out to the poor and disenfranchised of the community? Or even to those church members who are expecting

1. Kinnaman and Ells, *Leaders that Last*, 34.
2. Heller, *Your Body, His Temple*, 27–28.

to be alone for the holidays? A congregation's habitual practice around such questions will become its local tradition, and the tradition becomes expectation. Behind such traditions, however, is a more important question. What is the shared understanding of why Christmas is celebrated in the first place?

The easy answer, of course, is that Christmas is the celebration of the birth of Christ. Seasonal adornments from crèches to Christmas cards tend to idealize the scene. Baby Jesus is adorable, Mary is gorgeous, the shepherds are clean, and the animals are cute.

But this isn't reality. The situation of Jesus' birth was scandalously difficult, humble in the earthiest possible sense. We need to understand that, or we may miss the miracle. We need first to embrace the lowliness of the event, so that we can better appreciate the deep, mysterious event of God with us in the flesh.

Christmas, in other words, is about the *incarnation*. At Christmas, we are reminded to celebrate that God sent his Son to die for us—and rightly so. But Christmas means more than just the necessary prelude to Good Friday and Easter. We must celebrate that Jesus came not only to die for us, but to *live* for us, to live as one of us. The fact that God walked among us in a mortal body gives our own bodily existence both value and dignity.

There's no denying that in a sin-stained world, life in these bodies of ours can be a real pain, sometimes literally. But our physical existence is not some unfortunate accident; it is God's intention for us, a creative act that he himself pronounced as good (Gen 1:26–31). Jesus came to liberate us from being slaves to bodily sin (Rom 6:11–19), but not from bodily existence itself. His life on earth modeled what God had in mind for us all along. And in his resurrected state, he gave us a glimpse of our own future—one that is both glorious and bodily at the same time.

The point is that we need to live in ways that honor and respect the fact that by God's good design we are creatures of flesh and blood and bone. This is a particularly important message for pastors, who give so much of their energy to working with the souls and spirits of others that they give less attention to their own. Caring for their *bodies* may come way down the list of priorities, being considered of even lesser spiritual importance. But given the evidence of health concerns among pastors, it would behoove both clergy and congregations to rethink this. It should be part of our calling to be good stewards of the bodies God has given us.

Life in the Body

In 1986, Bill Cosby delighted his audience with a live performance on the perils of being forty-nine.[3] He recalled being an athletically fit teenager, playing football. He could run tirelessly, and eat like a horse while keeping a flat stomach. He would look at his overweight father, never imagining that the older man once had an athletic physique. But having reached the ripe old age of forty-nine, Cosby lamented he could no longer run without pain and no longer eat the way he wanted without accumulating a gut. And it meant starting to make the same grunting noises his father would make while getting into and out of a chair.

Ah, life in these sometimes broken-down bodies. Humorists find a mother lode of material in our dissatisfaction with our bodies, from pimples to gimpy knees to unruly hair. Paul Reiser quips that the first big mistake most of us make each day is looking in the mirror: "It's always a disappointment, no matter who you are. . . . Nobody looks in the mirror and goes, 'That's about right.'"[4] And in a culture endlessly obsessed with physical appearances, we look for ways to fix what we see. Books that tell us how to reshape our bodies routinely top the bestseller lists.[5] And over twelve million cosmetic plastic surgeries were performed in the U.S. in 2009. That includes almost a billion dollars worth of Botox injections.[6]

But appearance is not the point here; health is. We're not advocating that pastors should look like they just stepped out of the pages of a fitness or fashion magazine. Whatever our concerns about the way we look, it's wise to pay attention to our health. It's easy when we're young and comparatively fit to take our bodies for granted, eating whatever we want and going without sleep. Our bodies, however, won't let us do this forever. Not without a fight.

This is a theological issue; though it's not usually recognized as such. *Docetism* is the name of the ancient heresy that denied the physical reality of Jesus' bodily existence. An important part of Gnostic belief, it was denounced by the early church centuries ago. But as pastor Pete Scazzero has suggested, a more contemporary version of the heresy may still be with us: the refusal to acknowledge the reality of our own bodily existence. As suggested in chapter 5, this may take the form of ignoring our need for rest,

3. Cosby, *Bill Cosby*, 49.

4. Reiser, *Couplehood*, 158–59.

5. At the time of writing this sentence, the #1 and #3 top selling books at Amazon were about weight loss.

6. American Society of Plastic Surgeons, "Plastic Surgery Statistics."

and pastors may be among the worst offenders. Scazzero writes, "While I did not intellectually believe such an unbiblical notion, my life in God did not back up what I professed. I ignored my human limits and ran myself ragged to do more and more for God."[7]

The incarnation was not an accident, and neither is our existence as creatures of flesh and blood. There is no "Oops!" in the story of God's creation handiwork; instead, "God saw all that he had made, and it was very good" (Gen 1:31). Think about it: if God has declared his creation good, and given us dominion over it (Gen 1:28), does it make sense to think that God would be pleased if we neglected to care properly for our bodies?

It's true that living in a fallen world complicates matters. We do not yet possess the kind of resurrection body envisioned by Paul (e.g., 1 Cor 15:35–58)[8] and demonstrated by Jesus. Life in the body can be difficult; as Paul put it, we "groan inwardly as we wait eagerly for our adoption, the redemption of our bodies" (Rom 8:23, TNIV). But we have the Spirit. We don't groan as people who have no hope. God is in the midst of a grand restoration project, and we should do all we can to cooperate. And that means, in part, that we should treat our bodies in a way that points toward that eagerly anticipated future.

God has made us to be wondrous creatures. But as Rodney Clapp has suggested, the fallenness of this present world means that we are "tortured" wonders:

> The body as we now know it is weak: yes. The body is perishable: yes. It is corruptible and will rot: oh, yes. As such it can be a lot of trouble and bring disappointment: yes, again. Christian spirituality affirms all these possibilities as realities, but even more vigorously it refuses to give up on the body. . . . So we embodied souls, ensouled bodies, are wonders. But we are until the resurrection *tortured* wonders. We live in between, in and as bodies that before the resurrection can only slightly anticipate their full and grace-ripened spiritual capacities.[9]

Ideally, living in a way that actively looks forward to resurrection should encourage us into joyous stewardship. But it's not clear that even pastors think that way, to judge by the way some care for their health. As one male pastor posted on his blog:

7. Scazzero, *Emotionally Healthy Church*, 53.

8. Some interpret the idea of a "spiritual" body (v. 44) as meaning a "non-corporeal," but commentators generally agree that Paul's meaning is a physical body suited to the reality of a new age.

9. Clapp, *Tortured Wonders*, 47.

> Pastors think about their bodies and the earth in much the same way: they have expiration dates on them and God will one day make them new. But this type of fatalistic thinking omits a key feature: God gave us our bodies (and the earth) for us to be stewards over. If we are treating our bodies like people (allegedly) treat their rental cars then we have a stewardship issue.[10]

Do we have a moral obligation to treat rental cars with care and respect? If so, then what about the bodies God has given us? Our point is that self-care should be seen as a matter of stewardship, a mark of respect for God's good creation. As Lloyd Rediger has written to pastors: "Fitness is good stewardship. . . . You are the only person to whom God has entrusted the stewardship of your body."[11]

But the very mention of the idea of "self-care" raises the hackles of some ministers, as if it meant abandoning a heart of sacrificial ministry for narcissism and laziness.[12] To be sure, the temptations to self-preoccupation are everywhere. And there may well be harried pastors who use "self-care" as a defensive rallying cry, pushing congregations away and saying, "No more!" But we believe this is rarely the case. If anything, pastors know the sacrifices of ministry all too well, and find it difficult to assert or even recognize what they need. Overworked and overstressed, they are frequently candidates for burnout (see chapter 2).

All of this can be understood as a practical extension of a theology of Sabbath, as introduced in the last chapter. Jesus himself embraced a rhythm of work and rest. And we must always remember that our ministry is first and foremost God's ministry. Pastors can save neither the church nor the world—that's God's job, a glorious work in which we are privileged by grace to participate. In that attitude, pastors can find the freedom to engage in appropriate self-care, and congregations can be encouraged to help.

How Are Pastors Doing Physically?

We know that physicians keep records on their patients. But have you ever wondered how your family physician might describe your case? What

---

10. Raymond, "So Why Are Pastors Fat?"

11. Rediger, *Fit to Be a Pastor*, 69. For Rediger, "fitness" is an all-inclusive concept with physical, mental, and spiritual dimensions.

12. Oswald, *Clergy Self-Care*, 4.

would stand out if he or she were to summarize your physical condition to someone else? Imagine the following description:

> A 51-year-old male with symptoms of depression, the patient has high blood pressure and is overweight, presenting a heightened risk of heart disease and other illnesses. He works 60–70 hours a week in a sedentary job, does not currently engage in any physical exercise, and reports considerable work-related stress. Patient is married, with three children, one of whom expresses interest in following patient's career path. Patient expresses little enthusiasm for encouraging child to do so.[13]

This is physician Gwen Halaas's fictional composite of an average American pastor, as seen through a doctor's eyes. As the Director of Ministerial Health and Wellness for the Evangelical Lutheran Church of America, and a pastor's wife, she knows what she's talking about. Halaas is concerned not only for the well-being of pastors, but the congregations they serve. She writes:

> The fact that many of the church's leaders are overweight, inactive, depressed, and at increasing risk for heart disease and diabetes is a real concern. Taken in a context of a church in a time of declining membership, smaller and fewer congregations, older age at ordination than previously, and decreasing numbers preparing to serve congregations, this is an urgent situation.[14]

Her concerns may be based on ELCA statistics, but the larger point still holds: if pastors are not doing well physically, this is ultimately a problem for the church.

Even the popular press is beginning to notice. "Clergy sometimes neglect their own needs while helping others," declares the title of one recent news article.[15] No surprise there. But other articles cite specific health concerns uncovered by recent research. In 2010, for example, the *Los Angeles Times* reported on a large study by researchers at Duke University that captured health information from 95 percent of the United Methodist clergy in North Carolina, a sample of 1,726 male and female pastors.[16] To allow clergy to be compared to other people in the state, the researchers used the same questions asked each year by the Centers for Disease Con-

13. Cited in Wells, "Which Way to Clergy Health?"

14. Halaas, *Right Road*, 3–4.

15. David Olson, "Clergy."

16. Stein, "Some Clergy." A more complete report by the Duke research team can be found in Proeschold-Bell and LeGrand, "High Rates of Obesity."

trol and Prevention. The good news: the percentage of clergy who could be classified as "overweight" was about 5 percentage points lower than in the North Carolina population as a whole. The bad news: the *obesity* rates were 10–14 percentage points *higher*, such that only 21 percent of pastors were of normal weight. Clergy were also more likely to have been diagnosed with diabetes, arthritis, high blood pressure, and asthma. Among male clergy of the ages 35–44, 6 percent reported having had a heart attack at some time. That may not seem like much—until you realize that the figure for North Carolinian men of the same age was 1.5 percent.

Similar results were reported online in a 2003 study of 568 active senior pastors from across the U.S.[17] The sample had representatives of a variety of church sizes and Protestant denominations. A full 71 percent of the pastors surveyed judged themselves to be overweight, by an average of 32 pounds. Over a fifth of the pastors reported being overweight by 50 pounds or more. Why? Dietary habits may be one reason. Over half of the pastors reported eating fast food once or twice a week; a third ate fast food 3 or more times a week. Similarly, 41 percent reported that they knowingly ate unhealthy food at least 3 times a week.

Perhaps age is the culprit? We know that it's harder to stay fit and keep the weight off as we get older. But that doesn't seem to be what's happening here. As the president of the research firm that conducted the study noted,

> The youngest ministers are the heaviest, the most likely to skip meals, the most likely to eat unhealthy foods, the least likely to get exercise, the most likely to go without sufficient sleep, the least likely to take vitamins, the most likely to eat fast food, and the most likely to report problems sleeping. . . . It might be argued that these are eager young ministers out trying to change the world, or at least to build their careers. But it's tragic that they apparently are sacrificing their own health for these purposes.[18]

This is consistent with the idea that it's easier to take our bodies for granted when we're younger, to not have that kind of stewardship on the radar. Eventually, however, the bill for that kind of neglect will come due. Thus, as the *New York Times* recently reported,

> The findings have surfaced with ominous regularity over the last few years, and with little notice: Members of the clergy now suffer from obesity, hypertension and depression at rates higher

17. Ellison Research, "Just How Healthy?"
18. Sellers, quoted in Ellison Research, "Just How Healthy?"

than most Americans. In the last decade, their use of antidepressants has risen, while their life expectancy has fallen.[19]

What then? We're not trying to sell you on some kind of Christian diet or exercise program. Our point is that there are not only practical but also theological reasons why Christians should care for their physical health. If Sabbath rest is part of the good order of God's creation, then we shouldn't be surprised that overwork comes at a price. For pastors, this kind of stewardship takes on added significance, given their role as examples to the flock. Like it or not, when pastors preach self-discipline from the pulpit, people will filter that message (right or wrong!) through their perceptions of the pastor's own lifestyle.

This chapter, therefore, will briefly present information that we hope will be helpful in making good stewardship choices in three key areas of health: sleep, diet, and exercise. Volumes upon volumes have been written on these subjects, and we are not the experts—so please consult the resources in the notes, and make sure to talk to your doctor about any concerns this chapter may raise. Our modest goal is not to give you all the answers, but to motivate you to take these areas of self-care seriously.

Truth be told, much of what we say in this chapter may make us sound like your mother ("Go put on a sweater—I'm cold"). But frankly, Mom was probably right more often than we were willing to admit. Following up on the idea of Sabbath rest, then, we begin with the topic of sleep.

The Blessing of a Good Night's Sleep

In the Bible, restful sleep is a potent symbol of the peace of God's providential protection. The psalmist, for example, prays for deliverance from his distress, and in faith envisions God's answer: "In peace I will lie down and sleep, for you alone, LORD, make me dwell in safety" (Ps 4:8). Similar images of peace are found in the prophets (e.g., Ezek 34:25), where the ability to sleep in safety is a sign of God's covenant faithfulness to his people. It is also the symbol of a life in harmony with God's wisdom:

> My son, do not let wisdom and understanding out of your sight, preserve sound judgment and discretion; they will be life for you, an ornament to grace your neck. Then you will go on your way in safety, and your foot will not stumble. When you lie

19. Vitello, "Taking a Break."

down, you will not be afraid; when you lie down, your sleep will
be sweet. (Prov 3:21–24)

The writer of Ecclesiastes goes further, suggesting that those who obsess
over their earthly treasures can never rest:

> Whoever loves money never has enough; whoever loves wealth
> is never satisfied with their income. . . . The sleep of a laborer is
> sweet, whether they eat little or much, but as for the rich, their
> abundance permits them no sleep. (Eccl 5:10–12)

It would be exaggerating to call this "the biblical basis for getting a good
night's sleep." But we believe that just as Sabbath rest is part of God's design, so too is restful sleep.

So how well do pastors sleep? In the 2003 study cited earlier, 87 percent of pastors reported getting less sleep than they needed at least one
night a week. A striking 63 percent of pastors under the age of 45 said
this happened 3 or more times a week, compared to 41 percent of pastors
aged 45 to 59, and 27 percent of pastors over 60. Over half of pastors also
reported having trouble sleeping at least once a week. Over a third of pastors reported getting fewer than 7 hours of sleep each night; the overall
average was 6.8 hours.[20]

Those numbers have to be taken with a grain of salt. Ask people how
much sleep they're getting, and they'll probably give you an estimate of
how long they were in bed. But what matters, health-wise, is actual sleep
(especially deep sleep); the hours spent lying in bed awake don't count.
Experts believe that most people need at least 7.5–8 hours daily, and that
it's possible to accumulate a "sleep debt," such that the more sleep you lose,
the more you need.[21] There's a good chance, therefore, that many pastors
are chronically sleep-deprived, as are many of their congregants.[22]

If one has good sleep habits overall, the occasional late night won't
be a problem; the sleep debt will usually be repaid quickly. But a chronic
lack of sleep is associated with numerous health problems, from head-
aches and stomach ailments to diabetes, heart disease, and obesity.[23] And

---

20. Ellison Research, "Just How Healthy?"

21. Epstein and Mardon, *Good Night's Sleep*, 5.

22. A nationwide telephone poll of 1,000 respondents, estimates that the average
American sleeps less than 7 hours on weeknights, and just over 7 on the weekends.
National Sleep Foundation, "2009 Sleep in America Poll."

23. Epstein and Mardon, *Good Night's Sleep*, 5.

some therapists believe that people who are diagnosed with some form of mental illness may actually be suffering from sleep deprivation instead.[24]

If you think you may be suffering from not enough sleep, you may benefit from a full assessment at a sleep clinic, where potential problems like sleep apnea can be diagnosed.[25] Meanwhile, it may help to begin working on developing good sleep-promoting habits.[26] Here, for example, is a set of four simple guidelines from the National Sleep Foundation:[27]

- Try to have a standard relaxing bedtime routine and keep regular sleep times. Make sure your bedroom is dark, cool, and quiet and that your pillows, sleep surface, and coverings provide you with comfort.

- Exercise regularly, but finish your workout at least three hours before bedtime.

- Avoid foods and drinks high in caffeine (coffee, colas, and tea) for at least eight hours prior to bedtime, and avoid alcohol for a few hours before bedtime. Caffeine and alcohol disturb sleep.[28]

- Use your bedroom only for sleep and sex; if you do this, you will strengthen the association between bed and sleep. It is best to remove work materials, computers, and televisions from the sleep environment.

In other words, don't take a good night's sleep for granted; eliminate the habits that discourage it (e.g., don't read in bed), and build habits that encourage it (e.g., have a consistent and calming bedtime routine).

Insomnia appears to be a widespread problem. As the National Sleep Foundation reported in 2009, "Two out of every ten Americans sleep less than six hours a night . . . and nearly 90 percent report symptoms of insomnia at least a few nights a week in the past month."[29] What kept

24. E.g., Krakow, *Sound Sleep*.

25. Visit the National Sleep Foundation website at www.sleepfoundation.org to find a sleep specialist in your area.

26. See, e.g., Hart, *Sleep*; and Epstein and Mardon, *Good Night's Sleep*.

27. National Sleep Foundation, "One-Third of Americans."

28. Caffeine is a stimulant that creates something like a mild stress reaction in the body. Though individual effects vary, the half-life of caffeine is estimated to be about six hours; that means that six hours after you drink a cup of coffee, half its caffeine is still in your system.

Alcohol has a sedative effect at first, but later interferes with much-needed deeper stages of sleep; the problem worsens with continued alcohol use. National Institute on Alcohol Abuse and Alcoholism, *Alcohol Alert*.

29. National Sleep Foundation, "One-Third of Americans."

people awake at night? The most commonly cited worries had to do with the economy and personal finances, health, employment, and personal relationships[30]—in other words, the same concerns that many pastors have!

Sleep comes in cycles, and it's normal to wake up for a few minutes between them. But perhaps you're a worrier, a thinker. Sometimes, when you awaken, a thought will occur to you: something left undone during the day, something that needs to be done tomorrow. Suddenly you're wide awake. You look at the clock to see what time it is, then put your head back down and try to *will* yourself back to sleep. Needless to say, it doesn't work.

Sound familiar? Again, you may need to develop new habits. Sleep specialist Barry Krakow, for example, recommends that chronic clock watchers turn the clock toward the wall and let go of any attempts to figure out anything related to time, such as, *"What time is it? How much sleep did I get? How much can I still squeeze in before I have to get up?"*[31] Interestingly, Krakow also discusses this "time monitoring" behavior in the context of a larger sleep-robbing problem: at some level, *we don't want to sleep*, because unfinished business leaves us feeling that the day isn't really done yet.[32]

This brings us back again to the cultivation of a heart shaped by the rhythms of the Sabbath. As we've said before, the work of ministry itself is never really done. The peaceful sleep of Proverbs and the Psalms may require placing all the unfinished work of the day into the hands of the God who works even as we sleep. Pastors in particular might benefit from the practice of the *daily examen,* prayerfully reviewing the day, giving thanks where appropriate, and releasing their cares to God. As Paul exhorted the Philippians,

> Do not be anxious about anything, but in every situation, by prayer and petition, with thanksgiving, present your requests to God. And the peace of God, which transcends all understanding, will guard your hearts and your minds in Christ Jesus. (Phil 4:6–7)

Arch Hart specifically recommends that we end each day by prayerfully fostering gratitude, letting go of grudges, and focusing on God.[33] This is an excellent way to put Paul's words into practice as we anticipate a peaceful night's rest. Sleep on it!

30. National Sleep Foundation, "2009 Sleep in America," 17.

31. Krakow, *Sound Sleep*, 81.

32. Ibid., 72. He recommends his own strategies to achieve a sense of closure.

33. Hart, *Sleep*, 212–16.

Watch What You Put in Your Body

We've already seen some of the evidence suggesting that clergy don't have the best eating habits in the world, and that a variety of health problems may be the result. But again, we have no intention of promoting some kind of special "pastors' diet." Americans are already bombarded with a fusillade of diet advice, and this isn't simply about weight loss. The issue is stewardship, which applies to all pastors and persons regardless of weight. And we believe stewardship includes paying closer attention to what we put into our bodies—and then doing something about it.

How many of us say to ourselves, "I *know* I shouldn't eat this, but . . ."? (We warned you we were going to sound like your mother.) We pick up a donut and upbraid ourselves for a moment, almost as an assurance that we do, in fact, know better. But the moment is gone—and so is the donut!

So rather than try to tell you specifically what to eat, we present three principles of dietary stewardship and their implications. First, be intentional; change has to begin with your own personal commitment. Second, be informed; don't just settle for the hype—get the facts. And finally, recruit the help of others. Pastors and congregations can help each other, if they're willing to take together the courageous step of looking at what we eat as a spiritual issue.

Be Intentional

You may know some people who treat food as little more than fuel. They eat because they have to, without fanfare. For the rest of us, food may have a host of emotional associations. We have comfort foods that we eat when we're down; we have treats that we eat to reward ourselves. We celebrate with food, whether it's feasting with family, going out to eat with friends, or fellowshipping at a church potluck. Even Jesus, it seemed, enjoyed a good meal, so much so that his opponents considered him "a glutton and a drunkard" (Matt 11:19).[34]

Add to this a whole food industry that wants your money. Fast food franchises play on the adult sense of being too busy to cook, lure children with toys, and ply us with commercial images that suggest instant family happiness.[35] Convenience stores make it, well, *convenient* to pick up your

34. Though the greater objection was not what or how he ate, but with whom: the tax collectors and those they considered sinners.

35. E.g., Schlosser, *Fast Food Nation*.

favorite junk food while taking care of essentials like putting gas in your car. All this and other elements of American culture mean that eating in a consistently health-conscious way takes real *commitment*. It's much easier to develop bad habits than good ones.

For pastors, moreover, poor eating habits may be something of an occupational hazard. A busy schedule, particularly one involving visitation, may mean more eating out and eating on the run. Gwen Halaas cites one statistic estimating that "American restaurants serve on average 3,800 calories of food per person per day"—twice the recommended amount.[36] And what gets served to pastors who visit? If people bring gifts of food to the pastor to say thank you, what kind of food do they bring? We bet it's not carrot sticks.

It takes disciplined, prayerful intentionality to swim against the prevailing tide. This isn't some kind of dietary legalism, but the sober recognition that choices have consequences, and that our environment and habits conspire to make good choices more difficult. The good news is that once we start developing healthier habits, many of the choices become easier. But diligent commitment will always be needed.

Be Informed

If the first point is that we need to be more intentional about our food choices, the second is that our choices need to be well informed. There's a lot of market-driven dietary misinformation floating around out there, and ultimately, good stewardship involves at least an honest attempt to sort fact from fiction.

Let's start with this: be wary of the health claims splashed all over the boxes of manufactured foods. Remember, the food industry's number one goal is to turn a profit, not to make you healthy. They do what sells, and if the latest health craze helps them do that, so much the better for their profit margin.

In general, here's how it works. Researchers at a prestigious university discover some nutritional benefits to foods containing compound X. They publish their findings in a medical journal, appropriately saying that their conclusions are tentative, and that much more research is needed. But once the wire services get wind of the story, the race is on. Compound X becomes the next nutritional magic bullet. There isn't a shred of evidence showing that adding compound X artificially to food does anyone

36. Halaas, *Right Road*, 17.

any good, but it starts showing up in everything from supplements to potato chips. And we, who know that potato chips aren't health food, might actually start to think, "Hey, these chips are 'rich in Compound X'! They're actually *good* for me!" Wishful thinking. So widespread is this market strategy that one nutrition writer recommends that if you see a health claim on a product, that's enough reason *not* to buy it.[37] Being informed, then, includes being skeptical about trendy nutritional claims, especially those that seem market driven. *Caveat emptor!*

A related recommendation is this: don't take it for granted that the commonplace nutritional wisdom is true. It was once taken for granted that the vegetable-based unsaturated fat in margarine was a far healthier choice than the saturated fat in butter. But that was before scientists discovered the trans-fats in margarine that are so widely condemned today. And it's not simply a matter of waiting for some intrepid researcher to discover something we don't already know: much nutritional advice actually contradicts or ignores the science that is already available.[38]

In short, be skeptical of magic bullets, and don't assume that the prevailing wisdom is correct, as obvious as that wisdom might seem. Ask questions; seek out the science; get the facts. Make informed choices.

Recruit the Help of Others

As we've already suggested, part of what makes healthy eating difficult is that food is often at the center of social events. You get together to celebrate—and that often means eating large quantities of things that may not be good for you. Or, if you're assigned to bring food to an event, you probably want to bring something "special," which usually means sweet, rich, or both. Church socials and potlucks are no exception.

If you're serious about the stewardship of your body, at some point you will have to let others know. Pastors, someone put a lot of care into making that cheesecake, and they would be honored if you would have a nice big slice and rave about how wonderful it is (just don't describe it as "sinfully" rich)! It can be awkward to refuse—but a little less so if it's already known that you're being intentional about your health.

As we'll see in the next chapter, sometimes pastors need to ask for help from their congregations. Modeling a commitment to physical health in this way can also lay the foundation for others to embrace wellness. As

37. Pollan, *Defense*, 154–57.
38. E.g., Pollan, *Defense*; Taubes, *Why We Get Fat*.

one news release recently reported, "the number of health and wellness programs at church—from softball teams to diabetes screenings—often depends on the health habits of the man or woman at the pulpit."[39] In a study of pastors from across the U.S., researchers found that churches with some kind of health program were more likely to be led by pastors with better diets and less fatalistic attitudes about health, especially if the pastors had received health and wellness instruction as part of their training. Another important factor was denominational support: "If health as a priority comes down from the main organization, it can trickle down into the individual churches."[40] If physical health is important to the life of a congregation, and its ministry to the community, the pastor's own public commitment to self-care will be an important part of that picture.

So let people know what you're trying to do. Find yourself a trustworthy accountability partner. Encourage others to make intentional and informed choices about food themselves. Don't take this journey alone.

Getting the Exercise We Need

Much of what pastors (and seminary professors!) do is essentially sedentary: we sit for long hours reading, studying, or writing. When my (Cameron's) son was quite young, a friend asked him, "So what does your daddy do for a living?" Thinking about all the times he'd seen me planted in my recliner with a book, he confidently replied, "Nothing."

Our bodies need exercise, and we know it. Again, this is not about our appearance, but our health. The benefits of regular exercise are well documented, and include lowered risk of heart disease, stroke, high blood pressure, diabetes, metabolic syndrome, and certain types of cancer.[41] For older adults, strengthening and toning muscles can improve our balance and help prevent falls. And being more physically fit through exercise may even help ease our body's response to psychological stressors.[42] Do we need more reasons than that?

There are two kinds of exercise to consider: those that help you become aerobically fit, and those that strengthen your muscles. Most of the health benefits cited are the product of regular aerobic exercise: the kind that gets your heart pumping and can make you short of breath. Examples

39. Barcomb-Peterson, "Healthier Pastors."
40. Melissa Bopp, quoted in Barcomb-Peterson, "Healthier Pastors."
41. E.g., Centers for Disease Control and Prevention (CDC), "Fact Sheet."
42. Sapolsky, *Zebras*, 401.

include walking and jogging, riding a bike, sports like tennis and swimming, dancing, and even gardening. Federal activity guidelines define "moderate intensity" aerobics as that which still allows you to talk during the exercise, but not sing; "vigorous" means "you can't say more than a few words without pausing for a breath."[43] For optimum health benefits, they recommend 150 minutes of moderate aerobic exercise weekly, done in stretches of at least 10 minutes, and spread throughout the week. Vigorous aerobics counts double, dropping the overall requirement to 75 minutes a week. Some combination of moderate and vigorous exercise is also fine.

Muscle-strengthening exercises include weightlifting, the use of elastic resistance bands, and exercises like push-ups and sit-ups. The federal guidelines cited above recommend doing this kind of exercise at least twice a week, and working all the major muscle groups: arms and shoulders; hips and legs; back, abdomen, and chest. Many people go to health clubs for this purpose. But please be careful; if you're new to the equipment, it's easy to injure yourself by using it improperly! If you can afford it, get at least a few sessions with a trainer before diving into a new health club routine. Proper warm-up and stretching both before and after working your muscles can help prevent injury.[44] And as always, consult with your doctor first.

For sedentary folks, the thought of a regular exercise program can sound intimidating. Busy pastors may think, "Where am I supposed to find the time to do all this?" But the first question should be, "Does God really want me to be a better steward of my body, and if so, is regular exercise part of that stewardship?" We hope you're able to say yes to both questions.

But let's keep it realistic. We're not talking about going from couch potato to Olympic decathlete. You don't have to be a gym rat, pump iron by the ton, or train for a marathon. If you've fallen into a sedentary lifestyle, start simply by finding creative ways to get yourself moving more. Here, for example, are some simple ideas adapted from a list of suggestions by Gwen Halaas:

- Walk, jog, or bicycle, to work, school, the store, or church, instead of driving.

43. CDC, "Fact Sheet."

44. Rediger includes sample stretching exercises in *Fit to Be a Pastor*, 90–91, 170–72.

- Park the car farther away from your destination, or get off the bus one stop early.

- Take the stairs instead of the elevator or escalator.

- Walk the dog or play with the kids.

- Take mini-fitness breaks (e.g., go for a brisk walk) instead of coffee breaks.

- Take up gardening; do some fix-it jobs around the house.

- Exercise while watching TV.[45]

You can come up with your own ideas. The point is that health—and exercise!—is not an all-or-nothing affair. It needs to be a long-term lifestyle commitment, and that commitment may need to be built in stages. You need to find something that you will do, and will *keep doing*.[46] Covenanting with an exercise partner is a great way to stay motivated.

And as we suggested above in our discussion of making wise food choices, that motivation may benefit by going public. Here's one bold pastor's story:

> Three years ago . . . I was feeling fat and old. I was at a place where I was either going to just give in and not concern myself about it anymore or make a significant change. While preaching one Sunday morning on discipline, I looked at one of the men in my congregation who was a gymnast who talked often about physical conditioning. And before the whole congregation I said, "When I get back from India I want you to help me get into better shape."[47]

It worked for him, and he is now a dedicated fitness buff. Of course, that doesn't mean that every pastor needs to make an announcement during the Sunday service! But this is one way to get the help we need to stick with our intentions. You may think of others.

As Richard Swenson has written: "God gave us an amazing gift, and all we are required to do is feed it, water it, rest it, and move it."[48] May the church be a place where the gift is celebrated, and may we all learn to honor the bodies God gave us by taking wise care of them.

---

45. Halaas, *Right Road*, 15.

46. Department of Health and Human Services, "Be Active Your Way."

47. Berry, "One Pastor's Story."

48. Swenson, *Margin*, 108.

Postscript

To Pastors:

How important is your physical health to you? We mean *concretely*: what does your *lifestyle* say about your answer to the question? We understand the pressure of ministry, the demands you have to balance. And we know some pastors will push and push themselves until they drop. They never experience Sabbath rest. They sacrifice sleep, or allow their sleep to be interrupted. Physically exhausted, they retreat to their studies. Emotionally exhausted, they retreat from activity. They jump-start themselves with caffeine and sugar.

If this is you, please understand that we're not trying to add to your load of guilt. Quite the contrary: we hope that you will embrace the kind of Sabbath-like attitude that will give you the freedom to take care of yourself. Roy Oswald, for example, has said that "total health involves embracing our brokenness. Wholeness should never be seen as perfection, but rather an acknowledgment and acceptance of weakness."[49] It's both appropriate and necessary to embrace the limits that go with our bodily existence, and we'll expand on that idea in the next chapter. But we'd like to go Oswald one better—to recognize the bodies that we've been given as wondrous gifts of creation that need proper care.

We're not just talking about adding things to your already busy schedule. Self-care begins with developing new habits, with changing the way you do what you already do. How do you prepare for sleep, and guard those precious nighttime hours? What kind of food is sitting around your office, and what gets brought to meetings? How can you incorporate more movement into the routines you already have?

Start there and build outward. And again, if possible, don't go it alone. If you have one, talk to your staff about how to partner together for the sake of health. Enlist the expertise of relevant professionals in the congregation and in the community; hospitals often have health advocates who would be happy to help educate the flock. Above all, help the congregation understand self-care as an important part of every Christian's stewardship, and be a good role model yourself.

49. Oswald, *Clergy Self-Care*, 19.

To Congregations:

We hope you value not only your own physical health, but your pastor's! Even if your pastor doesn't *look* like he or she needs help in this area, there may be congregational habits that make the commitment to health more challenging. There are simple things you can do to be on the more encouraging side.

For example, just like everyone else, pastors need their sleep. Unlike most others, however, they're more likely to have that sleep interrupted by others. So don't call them in the late evening or in the middle of the night unless it *really* is an emergency! You may be worried about something and feel the urge to discuss it with your pastor at 3 a.m. But not only are you interrupting their sleep, you may be transferring your worries to them. So be considerate: even if you have to lose a little sleep yourself, if the matter can wait until office hours, let it wait.

Think about the "food culture" of your congregation. What role does food play in the social life of your church? Are people made fun of for trying to change their diet? We've seen it happen: at a men's breakfast, one intrepid soul was mercilessly teased just for asking if there was any decaffeinated coffee. Does this make it easier or harder for people, including your pastor, to make healthy choices? While we're not saying that the church potluck has to go, neither does it have to be a competition to see who can make the most popular dessert! Yes, it's hard to have such conversations when health choices are considered to be private matters. But unless such conversations can at least be started, it'll be an uphill climb for those in your midst who really want to be good stewards of their bodies.

Similar questions can be asked about exercise. The congregation needs to be a place where people of all levels of fitness can be encouraged toward better stewardship, without being shamed. Consider your pastor's health needs. Can you provide for a membership in a local health club, without taking it out of the pastor's compensation? Can you include some sessions with a personal trainer? How else can you support your pastor's commitment to exercise regularly?

If you're a health professional, talk with your pastor about possible initiatives your church might engage in for the wellness of the congregation and the larger community. Just remember: this mustn't become simply one more thing for the *pastor* to do; take responsibility for how you can bring your own gifts and expertise to any proposed ministry. Remember too that local hospitals often have staff who are happy to do health education. This can be an easier place to start. You don't have to begin with a full-fledged community program: start by developing a shared vision of how to practice the stewardship of our health, and build in small steps from there.

To Seminarians:

College students are notorious for poor health habits—living on little sleep and the cheapest and most convenient food they can find. If that's you, have you brought the same habits with you to seminary? We understand how the pressures of graduate school may lead to compromises in your self-care. But it's important to know how those compromises may affect you.

A simple example: do you cram all night before that final exam? Have you noticed that there comes a point where your eyes just seem to be scanning the pages, and nothing else is really going in? Current research suggests that sleep—especially dream sleep—is essential to the learning process (though sleeping during class is a clear exception to that rule). During the deeper stages of sleep, your brain consolidates what you've learned during the day. In other words, pulling an all-nighter of study is actually counterproductive.[50] Manage your time so that you don't have to depend on burning the midnight oil, and go to bed!

Similarly, if you find yourself being lethargic during the day, and unable to concentrate on your studies, it may well be a combination of sleep deprivation, a poor diet, and a lack of appropriate exercise. That double-shot latte with extra sugar might help you wake up in the morning, but it may also let you down with a crash later in the day. Medicating ourselves with food (that's what it is) quickly becomes a self-defeating cycle.

Cultivate a Sabbath-informed attitude toward your studies, and recognize that self-care is every bit as important to your ministry long-term as getting that A in New Testament Greek. Take a stand for your health, and talk to your classmates about doing the same.

50. Hart, *Sleep*, 51–52.

7

Embrace Wise Limits

Sometimes it can seem as if living within boundaries and limits is not in the best interest of the church. . . .Will anything get done? Will the church ever grow? Will everyone become self-absorbed narcissists living in isolation from one another if I teach this? . . .[P]eople in emotionally healthy churches trust in God's goodness by receiving his limits as gifts and expressions of his love.

—PETER SCAZZERO[1]

AH, HOME SWEET HOME. After a hard day at work, there's nothing like coming back to the place where we can kick off our shoes and be ourselves. Even after being away on the best of vacations, there's something comforting about coming back to our own bed and all the things that make our house a home.

I (Cameron) remember going camping with my wife, kids, and some good friends many years ago. The kids were still young, and we weren't exactly a camping kind of family. But it was an adventure, and we gamely set out for the California coastal redwoods. After several days of sleeping in a tent, hiking the trails, and cooking outdoors, we packed the car and got ready to head home. My wife turned to the kids as they settled into the back seat. "So," she asked cheerily, glad for the adventure to be over herself, "what do you miss most about home?" Without missing a beat, my son said simply, "Modern technology."

---

1. Scazzero, *Emotionally Healthy Church*, 150–51.

Home feels like our special haven, and we'll go to great lengths to keep it secure and comfortable. Home is our refuge. We don't expect people to walk in unannounced, as if they owned the place. That would be an intrusion. Even if we rent, we still expect the landlord to respect our privacy, to call before coming over to fix that leaky faucet, to ring the doorbell instead of just coming in. It's an unwritten, socially accepted rule: my home is my sanctuary; thou shalt not intrude without my permission. There are places where others can enter freely, and places where people must be invited in. Home is usually in the latter category.

As mentioned in our discussion of stress in chapter 2, stories of parsonage living frequently point to problems of intrusion. Without thoughtful planning and open conversation in advance, moving into a house owned by the church can present a minefield of conflicting expectations.[2] Overall, most pastors and their families don't live in parsonages (or "manses") anymore.[3] But the parsonage is symbolic of the sense of intrusion into their personal lives that many pastors and their families still experience. To use language that has become increasingly popular in recent years, it's a matter of *boundaries*.

We hear a lot about boundaries these days. Part of this comes from the influence of a popular series of books by psychologists Henry Cloud and John Townsend. Their original book, *Boundaries*, was published in 1992, followed by others directed toward parents and even dating couples.[4] But in its wider use, the word has come to signify different things to different people. The term has found a relatively receptive audience among Christians in general. Pastors themselves have learned to use the language, as the following quote demonstrates:

> Pastors need to set boundaries. The pastor and the people need to realize that the pastor can't solve all their problems. Without good boundaries, we take blame when things go wrong even when we had no responsibility in the matter.[5]

But what does it mean to say that pastors need "good boundaries"? In practical terms, the usage varies. Sometimes, it means protection against violations of the family's privacy. Sometimes it means setting limits on

2. If you are moving into a parsonage, be proactive; e.g., read Joyner, *Fish Bowl*.

3. One survey of 725 Presbyterian pastors, for example, found that 16 percent lived in manses. Research Services, PCUSA, "Findings."

4. Cloud and Townsend, *Boundaries*; *Boundaries with Kids*; *Boundaries in Dating*.

5. London and Wiseman, *Pastors at Greater Risk*, 65.

unrealistic expectations. Other times, it's about being clear whose responsibility is whose.

This is not as easy as it might seem at first, given the enthusiasm with which some people discuss the importance of boundaries. Start talking about boundaries in a church setting, for example, and a congregation can wonder:

Isn't the pastor just being selfish or shirking his or her job?

Don't we pay the pastor to be available?

Doesn't the pastor love us? Does he or she think we're too demanding?

Some church members may even think that boundaries apply to others, but not to them; after all, the pastor is their special friend, and the rules don't apply! Meanwhile, from the other side, pastors may think:

Am I being selfish? Is it inappropriate for me to think about boundaries?

Doesn't following the way of Jesus mean a life of pure self-sacrifice?

Isn't the church about community, deep friendship in God, life together?

Pastors may question whether the language of boundaries recasts the pastor-congregation relationship into something less like church and more like the relationship between a secular professional and a client. We believe they are right to do so. But we also believe that, rightly understood, the idea of boundaries has a much-needed place in the life of the church.

For these reasons, we believe it's important to briefly sort through the different meanings of the language of boundaries. These coincide with different kinds of intrusions that may be experienced between pastors and congregations. Drawing upon previous chapters, then, we will recast the notion of boundaries, practically and theologically, as a matter of protecting against unwarranted intrusions, embracing appropriate limits in a community of sanctified but imperfect people.

The Meaning of Boundaries

In the relationship between pastors and congregations, there are different roles, with different degrees and kinds of power, different responsibilities, and different levels of visibility. In what is commonly known as a "fishbowl" kind of existence, pastor's lives are necessarily public in a way that isn't true of others in the church. Members watch what they do, make judgments, and gossip among themselves. They talk about what kind of clothes pastors and their families wear. They talk about how the pastor's children behave. They talk about where the pastor lives, and what they drive.

After one Sunday morning service, for example, a member of our church followed me (Cameron) out to the parking lot. I don't remember what I had preached about that morning, but when I asked if I could help her with something, she replied that she just needed to see what kind of car I owned. When she saw my battered old Corolla, she smiled with satisfaction, waved, and walked away. Challenging people from the pulpit invites a different degree of scrutiny—it comes with the territory.

In this complicated relationship, then, we can distinguish three related types of situations for which the language of boundaries is used. We will refer to these as matters of social, emotional, and ethical boundaries, and will describe how each relates to intrusions that might be found in any local congregation.

Social Boundaries

Often with no sense of malice, and usually without awareness, the church makes inordinate demands on the life of the pastor. There are always more meetings to attend than people imagine. There are obligations to meet, programs to run, and people to visit, pray with, or counsel. The work of a pastor is never done; there is always more to do. Since the congregation pays a salary, pastors can be viewed as the hired hand, one who should be available at any moment, day or night. Understandably, church people want their pastors to be available in their time of need or crisis. From their perspective, their requests seem small. For pastors, however, each request stands in a long line with many others, and the demand can feel overwhelming at times.

This is, in part, because the pastor is not just a pastor, but a person with a life that is separate from the church. Remember when you were a kid, and you saw your elementary school teacher in some other context outside of school, like the grocery store or a restaurant? It could be disorienting: somehow, you just didn't think of your teachers doing anything else but teaching, as if they lived at school!

The same can be true of how people think about pastors: as if they had no life outside the church. One pastor recounted how he had been invited to dinner at the home of one the families in the church. After he left, the family's young daughter blurted out, "Mommy, that man looked just like Pastor Carl!"[6] But adults can become just as flustered when running into the pastor unexpectedly. Some will say, innocently, "Oh, hello, Pastor! I didn't know you shopped at this grocery store." But from the way it comes out, the pastor suspects that it never occurred to them that pastors shopped at *any* grocery store! Without a clear understanding that clergy have their own lives, homes, and families, it's too easy for congregations to intrude without even realizing it.

All of this points toward the first kind of boundary, a *social* one. Family therapists have long been concerned about how well the boundaries around social groups are maintained. It's a bit like the old (and rather ambiguous!) proverb, "Good fences make good neighbors." You may want some boundary to mark off the limits of your property, but a high and impenetrable stone wall would be excessive. The right kind of fence allows some privacy behind it, but also neighborly conversation across it.[7]

The congregation as a whole is a social group with its own wants and needs. Within each congregation are families, as well as a number of groups that come together for various reasons, including church administration, ministry, and fellowship. Pastors have their own needs and goals as individuals, as do their families. In other words, every local congregation is a complex mix of groups whose purposes may sometimes be at odds with each other. That's not sin; it's the nature of social groups. The question is, what kind of boundaries are appropriate to draw around these groups? What are the rules or guidelines for deciding who belongs to what group, or for knowing the lines and limits of responsibility and privilege?[8] Good order depends on getting these things clear.

Think, for example, of a church committee assigned to make a particular decision. Imagine the chaos of not knowing who was on the committee and who was not! Or you may know who's supposed to be on the

---

6. Quoted in Ulstein, *Pastors Off the Record*, 102.

7. Family therapists refer to this as the *permeability* of boundaries. *Clear* boundaries are better than ones that are too *rigid* (the stone wall) or too *diffuse* (so loose as to be functionally non-existent). See Minuchin, *Family Therapy*.

8. Minuchin defines boundaries as "the rules defining who participates and how" (*Family Therapy*, 53). Similarly, Kantor and Lehr describe boundaries as "strategies for interacting" at the place where two or more social systems meet (*Inside the Family*, 24). See also Lee and Balswick, *Glass House*, ch. 3.

committee, but have trouble closing the membership as people clamor to have their say. Once the membership is set, the group needs to be open to input, which means not defending the boundaries so rigidly that meetings happen in secret behind locked doors. That group would become disengaged from the congregation and do a poor job of representing the whole. But if they can't put a limit on how much input to allow, the committee will become too enmeshed with the congregation to take a stand. Decisions may never get made, because the group fears offending anyone.

In other words, any complex system has subgroups within it, each with its own functions and purposes. The groups must stay open to input from each other, but good order is violated when one group tries to impose its will on another (even if it's done nicely) or can't take an independent stand when necessary.

Pragmatically speaking, then, one way of keeping good social boundaries in the church is to set limits on what's expected of the pastor and how expectations are communicated. A pastor once told the church board that he no longer wished to mow the lawn at the church, and would like the church to hire a gardener. The board chair replied, "The former pastor always mowed the lawn at church." Undeterred, the new pastor retorted, "I know. I asked him. But *he* doesn't want to mow the lawn anymore either."

As we've already insisted, it's not that pastors are lazy. Because of the calling that drew them into ministry in the first place, pastors care and want to serve. They want to be involved in the lives of their people. But as we have noted again and again, this can be unending and overwhelming. Wise limits are needed. As Richard Swenson has written,

> Boundaries are about establishing a perimeter around the personal and private spaces of our lives and not letting the world come crashing in uninvited. This is not an issue of selfishness but instead of self-care.[9]

All Christians are real people with real needs—the need for Sabbath rest and reflection, for downtime, for time with family. These things may be even more important for church leaders—especially pastors—because the congregation makes more demands upon them. Spiritually healthy congregations understand that proper care of a church's leaders ultimately serves the unity of the whole, and embrace limits appropriate to that care. This is but one concrete way to embody Paul's admonition to the Philippians: "Do nothing out of selfish ambition or vain conceit. Rather, in

9. Swenson, *Margin*, 91.

humility value others above yourselves, not looking to your own interests but each of you to the interests of others" (Phil 2:3–4).

As we will see in chapter 9, it is particularly important to safeguard the boundary between the church and the pastor's family. Again, this is not a matter of setting up an impenetrable wall, nor exempting the family from participating in the life of the church! But too often, the ever-present needs of a congregation are allowed to intrude upon the pastor's family in a way that no other family in the church would allow.

Pastors themselves must bear much of the responsibility for balancing their priorities and making wise decisions, carefully weighing the demands of their role against the importance of self-care and of spending time with their family. I (Kurt) have suspended a family vacation to perform a funeral, and other times I have remained on vacation, leaving others to officiate.[10] It's a difficult place to be and a tough decision to make. The way pastors make these decisions says a lot about their priorities, their personal needs, and their style and philosophy of ministry.

And sometimes pastors must take steps to protect their families from the inappropriate expectations placed on their spouses and children. One Sunday after church, my then-fifth-grade son told me that he was asked to pray in Sunday school. The teacher had said, "You're the pastor's kid; you can lead the class in prayer." I immediately went to that Sunday school teacher and said, "You don't ask the plumber's son to fix your leaky faucet. Don't ask my kid to pray just because I'm the pastor."

It was an innocent comment on the teacher's part, but it was important for my son to know that there were no expectations on him to be anything because of *my* calling. Of course, we had high expectations for him as a young man, as a follower of Jesus, but not because of being a pastor's kid. We worked very hard to help our kids understand that my calling to be a pastor did not automatically mean a similar life demand placed on the rest of the family.

Churches can also place a lot of expectations on the pastor's spouse. Some spouses have a shared sense of call to be in a leadership role in a congregation, a call nearly equal to the pastor's—but many don't, and this can't be assumed. When we were looking for our first pastoral placement, I entered into conversation with a church for a youth pastor position. In our correspondence, the pastor asked a telling question: "What instrument does your wife play, and what age Sunday school does she teach?" He had high expectations for the unpaid role my wife would play! I wrote

10. The stories in the remainder of this section are Kurt's.

back, "My wife has a master's degree in counseling. She's supportive of my church work, and will be involved in the church, but at her own pace," as should be expected of any committed member of the congregation. The pastor replied that the job was no longer available, citing a sudden budget crisis. He also mentioned that the church had previously had a youth minister "with a wife like yours" (whatever that meant), adding that "he's working in a factory today"(!).

We don't want to paint a one-sided, negative portrait of pastors having to defend their turf against intrusive congregations; churches can also be incredibly loving and supportive (a topic we will turn to in the next chapter). But one of the major practical expressions of the idea of social boundaries is that expectations of the pastor and of the pastor's family need to be dealt with honestly and openly, without unexamined assumptions of who must do what. How family members are to be involved in the life of the congregation is for the family to decide, not something to be imposed as an expectation from the outside.

Emotional Boundaries

A second sense of boundaries involves the *emotional* reactions of individuals as they navigate social waters. This is the primary meaning promoted by Cloud and Townsend's work.[11] Social boundaries, in the sense described above, can be thought of as a matter of good order. We need to know who has the power to make what decisions, and so on, for a complex group to operate smoothly. In short, it's an organizational issue.

But as anyone who's spent time in organizations knows, people don't always discuss these things calmly. Anxieties get triggered; tempers flare; defensive walls go up. Consider, for example, the emotional sensitivities that dominate the following explanation of boundaries from pastor Pete Scazzero:

> People with poor boundaries feel compelled to do what others
> want even though it is not what they want to do. They are afraid
> of disappointing someone or being criticized. We want others to
> like us, and we surely don't want to be seen as selfish.[12]

11. Based on the contemporary psychoanalytic perspective known as *object relations theory*, especially Mahler et al., *Psychological Birth*.

12. Scazzero, *Emotionally Healthy Church*, 147.

Pastors in particular must learn—sometimes the hard way—the difference between being a servant and being a doormat. Some, being by nature "people pleasers," find it hard to set appropriate limits.

Personal, emotional sensitivities, in other words, may make it hard to establish or maintain clear social boundaries. There are anxious undercurrents to some instances of a congregation's intrusions on a pastor's private life; the felt message is, "We can't survive without you!" That would be a problem of emotional boundaries from the congregation's side. Church members' unacknowledged and unresolved anxieties can leak into their interactions with the pastor, masked by arguments about the *pastor's* responsibilities.

From the other side, however, some pastors have a strong need to be needed. They can't imagine going away on vacation without the church collapsing. If they do go, they call to check up on things, to the annoyance of both their families and church leaders. Some pastors appear to delegate responsibility and authority, but keep taking back the reins. And eventually, in a congregational catch-22, pastors who can't let go for personal reasons may find that they've created systems where they can't let go for organizational reasons.

Some workaholic pastors glory in their busyness, as if this conferred its own kind of saintliness. They aren't forced to work that way by their congregation. They do this, supposedly, to show their dedication. But what else is going on behind the scenes? Are they avoiding something in their private lives, throwing themselves into their work instead? Do they have such a low view of themselves that they need to work insane hours and be at everyone's beck and call just to prove to others—and to themselves—that they're worthy or valuable people? And some pastors are so concerned about the success of their church that they become like gamblers who just can't stop: they bet on one more call, one more meeting, to make everything all right. This is a dangerous place to be.

Pastors give themselves to their congregations. But emotional vulnerabilities on both sides can perpetuate a dysfunctional dance of unreasonable demands and anxious overwork, devoid of Sabbath rest. Pastors need to learn to say no, to know and embrace their limits, even when the congregation continues to cry out, "Take care of me now!" Pastors do this best when they remember they're not God. The church, the ministry, all belongs to a God who never sleeps.

Saying no will make some people mad. But pastors need to say it when appropriate, and congregations need to hear it. People may talk about how the pastor isn't being nice. But as Bill Easum has suggested, sometimes we have to be not nice for the sake of the gospel.[13] Sometimes the right thing to do is the toughest thing to do.

Ethical Boundaries

There is one other boundary area to be discussed. As we've seen, congregations may make intrusive demands on pastors, and many pastors have difficulty learning to say no. But it's also possible for the pastor to be the intruder. Pastors don't like to talk about this, but it is vital to the life of the church.

Pastors have power and authority in the lives of congregants: the spiritual power of one who preaches the Word; the emotional power of one who has access into the most personal places in people's lives. All of this must be held in sacred trust. When that power is abused, the pain and betrayal that results can propel people out of the church and far from God. We've heard or read the stories of clergy abuse of children, of pastors getting sexually involved with parishioners, or of a whole host of financial improprieties.

But the temptation for pastors to misuse their position or authority may also come in more subtle ways. During a sermon, I (Kurt) once told the story of how I dodged a speeding ticket by flashing my police chaplain identification. The point of the story was undeserved grace: I deserved a ticket, but I didn't get one. Later, I received an angry note from someone in the congregation. Her son had just obtained his driver's license, and here I was in the pulpit, talking about speeding and intimidating a police officer! I know officers, and they're not often intimidated by clergy, but she was right: I had crossed the line.

This is a matter of *ethical* boundaries. In chapter 4, we mentioned how part of the definition of a "professional" includes abiding by a code of conduct. This is because professionals, by virtue of their expertise, have power over others that can be abused. Ethical codes establish the limits of proper behavior to help protect the vulnerable. Christians know that merely following rules does not constitute the whole of a moral life. But they also understand the reality of sin: no one, not even a minister of the gospel, is immune to temptation. Holding to some concrete set of limits is a wise safeguard.

13. Easum, "On Not Being Nice."

Though some denominations offer their own guidelines, there is no universal ethical code for pastors. It goes without saying that Scripture is the norm for all believers. But pastors should also reflect upon existing ethical codes (denominational websites are one source for these) for help in setting boundaries that are specific to the professional side of the pastorate. For example, two perennial issues in ethics codes have to do with confidentiality and sexuality. Only in situations where a person is an immediate danger to themselves or to others will a pastor dare to break a confidence with another person. Sexual intimacy with a parishioner is strictly out of bounds. But beyond that, wise pastors will also set behavioral boundaries that help guard against any impropriety with the opposite sex. Some male pastors, for example, when counseling women, will leave their office doors open, or include another woman (e.g., his wife or a female staff person) in the session. When saying hello or goodbye, they observe careful limits on physical touch; handshakes or "side-hugs" are safer than full face-to-face hugs.

In short, pastors must be prudent given their station of power. Jesus' words and example are crucial: pastors are to be servants, not lording their authority over others (Mark 10:45); their position is one of humility and surrender (Phil 2:5–11). Clergy never use their God-given pastoral office or the pulpit as a place to push their personal agendas. Instead, they work diligently to uphold the trust that others place in them.

Toward a Theology of Boundaries

Applying the idea of boundaries to the ministry context must be done with wisdom and grace. A major goal of this book is to support both pastors and congregations by strengthening the mutual understanding between them.

Pastors are part of a church family, and as with any family, there will be sacrifice and inconvenience. Recognizing that sacrifice, some resist applying the language of boundaries to the pastor-congregation relationship. The practical tension can be heard in this quote from an interview with Eugene Peterson:

> For the most part, I never felt hassled or pushed or had demands put on me that were inappropriate. To live this kind of life . . . you do have to be wise and careful, so that you aren't exploited by neurotic or even psychotic people. You can't be naively open all the time to everybody. There's got to be some protection. But

that being said, from the very beginning I reacted against the professional model of keeping the boundaries clearly defined. I found other ways to protect myself from exploitation. . . . [T]he major one was keeping a Sabbath.[14]

Some pastors might find that first line hard to believe. *Never* hassled? No inappropriate demands, ever? His statement stands in stark contrast to one from veteran pastor Gary Kinnaman: "Why does it feel like the people we're serving are killing us?"[15]

But there's an unspecified amount of wiggle room in that phrase, "For the most part." Whatever his own experience, Peterson openly recognizes that pastors can be exploited, and that to deny this would be both unwise and naive. Some concept of protective boundaries is both beneficial and necessary. The pastoral rat race, after all, is not a noble one. As one re-search team has written,

> Clergy often have a more difficult time than people in other occupations claiming private space for themselves away from the demands of the church job. . . . [M]any parish ministers are expected and expect themselves not to have a life that is dis-tinct from their church work. This makes it difficult for clergy to find sufficient personal, family, or social time away from the demands of the church to enable them to be whole, healthy individuals.[16]

Does that describe your situation as a pastor? You can't continue to min-ister without wise limits, at the mercy of every demand, whatever the cost to your physical, spiritual, and emotional health, or the well-being of your family.

Yet the question remains: is what Peterson calls the "professional model" of boundaries the right one, theologically, for the church? Else-where in the interview, he explains that he grew up in a small town in which his father, a butcher, was on a first-name basis with all his custom-ers. In such a tightly-knit community, there was no sharp line between work and home, a sensibility that Peterson brought to his pastoral work from the beginning. Instead of merely imposing a set of rules from the outside, he was bold enough to engage his congregation in honest conver-sations about what he needed from them as their pastor: "I want to help

14. Wood, "Best Life," 21.

15. Kinnaman and Ells, *Leaders that Last*, 14.

16. Zikmund et al., *Clergy Women*, 23.

you live your Christian life, but I need your help too."[17] And he reports that when the congregation understood what he needed and why, they not only cooperated, but sometimes gave him more than he asked.

Pastors, there is much to learn from his example. Boundary-making, in other words, is ideally about working together with your congregation to hammer out appropriate mutual expectations. We know—some of you can't imagine having the conversations that Peterson had with his flock; it's all you can do to figure out how and when to say no. But if you're going to establish boundaries, do it for the right reasons. Peterson's experience helps point the way, by suggesting the Sabbath as the touchstone for a renewed concept of boundaries in ministry.

In chapter 5, we argued that the Sabbath is not merely a day off for the pastor, but a blessed day of rest for all God's people. Keeping the day holy requires setting limits that protect sacred time from the intrusion of the mundane. There is a positive purpose to appropriate limits, in which boundaries "help us prioritize and protect what matters to us."[18] The question of what matters to us is the key: to whom does it matter, and why? Ultimately, the boundaries that are appropriate to the body of Christ are not grounded in the pastor's no, but in the congregation's yes—a yes to wise limits that represent shared priorities for the sake of the church's spiritual health and its mission to the world.

The Way Forward

Thus, there are different ways of thinking about the notion of boundaries, describing different limits that are important to the life and well-being of a congregation. Because we must work together, we need to set social limits that honor the needs, gifts, and responsibilities of others in the body of Christ. Because we are emotionally vulnerable in a myriad of ways, we need limits that respect the sanctity of each individual, so that no one is pressured into being the means to someone else's ends. Because we are called to be representatives of Jesus through a life of holiness, we need moral limits that help us define the character and behaviors appropriate to such a people.

Understood in this way, establishing good boundaries isn't about pastors—or anyone else in the church, for that matter—drawing lines in the sand that shout, "Leave me alone!" It's not about individuals selfishly

17. Wood, " Best Life," 20.

18. Wilson and Hoffman, *Preventing Ministry Failure*, 140.

asserting their independence against the group. In fact, it's quite the opposite. Congregations that set good boundaries do it as something akin to a community-wide spiritual discipline. Recognizing how individuals and groups often pull against the good of the whole, they set limits that serve a shared vision of the kind of community that God is calling them to be. It is in that spirit that Cloud and Townsend are able to assert that boundaries "are not built in a vacuum; creating boundaries always involves a support network."[19] Toward such a congregational vision, we offer three general suggestions, each building on the one before.

Be Honest and Clear about Your Own Vulnerabilities and Limitations

Part of this has to do with knowing the sensitive areas in which we are most likely to take offense too quickly. Some church members, for example, are primed to feel personally rejected anytime a pastor says no. Some pastors take every verbal challenge as a personal threat to their authority. There can be a grain of truth in these perceptions; as the saying goes, just because you're paranoid doesn't mean they're *not* out to get you! The problem is that our knee-jerk reactions automatically make others into villains, and they will be quick to return the favor. Honestly owning up to the ways we typically overreact will help us manage our defensiveness, listen, and avoid unnecessary conflict (more on this in chapter 8).

Being clear about limitations also means recognizing that one person, or even a handful, can't do everything a congregation needs. That's not simply a practical point about limitations of time or energy; it's a theological one, grounded in the fact that God's design for the church is that "there are many parts, but one body" (1 Cor 12:20). And that means that no one should try to do it all, and no one should be expected to do it all—not even the pastor. It may seem heroic when a faithful few pick up the slack for idle members of a congregation. But the activity of the few quickly becomes enmeshed with the passivity of the many. Thus, the more active members of the community need to think carefully about how to leave space for the contribution of others.

19. Cloud and Townsend, *Boundaries*, 37.

Communicate Consistently about What's Important

As management expert Stephen Covey has memorably put it, "The main thing is to keep the main thing the main thing."[20] It's easy to get so wrapped up in all the planning and execution of church programs and activities that they become ends in themselves. If an event comes off without a hitch and is well attended, it's considered a success. That's certainly not a bad thing. But is it the main thing? How often have we heard of famous Christian leaders who have had a significant impact on the church and the world, but left their families in shambles?

Think about it from a purely organizational standpoint. Who decides the pastor's job description? Or perhaps we should phrase that differently, since pastors only rarely seem to be given clear job descriptions: who decides what is or isn't the pastor's responsibility? An interesting exercise is to have a pastor bullet-point a job description, and then have the church board do the same—often the lists look very different.

I (Cameron) remember meeting on a Saturday morning with all of the staff and lay leaders of a local congregation to discuss their ministry goals. About sixty people were assembled. One of the first questions I asked them was, "How many of you know that your church has a mission statement?" As expected, everyone in the room raised a hand. But then came the obvious next question: "And how many of you know what it says?" This time, only four hands went up—those of the pastor, his wife, and two people who helped write the mission statement. So now, when someone calls me to speak at their church, I often ask, "How will what you want me to do help fulfill your congregation's mission?" The typical response is a long pause, followed by something like, "Wow, that's a great question. Let me talk to our people and I'll get back to you." Usually, that's the last I hear from them.

What's wrong with this picture? And what would happen if the same questions were asked of the leaders in *your* congregation? A conscious awareness of the mission of the church in general and of the congregation in particular should be shot through every ministry discussion. Without a shared sense of mission and the corresponding priorities, the ministry activities of a congregation can become a loose collection of pet projects. Each and every project may be worthwhile in itself, but when people don't have a clear sense of the whole, discussions about resources turn into turf

20. Covey et al., *First Things First.*

wars, with pastors sometimes caught in the middle. As Wilson and Hoffmann have argued,

> Ministers living from crisis to crisis lead unfulfilled lives. Aligning our weekly and daily tasks to be consistent with the things we value most is critical for living out a Christ-centered calling. . . . One person's sense of urgency does not change another person's sense of calling.[21]

And as we have already suggested, one of the key areas of value for any congregation centers on the question of what kind of people God is calling us to be. Let us set our priorities by the light of a shared vision of the aspects of Christlikeness being formed in our community.

Identify and Embrace the Limits that Embody Those Priorities

This point necessarily comes last. Boundary-making shouldn't be just a psychological principle slapped onto the life of a congregation. For our boundaries to honor God, they must grow organically out of our desire to do his will, our willingness to humbly recognize our vulnerabilities, our proper place in the body, and our ongoing conversation about what it means to partner with others—*really* partner—in the cause of the gospel.

We won't try to replicate in miniature the advice that other authors have already given about boundaries. Our goal in this chapter has been more general: to create what we hope is a proper perspective for using boundary advice in a congregational context. We've argued that there are different ways of understanding boundaries, each of which has its place. And believe it or not, we think we can boil the whole discussion down into one key question.

It starts with the assumption that the members of a congregation are willing to embrace their calling to grow in Christlikeness, and to think humbly about their proper role in working alongside others. As any pastor would agree, such an assumption is not to be taken for granted! But if there is any such mutuality to build upon, then the question of boundaries is this: *What rules or guidelines do we need to agree to in our lives together to encourage good order, and to set protective limits on our self-centered and thoughtless ways?*

The possible applications are far ranging. How should we behave with each other in our various roles? How are decisions to be made, and

---

21. Wilson and Hoffmann, *Preventing Ministry Failure*, 149, 151.

who makes them? How do we respect the needs of individuals and groups, and how are these needs communicated? The point, of course, is not that every congregation must have a 200-page policy manual. It's that we must care enough about unity and mutual respect to be willing to risk the hard conversations, and to work toward the common good.

Sometimes, we simply need to *have* those conversations in the first place, to clear the air and correct any misperceptions. There may be sufficient trust to end the conversation with nothing more than a handshake or a mutual sense of having been truly heard. When necessary, however, agreements can be formalized to help fend off future misunderstandings. Either way, the goal is to embrace and honor the kind of wise limits that help all of our imperfect congregations to more consistently embody what it means to be God's church.

Postscript

To Pastors:

Even if setting wise limits is necessary, it can be complicated. There is so much to do to keep a church in good working order, often with too few resources. Perhaps the members of your congregation have become accustomed to being passive spectators instead of active participants. Time and time again you—or a faithful and overworked few—have bailed them out by doing it all yourself. Or you've already tried to establish some boundaries, and it hasn't gone well. Some folks seem to think you have all the free time you could possibly need, and even doubt your commitment to the ministry when you try to set limits for yourself or your family. Or maybe you yourself question the legitimacy of limits in the first place. After all, when you look at the cross, you realize that whatever sacrifices you've had to make in the ministry, it hasn't been "to the point of shedding your blood" (Heb 12:4)! So shouldn't we all just quit whining and get on with the ministry?

We agree that the ordinary sacrifices of congregational ministry pale in comparison to the cross, and that it's good to keep things in that perspective. Indeed, it is precisely because of the cross that Christians must learn what it means to be the kind of church for which he died. Thus, whatever your situation, we encourage you to approach the issue of boundaries from core convictions about God's intention for the church and your own vocation. We know we're preaching to the choir when we say that the church's true identity is expressed in the way life is done together, and that gifts and responsibilities are not all located in one person. But even if *you* believe that, the challenge may be in getting others to embrace it as well.

And *that*, we believe, is the key. Boundary making, ideally, should be a communal process, grounded in a shared vision of what's important for the congregation as a whole. You may be able to negotiate some social boundaries, for example, to protect your time and privacy, but unless the congregation understands why such boundaries are important, they may be an ongoing source of contention.

Don't just set boundaries independently; talk about what limits are needed to serve the common good. As a spiritual leader, for example, you must model good moral boundaries. But you should also help people understand the reasons for them, and encourage them to embrace similar limits as a way of living out the reality of their sanctification. Teach about the organizational boundaries needed to help people minister in unity. Extending outward from a Sabbath-shaped vision of work and vocation, decide what limits you need to safeguard your physical, spiritual, emotional, and family health. Teach others why these values are important to you, and help them establish similar priorities that are appropriate to their situation.

And finally, think honestly about the personal and emotional sensitivities you bring to the congregational mix (for example, see the postscript to seminarians below). Privately, you can learn to monitor your reactions and ask God to help you do a better job of taking responsibility for your contribution to church conflict. Beyond this, consider what level of honest self-disclosure on your part might help others also take responsibility for their contributions.

We don't make that last suggestion lightly. Indeed, we realize that all of these recommendations involve varying degrees of vulnerability. We can't tell you exactly what conversations to have, or with whom to have them. Careful and prayerful reflection is needed. But our hope, once again, is that whatever you do, it will be grounded in your core convictions about the church and what God has called you to do.

To Congregations:

Your pastor needs your help, even if he or she doesn't ask for it. As we've said before, the most helpful thing you can do is to take with utter seriousness your own calling to be the church. We believe that embracing wise limits through appropriate boundaries is part of that calling. This isn't just about the boundaries that need to be drawn for the sake of your pastor, though it includes that—it's about the limits needed for the health and viability of the whole community.

It should be obvious how important moral boundaries are to the life of a community that seeks to display the character of Christ. But this needs to be more than an abstract conviction; it needs to be translated into concrete commitments to which everyone is accountable. Imagine what would happen, for example, if everyone understood what makes gossip sinful, and covenanted together to eliminate it from their speech? Some of the most nagging, chronic problems of congregations would wither away from that change alone.

What about social boundaries? How do these serve the good of the whole? Using the pastor's vacation time as an example, a congregation that understands the value of clear social boundaries will think like this: "We want and need our pastor to have a solid family life: a strong marriage and thriving kids. We'd want that for any family in the church—but we also realize the extra burden that comes with being the pastor's family. Getting some vacation time together, away from the responsibilities of the church, will help them stay strong, so we need to respect that boundary. That includes having clearly assigned roles and responsibilities that will help us to deal with anything that might come up when the pastor's gone. That way, we'll only need to contact the pastor if there's a *real* emergency—and we'll get clear in advance what constitutes a real emergency, and what doesn't." The same kind of logic can be applied by extension to the pastor's other needs, and the needs of other leaders in the congregation.

Finally, emotional vulnerability is part of our common humanity. No one is exempt. In Christ's name, and for his sake, work together toward a climate in which it is safe for all to humbly recognize their own foibles, and to learn compassion and patience for the foibles of others. And that includes accepting that your pastor has weaknesses too, which are just as deserving of your forbearance and grace.

To Seminarians:

We hope that in this and previous chapters, we've stimulated you to anticipate the personal and interpersonal challenges you're likely to face in ministry. If you aren't currently engaged in pastoral work, you may not be experiencing pressures related to moral and social boundaries. But don't wait until later to start thinking these issues through. Ethical violations often happen *without* thinking, and you don't want to put yourself in too many situations where you have to figure out the proper policy on the spot. Likewise, the time to discuss and negotiate at least some social boundaries may be during the interview and hiring process, so it's helpful to think carefully about what you or your family need beforehand.

Perhaps most importantly of all, be proactive in examining your emotional boundaries. Do you know your particular areas of sensitivity? What is it that pushes your buttons? Are you wired with a need to be liked, so that it's hard to say no? A need to belong, so that disagreement feels like rejection? A need to be in charge, so you can dampen your anxiety about how things will turn out? A need to be admired, so that even constructive criticism feels like a personal attack?

We're not saying, of course, that there's anything intrinsically wrong with wanting to be liked, to feel like you belong, and so on. We're talking about being aware of the ways you typically overreact in relationship to others. That overreaction may be directed outward, in sarcasm and anger, or inward, in self-recrimination and depression. If you don't know these things about yourself, it will be too easy to unilaterally blame the congregation for your distress. You have an opportunity now, while still in seminary, to deepen your self-awareness before you encounter the demands of ministry. Take advantage of it—don't wait for a congregation to start pushing your buttons to figure it out!

8

Nurture Healthy Relationships

The starting point for thinking about the church is to recognize that it is already a community that possesses an essential oneness. . . .[It] is as if God says to the diversity of churches in any context, "You are one. Now learn how to affirm each other's distinctiveness while you work out your differences." . . . Every part of the church must be zealous for the life, health, vitality, and unity of the whole.

—CRAIG VAN GELDER[1]

EVEN THE BEST AND most successful pastors and congregations are no strangers to conflict. Any change to the status quo, even a "good" one, may bring its own kind of tension and pain. That's not necessarily a bad thing—it's just reality. People don't like change. And people don't stop having emotions when they become Christians. Moreover, their emotional responses to situations can cause problems in the church. Here's a famous example. You may already know the story, but for now we'll hold back the names.

Perry was one of the lead pastors at First Church of Hometown, a well-known congregation with multiple staff and an active missions program. Patrick, one of the missionaries First Church supported, was having tremendous success on the field, working among the people of Altertown, who had only recently heard the gospel. First Church had already sent one missionary there, Bill, who had in turn recruited Patrick to the work. The newly planted church was growing steadily under Patrick's and Bill's

1. Van Gelder, *Essence of the Church*, 122.

leadership, and the staff back in Hometown acknowledged that their ministry was being blessed by God. At one point, Perry decided to visit the new church, and was delighted to see how the mission was progressing. He gladly joined in the spirit of fellowship among the converts, experiencing their culture firsthand.

Soon after, a whole delegation arrived from Hometown. They came, supposedly, representing Jared, another of the lead pastors. This group was more religiously conservative than Perry; they tended to worry about whether the faith was being compromised by the kind of cultural accommodation that always seemed to happen on the mission field. Perry knew this, and their presence made him anxious. He began to second-guess himself. Was he wrong to have jumped into fellowship with these new believers so quickly? What would Jared and his people say? Uncertain what to do, he broke off contact with the Altertonian converts. This was too much for Patrick, who was incensed at Perry's hypocrisy. He confronted Perry publicly for being so two-faced, for turning a gospel of grace back into a religion of works.

Do you recognize the story?

Though we've changed the details a bit, this is essentially the story of the confrontation between Peter and Paul in Antioch, as told in Galatians 2:11–14 (see also Acts 11:19–26). For Paul, the point of telling the story is to chide the Galatian believers for making the same mistake that Peter did: abandoning the gospel of justification by faith in a crucified Christ for a dead religion of justification by works.

For our purposes here, the point of telling the story is to notice *why* Peter made his hypocritical *faux pas*. Perhaps his understanding of the full implications of grace was still under construction, hence Paul's theological challenge. But the more immediate explanation seems to be that Peter succumbed to pressure, real or imagined, from the group that had come from the Jerusalem church, representing James. Note that Paul doesn't say that the Jerusalem delegation badgered Peter into withdrawing from sharing a table with Gentiles; he only says that Peter drew back because he was afraid. In other words, the delegation didn't necessarily have to say or do anything to get Peter to back down. Their mere presence, and Peter's fear of what they might think or say, was enough.

This is Peter, the Rock: Peter, who galvanized the crowds in Jerusalem with his sermon at Pentecost (Acts 2:14–41), faced down the Sanhedrin in the power of the Holy Spirit (Acts 4:8–12; 5:27–32), and boldly condemned Ananias and Sapphira for their public deception (Acts 5:1–11).

Can this be the same Peter who embarrassed himself in Antioch because he was afraid of what others might think? Peter courageously and faithfully faced torture, prison, and death in the name of the Jesus—then caved under peer pressure.

In our own inconstancy, we're no different. One moment we're faithful. The next moment, we let our anxieties get the better of us, and react to situations in less than ideal ways. This is part of our vulnerability as embodied beings. An important part of what it means to be faithful, then, is to acknowledge our emotions and do a better job of tending our relationships. In this chapter, we'll look at the role emotions play in the life of a congregation, especially when it comes to understanding the conflicts that inevitably arise. But first things first: before we deal with unhealthy patterns of relationship, let's consider what it means for a church to be healthy.

What Is a "Healthy" Church?

In this book, we have already used the terms "health" or "healthy" several times. These are words we tend to take for granted, though they may mean different things to different people. Sometimes the words refer to the physical aspects of well-being, or they may point to emotional, spiritual, and relational aspects. But what do they mean when applied to a local congregation? It would seem oddly inappropriate, for example, to define a healthy church as one in which all the members lacked medical or psychiatric symptoms!

Some people, when speaking of a healthy church, mean something like "successful," as when a congregation is growing numerically. The assumption, apparently, is that healthy things necessarily grow. But is that always the case? If a church's attendance and membership aren't growing, does that mean it's not healthy? Many pastors would actually say that their congregations became spiritually healthier when the membership *declined* in specific ways, as when the chronically disgruntled leave, and those who remain become more focused. Thus, numerical measures of success may be a poor index of a congregation's health. What are the alternatives?

Over a year ago, I (Cameron) was diagnosed with a chronic Epstein-Barr infection. The virus is quite common; some medical experts believe that up to 95 percent of the population may have it lying dormant somewhere in their cells. In some people, unpredictably, the virus activates, causing a variety of symptoms from mild to severe. Mine, thankfully, are mild; for me, it's like having a case of jetlag, 24/7. I can be in the pulpit, preaching with energy and enthusiasm—then I have to pause while my mind goes blank for a moment. People think I'm pausing for dramatic effect, but in reality I'm waiting for my brain to get back on track!

Concerned friends and colleagues often inquire after my health. It's hard to answer the question: I can only say how I'm feeling that day, knowing that invisible processes are at work in my body. How I feel tomorrow may be quite different. Sometimes, what they want to know is: *Is it gone yet? Are you back to being healthy?* I remind them that though the virus may one day go dormant again, it will never be completely gone. My "new normal," therefore, is to practice healthy habits that support my immune system, and then take each day as it comes.

We believe it's helpful to think of congregational health in much the same way. As Peter Steinke has written, "A healthy congregation is one that actively and responsibly addresses or heals its disturbances, not one with an absence of troubles."[2] Problems that may be lying dormant in the system today may unexpectedly go viral tomorrow, as one person's anxiety erupts and is passed on to others. Instead of defining healthy congregations by a mere absence of symptoms, we should focus instead on what it takes to have a strong immune system, one that is able to respond effectively to the inevitable difficulties that arise in any complex group.[3]

Such an understanding of health is more compatible with a missional, purpose-oriented way of thinking. Again, to quote Steinke, "Health is not an end but a means to fulfill the purpose of life. . . . Health is a process, not a thing or state. . . . Health is a direction, not a destination."[4] Thus, the question of health is not simply "How are you doing?" but "Where are you going?" A congregation isn't healthy because it's problem free; that is at best a temporary—though blessed!—state. Rather, a healthy congregation is one that knows its mission and is actively pursuing it. Problems may come up in the process of that pursuit, knocking the group off balance and off course for a time. But the healthy church shows its resilience in how it responds to these disruptions, righting itself and finding its way.

This is why we should pay attention to emotional processes in congregations. It's not a matter of holding up some psychological scorecard to the group, as if some definition of emotional health were an end in itself. But emotional undercurrents can easily distract a congregation from

2. Steinke, *Healthy Congregations*, 13.

3. The immunity metaphor is from Steinke, *Healthy Congregations*, ch. 8.

4. Steinke, *Healthy Congregations*, xiv, 27.

its mission. Pastors who fear offending powerful members of the church, for example, are wary of preaching prophetically. Congregations torn by conflict are a poor witness for the gospel, and the conflict itself absorbs so much of the people's energy that nothing is left for the real work of the church.

But we're getting ahead of ourselves. We don't want to promote a crisis-oriented way of thinking that emphasizes problems and how to fix them. Too often, that already characterizes the woeful way we treat our physical bodies. We take them for granted, don't rest them enough, and stuff them full of garbage. We don't pay serious attention to our health until there's a problem—sometimes not even then! And we prefer quick fixes to lifestyle changes: *Doctor, can't you just give me a pill for that?*

Do we treat the body of Christ the same way? As we said in chapter 3, the church *is* the body of Christ. We don't have a choice about this—it's the God-given reality of who we are. But we are responsible for what *kind* of body we are. Is the body healthy? What are we doing to keep its immune system strong? In other words, it's not enough to look for quick fixes to solve church conflict. First and foremost, a healthy congregation is one in which people have learned to care for one another, to love one another with the love of Christ.

Being a Congregation That Cares

Most Christians are familiar with these words of Jesus: "A new command I give you: Love one another. As I have loved you, so you must love one another. By this everyone will know that you are my disciples, if you love one another" (John 13:34–35). Three times he says it: love one another. But do we remember the context in which these words were spoken?

This is the night of Jesus' betrayal. The disciples are gathered for their evening meal. Jesus knows what's coming; he knows that he must leave them soon, by way of the cross. What will be his final words to them? How can he convey his deepest desire for who they will become as disciples? He rises, girds himself with a towel, and begins to wash their feet. This, he tells them, is how they are to treat one another—with loving and lowly service.

Then he drops a bombshell. One of the Twelve is going to betray him. This is the scene da Vinci paints in his *The Last Supper*: Jesus makes his announcement, and the disciples react with surprise, horror, and confusion. And it's in this context, when Judas goes off into the night, that Jesus commands them to love one another.

Peter seems not to hear the command, only the news that Jesus is leaving. "Where are you going?," he demands. "I'm going with you, even if I have to die."

Jesus' response is a poignant one: "Really, Peter? Will you really? I tell you that before the night is over, you will have disowned me three times."

The commandment to love is not an idle one. Sandwiched between the betrayals of Judas and Peter, given in full view of the cross, it's a hard-nosed directive of what the church must do—what the church must *be*—in the face of human selfishness and sin.

What does this mutual love between believers look like? In passage after passage, Paul plays it out for us: we are to accept one another as Christ has accepted us (Rom 15:7), to serve one another humbly in the Spirit (Gal 5:13), to be patient and forgiving with one another (Eph 4:2, 32; Col 3:13), and to comfort one another with assurances about our future in Christ (1 Thess 4:18; 5:11). With a sincere love, living in harmony, we are to show devotion and honor toward each other, share with those in need, be hospitable, rejoice with those who rejoice, and mourn with those who mourn (Rom 12:9–16). This is how people will know that we really follow Jesus, and that his Spirit is alive and well in a local congregation.

We see this in action when members of a church reach out to support each other in time of need. People pray for each other's concerns and stay in touch, offering encouragement and solace. A collection is taken to help a family pay the rent when someone is laid off from work. A parent goes into the hospital, and friends rally to provide meals and to shuttle the kids to school. Even when there are difficulties to be ironed out in a congregation, such glimpses of grace can still be seen. These should be received with thanks.

Again, the church is the body of Christ. When the body is healthy, it is characterized by mutual concern, love, and support. The pastor is also a member of the body, albeit one with a far more public role. Pastors may have particular gifts that set them apart for specific kinds of service. But these gifts come from the same Spirit that all the members of the body share, by the grace of the same God (1 Cor 12:4–6). So here's the question: can the pastor count on the same kind of love and support as others in body? When pastors or their families have needs, who rises to meet them? Is it even safe for pastors to admit they have needs in the first place?

In her memoir of growing up in Kentucky as the daughter of a Southern Baptist pastor, Elizabeth Emerson Hancock recalls the day her father told her that he was leaving the ministry. The family was coming from her grandmother's funeral service, a disappointing affair that confirmed that the people of the congregation, though saying the appropriately pious things, simply could not or would not give the family the emotional support they needed.

Elizabeth's father tried to break the news to her gently. He began with a story from her childhood, in which she had found a badly wounded kitten and brought to it her father, saying with simple and unquestioning faith, "Fix, Daddy." But he already knew the kitten couldn't be saved. He had the vet put the suffering creature to sleep, and concocted a story for Elizabeth that the kitten had been sent to a poor and deserving family that had more room to keep pets.

Telling the story, this time including the parts she didn't remember, was her father's way of answering her question of why he no longer wanted to be a pastor. He explained:

> [It's] twenty years of a hundred and twenty people a day coming to your door, without a reservation in the world, saying "Daddy, fix." And you want to, you really do. You always try. But eventually you get tired. And eventually, you decide it's time to devote more energy to fixing things in your own house.[5]

He was wrung out, emotionally drained. There were so many needs in the congregation, so many expectations. And although he was required to serve them in their times of grief, he had no one to support him in his own.

As William Willimon has written, "pastors are some of the loneliest people in the church."[6] This can happen for structural reasons, especially as churches grow. Feeling the push to chase numbers, pastors may bask in adulation when they succeed, but live in constant fear of failure.[7] With whom can they be honest? With whom can they talk freely? It's no wonder that some church experts insist that "Most people in full-time ministry do not have close personal friendships and consequently are alarmingly lonely and dangerously vulnerable."[8]

As much as we might believe in the priesthood of believers and all the "one another" commandments of Scripture, the daily reality of pastors is to be relegated to a different category of humanity, one that often isolates

5. Hancock, *Trespassers*, 263.
6. Willimon, *Calling and Character*, 83.
7. Galli, "Most Risky Profession."
8. Kinnaman and Ells, *Leaders that Last*, 10.

them from the care of others. Their perceived role can create a social and emotional gulf between helper and helped, shepherd and sheep.[9]

That gap, moreover, can be reinforced from both sides. As we have argued, congregations often view clergy through the lenses of unrealistic expectations. Because of this, a minister's need for emotional support is easily overlooked. As one pastor remarked,

> Most think the pastor needs no encouragement or affirmation but think that we should always be aware of [*their* needs] for encouragement and affirmation. In thirty years of pastoring, I would say that no more than a dozen times have people shown awareness.[10]

But from their side, pastors may also be reluctant to seek support. Sometimes it's because they've experienced the pain of being vulnerable with church members only to become the object of gossip. Other times, however, their own personal history gets in the way:

> It's difficult for me to ask for help because of my nature. I don't like to admit weakness. I don't like to be vulnerable. . . . My theology tells me "no," that's not right. . . . [But my] theology breaks down, because I don't want people to see that I am a hurting person.[11]

For this pastor, unfortunately, emotional and cultural training trump theology. Family histories can shape how pastors deal with their own emotional needs and those of others.[12] And while pastors' reticence to ask for support may reflect cultural norms of self-sufficiency,[13] it's not just about American individualism; the values of other cultures can also reinforce the hierarchical expectations that set clergy apart from those they serve.

Why does it matter? At a general level, social support is not only good for our emotional well-being, but our physical health as well, including immune function and how we handle stress.[14] We're social beings by nature, and as Esther Sternberg has observed, the quality of our relationships registers in our bodies:

9. E.g., Gilbert, *Who Ministers to Ministers?*, 34–37.

10. Quoted in Stone, *Ministry Killers*, 103.

11. Quoted in Gilbert, *Who Ministers to Ministers?*, 30.

12. For a discussion of how pastors can do their own family-of-origin work, see Richardson, *Becoming a Healthier Pastor*.

13. Gilbert, *Who Ministers to Ministers?*, ch. 4.

14. E.g., Uchino et al., "Social Support and Physiological Processes."

there are positive and negative effects of our social world on health. Too little interaction—loneliness—and we can wither; too much negative social interaction, and our stress response goes into overdrive. But a rich and varied fabric of positive relationships can be the strongest net to save us in our times of deepest need.[15]

We all need supportive friends, families, and colleagues. Under the pressure of stress and burnout, we need people who can help us cope by lending a hand, offering a listening ear, helping us to see things in a new light, or just plain getting us to laugh.[16]

More specifically, there's evidence of the importance of social support in pastors' lives.[17] Family support is particularly important (a topic we will return to in the final chapter). Pastors may also have friends from a time before they entered the ministry. Such friends are able to see them as people first and pastors second, and can provide a welcome place for clergy to relax and be themselves.

Many clergy also seek support from each other, where there is already some shared understanding of the burdens of ministry. As Lillian Daniel has written, "Ministers without collegial friendships have no one to bring them back."[18] Pastors need safe places to vent, to cry, to express doubt. It doesn't happen as often as it should. In part, this is due to a variety of challenges, including an implicit competitiveness that makes it difficult to be honest. Pastors, no less than other professionals, dislike feeling foolish in front of their peers.[19] When they get past such defenses, though, pastors often find the support of colleagues to be a lifeline to sanity.[20]

When I (Kurt) was pastoring, for example, I made a phone call every month to my best ministry friend. We took turns reminding each other why we do what we do, sharing the joys and the hardships of our calling.

15. Sternberg, *Balance Within*, 157.

16. Maslach, *Burnout*, 183–90.

17. E.g., Chandler, "Pastoral Burnout"; Ellison et al., "Religious Resources"; Lee, "Patterns of Stress"; Lee and Iverson-Gilbert, "Demand, Support, and Perception."

18. Daniel and Copenhaver, *Odd and Wondrous Calling*, 40.

19. Other obstacles include: unwillingness to offer support to anyone else, even other pastors; reticence to be reminded of their own pain by other pastors' stories; lack of trust that others will keep matters confidential; concern that the support will be only superficial. See Gilbert, *Who Ministers to Ministers?*, 57.

20. In a recent survey of 725 Presbyterian (PCUSA) clergy, nearly three fourths had participated in a peer support group in the last five years; 23 percent had participated in some other kind of support group. Almost all found them at least helpful; over half (54 percent) said they were "very helpful." See Research Services, PCUSA, "Findings."

That monthly call was essential to my pastoral health. Now, as the director of a Doctor of Ministry program, one of my favorite things to see is what happens among pastors outside the classroom. Around the table at mealtimes, students begin to share stories of their lives and ministries with each other. And in doing so, they realize that they are not alone, that they are not the only ones who feel crazy! This is one of the reasons I am so passionate about the importance of lifelong learning, whether at a conference or in a Doctor of Ministry program. It's not just about the skills and knowledge learned, but also about making personal connections with other pastors.

And for those in denominations that have a more centralized structure, the denomination itself can be an important source of support. Here, too, there are challenges. Many pastors are reticent to take advantage of services offered by their denominations, particularly if it means talking about their difficulties with someone who may be involved with future placement decisions. But one recent study suggests that many helpful support services are available, and pastors are taking advantage of them. In fact, they are asking denominational leaders for more: more awareness of their individual needs for support, more information about services already available, more access to confidential mental health care, and more leadership in creating system-wide policies for time off and sabbatical leave.[21]

Our emphasis here, however, is on the pastor-congregation relationship. Can pastors have supportive friendships from among the people of their own congregations? Again, some of the research evidence says yes.[22] But many clergy have been taught to avoid this, and for good reason. For all the talk of the priesthood of believers and the unity of the body amidst the diversity of gifts, the fact of the matter is that pastors are different. By virtue of their calling, profession, and office, they are uniquely set apart in the eyes of the congregation—perhaps even more so in traditions that emphasize the priestly aspects of the ministry.

Because of their differentness, what pastors say and do socially more easily becomes a bone of contention. For instance, there's the problem of perceived favoritism. Members of a congregation may have their cliques, and no one gives it a second thought. But if the pastor appears to be too chummy with a select few, others will secretly (or not so secretly!) resent

21. Trihub et al., "Denominational Support."

22. E.g., Krause et al., "Church-Based Emotional Support." Female clergy may be more successful than their male counterparts in establishing supportive relationships with members of their congregations. See McDuff and Mueller, "Social Support."

not being part of the pastor's "in-group." And as mentioned earlier, many pastors and their spouses have been badly burned by privately airing their complaints with a member of the church only to have those complaints distorted and made public. Such things happen often enough that a rule against having friends in your own congregation has become common wisdom among many pastors, and even in some seminary classrooms.

It's true that there's a risk to sharing thoughts and feelings that we want kept confidential. Pastors must always exercise wisdom and discretion. Given the pastor's position, it can actually be too great a burden for most parishioners to carry a pastor's confidences. Moreover, when a congregation is in the midst of conflict, relationships are typically unstable and emotionally volatile. This may be the time when a pastor has the greatest need to let off some steam! But it's also the time when it's most dangerous to do so, and the consequences are the most unpredictable.

So even if pastors sometimes wish they could be "just folks" with the congregation, they know they're not. It can feel unfair, and often makes the pastoral calling a particularly lonely one. Deep, trusting soul friendships are rare enough for anyone, but they are probably even rarer in the pastorate.

Rare, but not impossible. Some clergy do have church members as good friends, and they cherish those relationships. But they will tell you that this didn't happen overnight; it required a dogged persistence and a willingness to risk, little by little, until the trustworthiness of the relationship could be reasonably assured. And even then, the possibility of betrayal is never completely banished.

We believe that it is possible for pastors to have friends in the congregation (and we'll suggest a few basic and cautionary guidelines in the postscript). But that doesn't necessarily mean that the pastor must have confidants in the congregation. The larger point is that the pastor needs—and deserves!—loving and empathetic support and care, just as any other member of the body does:

> A church must minister to its minister for Christ's sake and not because the pastor maintained a good approval rating. . . . The work of the church must always be redemptive in every aspect, especially in its treatment of pastors. Only when churches care for their pastors can they bring security to the sheep. And only then will the church encourage the best of its pastor's potential, since no one ever works well in fear and insecurity.[23]

23. Susek, *Firestorm*, 192.

The congregation that is best at supporting its pastor will be one where people understand their own calling to be the body of Christ, with a shared vision of the kind of care believers should extend to one another.

And this congregation will also be the one in which conflict is most readily and thoroughly resolved.

Emotions and Conflict

A healthy congregation, then, is one that seeks to be the caring and supportive body of believers that Christ has called them to be. A natural extension of that principle is this: "Healthy congregations use their resources and strengths to manage conflict. They do not let conflict fester."[24] Note the language: it is assumed that conflict will happen. What marks the maturity of a congregation is not whether conflict occurs, but how wisely it is handled.

How common is church conflict? A recent study of large church pastors by the Leadership Network gives some indication. Pastors were asked, "Over the past two years, has there been conflict in this congregation?" Of 384 pastors of churches with 500–5,000 attendees, 29.4 percent answered, "No conflict." That means, of course, that over 70 percent of the rest of the pastors saw at least minor conflict in their churches in the past two years. Moreover, over 11 percent of the pastors reported that they had experienced the more serious kind of conflict that resulted in leaders or other people leaving the church.[25] Our guess would be that most of these major conflicts didn't start out that way; they grew gradually from smaller seeds of discontent.

The late rabbi and family therapist Ed Friedman has famously said that of all the different social systems in which one might work, "the one that functions most like a family is the church or synagogue."[26] The Bible speaks of Christians as brothers and sisters in Christ. When we speak of

24. Steinke, *Healthy Congregations*, 29.

25. Bird, "Teacher First." The figures we've reported have been recalculated from the numbers presented on pages A1 and A8 of the appendix, excluding pastors with churches of over 5,000 attendees.

26. Friedman, *Generation to Generation*, 197. Friedman was a student of family therapist Murray Bowen. Others have applied Bowen's theory to church dynamics, e.g., Richardson, *Becoming a Healthier Pastor*. For a simple introduction to the theory, see Gilbert, *Eight Concepts*; for a more in-depth treatment, see Kerr and Bowen, *Family Evaluation*.

our "church family," we usually do so with warmth and affection. But siblings also fight, sometimes cruelly.

Pastors can be the targets of unreasonable anger. Sometimes, the reason is a simple misunderstanding. I (Kurt) once received a phone call from the wife of the gardener/custodian at our church. She yelled at me for "mistreating her husband." His job description included doing light maintenance around the church, so I had him doing minor chores on a regular basis. But for some reason, they were becoming increasingly angry with me. When the wife called, I finally found out why. They had thought that "light maintenance" meant that he was only responsible for changing light bulbs! Every time I asked the gardener to do other work, he seethed. Happily, once we cleared up the misunderstanding, it became our in-joke.

Pastors themselves, because of their office, are often the targets of their parishioners' vendettas. We know of one case, for example, in which a woman asked to meet with her pastor. Being a wise and careful man, he met with her in a public place, together with his wife. At one point in the conversation, the wife excused herself to use the restroom. In those short moments another member of the congregation happened by, saw the pastor and the other woman together, and promptly went home to mount a public campaign defaming the pastor and demanding that he be ousted.

The ministry literature is littered with unfortunate stories like these. Small matters that are left to simmer can boil over with astonishing suddenness. Often the pastor feels mystified, blindsided, and betrayed. Sometimes, the stories end well, on a note of reconciliation, forgiveness, and spiritual growth. But not always. Unresolved conflict, and the pain it inflicts, can drive gifted pastors out of the ministry. In a study of nearly 1,000 ex-pastors from five denominations, well over a third reported experiencing major conflict in their final two years of ministry. Conflict, in fact, "was the main reason ministers left—conflict with parishioners, with other staff members, or with denominational officials."[27]

Congregations are complicated social systems, and the conflicts within them are similarly complex, fueled by a number of spiritual, emotional, and situational factors. We can't give you a how-to primer on managing church conflict, but others have already done so, and we've listed some helpful sources in the notes.[28] Our emphasis, again, is to encourage

27. Hoge and Wenger, *Pastors in Transition*, 29, 77.

28. Ibid., 244, recommend the following: Dobson et al., *Mastering Conflict*; Halverstadt, *Managing Church Conflict*; Lott, *Conflict Management*; Rediger, *Clergy Killers*; Susek, *Firestorm*. Also helpful are Haugk, *Antagonists*, and Shelley, *Well-Intentioned Dragons*.

mutual understanding for the benefit of both pastors and congregations. To that end, we'll explore the role of emotions in church conflict, and what it might mean to proactively promote a strong congregational immune system.

The first thing to remember is that conflict in the church is seldom just an intellectual disagreement about the facts. Pastors who have been unjustly accused know this. Going to their accusers with the facts of the matter doesn't usually make them say, "Oh? Then we've made a terrible mistake! Please forgive us." They may back off for a time, but only until the next accusation can be brought, even more insistently. It's not just about the facts, but the emotions that drive how events and ministry decisions are interpreted. On the surface, we may be having what seems to be a disagreement about what the Bible teaches. But this quickly turns into an ugly confrontation when we use Scripture to bludgeon people into submission, or to demonize them when they don't cooperate.

In healthy relationships, simple disagreements can be resolved, because people are able to remain calm and listen—*really* listen, which means understanding and considering each other's point of view without getting defensive. But disagreements easily flare into conflicts when our emotions begin to kick into high gear. Think back to chapter 2 and the biology of our stress reactions: when we're threatened, our bodies respond automatically, shaping not only what we do, but how we think and feel. In the heat of the moment, we tend to rely upon what Hugh Halverstadt calls our "gut theologies of conflict," the ingrained habits and beliefs formed in our families of origin:

> Early family life is everyone's first school of theology. In family
> fights we acquire our basic attitudes and beliefs about conflict.
> What happened to us, how authority figures behaved and dealt
> with us, and what we were told or not told about it all generated
> our gut theologies of conflict.[29]

Such theologies may be shaped by past experiences with abusive religious authorities, such that even the hint of conflict will be enough to evoke anger and fear. Or they may include the idea that because Christians are supposed to love one another, they must never disagree. Instead of actively making peace (Matt 5:9), we maintain a kind of pseudo-peace by avoiding conflict and driving disagreements underground. But they seldom stay there. Unless the accompanying emotions are dealt with, people are more

---

29. Halverstadt, *Managing Church Conflict*, 22.

likely to keep a "record of wrongs" (1 Cor 13:5), making a destructive overreaction to the next disagreement even more likely.

In other words, we do not come to conflict situations as blank slates, but as people with personal histories, including areas of particular sensitivity, which have aptly been called "emotional allergies."[30] This is true of both pastors and church members. We all have normal needs, for example, to have a place to belong, where we are accepted and affirmed, or to feel like we have some control over what happens to us. But if we've been repeatedly hurt or disappointed in these areas, we may overreact to signs that we will be hurt again.

And unfortunately, it doesn't stop there. Because a church family is a web of social connections, problems in one relationship may quickly spread to others. We're reminded of the metaphor used by the apostle James to teach about the deadly power of the tongue:

> Consider what a great forest is set on fire by a small spark. The tongue also is a fire, a world of evil among the parts of the body. It corrupts the whole body, sets the whole course of one's life on fire, and is itself set on fire by hell. . . . With the tongue we praise our Lord and Father, and with it we curse human beings, who have been made in God's likeness. Out of the same mouth come praise and cursing. My brothers and sisters, this should not be. (Jas 3:5–6, 9–10)

James could easily be describing the spiritual and emotional state of some of our own congregations—in which people publicly praise God in worship, then privately cut others down with words. These can be the sparks that ignite a firestorm of conflict,[31] because whether we realize it or not, congregations are loaded with emotional tinder.

One of the chief ways the fire spreads is by gossip. The book of Proverbs teaches that gossip starts conflict and separates friends (Prov 16:28). We are drawn to gossip "like choice morsels" and are ensnared by it (Prov 18:7–8). Paul goes further: he considers gossip to be the sign of a depraved mind, right up there with "envy, murder, strife, deceit and malice" (Rom 1:28–29). But if the truth be told, we enjoy the sense of superiority that comes from telling about someone else's faults, or the camaraderie that comes from sharing a scandalous secret. We implicitly put ourselves in a

30. Christensen and Jacobson use the term "psychological allergies" to discuss how needs for security, freedom, admiration, approval, and control play out in our relationships. *Reconcilable Differences*, 8off.

31. Susek, *Firestorm*.

more positive light by putting someone else in a negative one. And even if at some level we know we're gossiping, we find ways to kid ourselves and others that we're not. We might, for example, give gossip an air of religious respectability by calling it a prayer request. But God knows better. And if we were honest with ourselves, so would we.

Congregations who have been through it know: gossip, misunderstanding, and misinformation spread like wildfire among anxious people who haven't learned constructive ways to handle disagreement and conflict. We don't mean to be alarmist, but it needs to be said: any church may be just a matter of months away from its own demise. This is true even of those churches that seem to be successful and growing.

In fact, churches that are growing rapidly may be at special risk. The atmosphere of excitement and enthusiasm makes it more difficult for people to express their reservations about the changes that necessarily accompany growth.[32] They begin to think, "This doesn't feel like my church anymore." If they voice their discomfort, they may be dismissed (nicely, if possible!) as old-fashioned, obstructionist sticks-in-the-mud. So they murmur in the background. Some begin to gather a following, establishing a power base. When disagreements can't be worked out calmly and directly, factions of like-minded people begin to form. Groups unite against each other, or against a scapegoat—often the pastor—who is seen as the cause of all the congregation's ills.[33] These emotional dynamics smolder away until something—a controversial decision, a remark taken out of context—suddenly fans the embers into flame.

In a sense, this is a congregational corollary to the prophet Samuel's statement that "The LORD does not look at the things people look at. People look at the outward appearance, but the LORD looks at the heart" (1 Sam 16:7). It's too easy to become enamored of secular models of success that may lull us into thinking that our congregation is enjoying God's favor. But are we blind to the relational cancer eating it away from the inside?

We doubt that there has ever been, or ever will be, a congregation that has lived in perfect unity of mind and spirit. That's the reality of living on this side of Jesus' return. But that shouldn't stop us from doing everything we can to live in the unity made possible by the Holy Spirit. That is, after all, one way of putting Paul's council to troubled churches:

32. Galindo, *Hidden Lives*, especially ch. 5.
33. Lee and Balswick, *Glass House*, 48–53.

you all share the Spirit of Christ; this is the deepest reality of who you are; now live like it!

In Proverbs 26:21 we read, "As charcoal to embers and as wood to fire, so is a quarrelsome person for kindling strife." This is no surprise. But there is also great wisdom in the preceding verse: "Without wood a fire goes out; without a gossip a quarrel dies down." Firefighters don't just try to extinguish a forest fire directly; they starve it by removing the fuel. That doesn't mean identifying and rooting out the "troublemakers"! We're *all* troublemakers, each in our own way. Rather, it means striving together to be the kind of Spirit-filled, mature community in which fires don't easily take hold.

Or, to return to our earlier metaphor, it means building a strong congregational immune system. As Steinke has written,

> disease is a transaction between the invading microbe and the condition of the person. . . . All anxiety needs a host-cell, a co-contributor. We easily overlook how two sides give rise to and maintain a problem through mutual functioning.[34]

In other words, as people, we will continue to have our emotional sensitivities and gut responses to conflict. We will continue to populate local congregations. And we will continue to be susceptible to the infectious nature of anxiety. But we don't have to let the infection spread. We can consciously cultivate the kind of mutual love and support that makes it safer to disagree. We can hold one another accountable to shared practical principles that embody more godly ways to handle conflict. Halverstadt, for example, recommends that churches adhere to the following commitments of attitude and conduct:

- Exercise self-control when interacting with others.
- No one here is perfect. Mistakes are human and forgivable.
- No one here is superior or inferior. Everyone is valuable.
- When differences arise, there will be no labeling and no personal attacks.
- Speak for and be yourself.
- No personalizing of issues. Address behaviors, not persons.
- Conflicts are problems to be solved, not contests to be won.[35]

34. Steinke, *Healthy Congregations*, 19.
35. Halverstadt, *Managing Church Conflict*, 65.

That may not be your preferred list, but it's a good place to start. Principles like these respect the dignity of each member of the body, respond to human fallibility with grace, and work toward unity by putting limits around the things that divide. But in the end, what makes for a healthy church is not just how we respond to the conflicts that erupt, but the kind of relationships we cultivate before an eruption happens.

Postscript

To Pastors:

Perhaps it feels like you spend most of your waking hours supporting others. Who supports you? Ultimately, of course, you depend upon God—but like the people of your congregation, God has created you for community, to be a member of a local body where people care for one another in the name of Jesus. Are you too busy for friendship? We ask you to meditate again on the meaning of Sabbath and its implications for your busyness and self-care. Are you skeptical about having friends in the congregation? We understand why! But we also ask you to consider the following suggestions:

- *You can be friendly without having to be everyone's friend.* Some people may want a special friendship with you, for their own reasons. But most just want to know if you accept them. They'll read your tone of voice, facial expressions, and body language. Cultivate a compassion for others that expresses itself as genuine warmth. If others see this, they're less likely to be concerned about who your "real" friends are.

- *Remember that friends don't have to be "all-purpose."* The person with whom you share an interest does not have to be the person with whom you share a confidence. There are many people with whom you can simply enjoy a laugh without their also having to be an outlet for your frustrations.

- *Never trash one member of the congregation to another, even in confidence.* This should go without saying. After all, you wouldn't want the people of your church doing this either!

- *Only share your frustrations with people who understand and accept that you have weaknesses, who are honest about their own, and who are willing to confront you lovingly when necessary.* These are characteristics of people who are better able to handle the tough stuff. This kind of friendship needs to be cultivated over time, but is precious as gold in the long term.

- *Don't rely upon your family as your sole source of support.* As we'll discuss in the next chapter, the ministry environment can be stressful for your spouse and children, too—having to be your sole emotional support may make their own burdens harder to bear. Friendships with other pastors can be invaluable; see what resources your denomination may have to offer.

Be proactive in dealing with conflict and disagreement. Don't assume that everything is fine just because people are not disagreeing with you to your face. Call the community to embrace standards of conduct, give them the biblical reasons, and encourage mutual accountability—yourself included. Above all, be aware of your own areas of emotional sensitivity so that you can better manage your own reactivity. As Ronald Richardson has said,

> The job of effective church leaders is to help keep down the level of anxiety in the emotional system of the congregation. . . . They do this primarily by managing their own anxiety, and then, secondarily, by staying in meaningful contact with other key players in the situation. They do not tell others to "be calm." They simply bring their own calmness to the situation.[36]

This, in itself, won't "solve" conflict. But it will help insure that you aren't the one through whom the infection is passed. And at the very least, it will give people less to gossip about!

If you've already been deeply wounded by your church, we know how hard it is to imagine remaining in the ministry. There is a way back, but the road may be a long and arduous one. Begin by prayerfully reading and reflecting on the books about conflict listed in the notes. Guard your integrity; hold tight to your confession and calling. There may come a time when you decide the wisest course is to leave the pastorate altogether. But even as you consider it, we hope you can stay open to the possibility of God's redeeming and renewing grace breaking through your misery. Our prayers are with you!

36. Richardson, *Healthier Church*, 51.

To Congregations:

We hope that this chapter has encouraged you to take your pastor's need for support with all seriousness. Some ministers seem to have it all together, but that may in part be the projection of the image they feel is necessary. God has called us to be the body of Christ (Rom 12:5; 1 Cor 12:27), and Christ—not your pastor—is the head (Eph 4:15; Col 1:18). So extend to him or her the same loving consideration and concern that you would to any member of the community.

What, pragmatically, can you do to show your support? Here's a sample list of suggestions adapted from a summary of comments by pastors:[37]

- Refuse to engage in gossip about your pastor; when appropriate, rise to your pastor's defense when he or she is verbally attacked.

- Show your pastor that you understand the challenges of the role.

- Take the time to send personal notes or cards expressing honest and concrete appreciation, and/or asking how you can support your pastor in prayer.

- Notice when the family has a need or crisis, and reach out in a practical way (e.g., meals, housecleaning, accompanying family members to the hospital, etc.).

In general, remember that "whatever you say to your minister has the power and the potential to build them up spiritually and emotionally or chip away at their will to serve."[38]

Equally important is what you say *about* your pastor to others. Seemingly innocent jokes made at the pastor's expense, for example, are often thinly disguised complaints. Do you laugh at those jokes, even if you don't share the underlying complaint? We're not asking you to be humorless killjoys, but to recognize how that kind of humor reinforces a congregational culture in which potential problems aren't dealt with constructively. What other way can you respond that would encourage honesty and respect?

In short, complaints are particularly contagious, so guard your words carefully. With your pastor's help, cultivate lay leaders who have a strong vision of the church as a body, and who are committed in word and deed to patterns of healthy relationship. If, heaven forbid, you already find yourself in a rapidly deteriorating church crisis, get outside help immediately. Your

37. Stone, *Ministry Killers*, 101–2.

38. Dobson, *Caring for Your Pastor*, 99. The quote has been altered to be gender-neutral.

denomination should be able to recommend an outside consultant that understands the unique spiritual and social dimensions of church conflict.

To Seminarians:

The graduate school experience is full of promise. Your education is meant to prepare you for the professional side of ministry, and you may take up your first church appointment with eager expectation. The people who have hired you may commend both your energy and your vision. But here's a hard reality: whatever they may say to recruit you as a pastor, people often resist change. We're not talking about open deceit; rather, it's the understandable ambivalence of anxious people who have both hopes for the future *and* lingering concerns about the past. People won't be more receptive to your ideas just because you say them more forcefully. View this as part of your practical training. As church conflict expert Ron Susek has said,

> Don't assume that seminaries create pastors. They don't because they can't. Seminaries can only provide the tools for becoming a pastor. The church, more than any human factor, will determine the shaping of a pastor.[39]

Thus, it's wise to sit loosely to your vision while you adjust to the local culture and history of the congregation you're about to serve. During the interview process, for example, you might want to find out why the previous pastor left; eventually, you will inherit the conflicts that remain unresolved. So while you're still in seminary, if someone isn't teaching you communication and conflict-resolution skills, go get the training yourself—you'll be glad you did. Such training can't always prevent conflict from happening; you simply don't have that much control. But given your office, you do have *some* control, and these skills will give you a better chance of managing your own anxiety to the benefit of all.

Begin now to plan where you can get ongoing social support. It may be hard for you to imagine, at this stage, the reality of the congregational dynamics we're describing in this book. The simple truth is that pastoral ministry isn't something you should try do without support, without the resource of having someone you can speak to honestly. And as we've suggested to pastors above, you can't rely on getting all your support needs met by your family or spouse.

---

39. Susek, *Firestorm*, 187.

So again, plan ahead, while you have the chance. Look into what's available through your denomination. Don't let yourself fall bit by bit into isolation and loneliness. Some seminarians band together during graduate school and keep their relationship going after graduation, even when their ministries disperse them to different denominations and different regions of the country. You can keep in touch by phone or email—we even know a group that has a yearly ritual of meeting together for a retreat! Whatever creative idea you come up with, do something now to make sure you'll have the support you need later.

9

Make Your Family a Priority

Profound commitment in marriage . . . is not a compromise of our pledge to "seek first the Kingdom of God."

–Richard John Neuhaus[1]

Up to this point, we've focused primarily on the relationship between the pastor and the congregation, with only a few comments here and there about the experience of being a pastor's spouse or child. It's time to be more explicit in this final chapter, for these experiences deserve specific and separate treatment.

Much of what has already been said about pastors applies by extension to their families. Ministers, as we've seen, have a very public role in which their lives are subjected to constant scrutiny. They are expected to live up to a variety of congregational expectations. Likewise, the spouses and children of ministers routinely complain of living in a fishbowl—the sense of being under the congregation's ever-present watchful gaze.

Do church members understand what it means to live or to grow up in a minister's family? The stories that spouses and children tell reveal both joy and heartache. On the one hand, a congregation that interacts in healthy ways can create a wonderful, life-giving environment in which the pastor's family feels loved and cherished. On the other hand, the opposite is also true: trouble in the pastor-congregation relationship easily

---

1. Neuhaus, *Freedom for Ministry*, 58.

spills over into the family, creating a stressful environment of confusion, anxiety, and resentment.

Anne Jackson, for example, was raised as a "PK," a preacher's kid. She recalls her father's second pastorate, at a small church in rural west Texas. Though she was only in the fourth grade, Anne began to notice how upset her father was after the monthly deacon's meeting. Being naturally curious, she decided to find out what was going on.

She set up an elaborate scheme to spy on the next meeting, pretending to go to bed and then sneaking out of her parsonage bedroom to eavesdrop from a closet adjacent to the room where the deacons met. That night, there was a confrontation over her father's request for vacation time. Anne recognized the music minister's voice, and was taken aback by how hostile he sounded. She had no idea that the deacons she respected so much could argue in this way.

Then, from out of the blue, the same man called her father a liar, and threatened to ask for his resignation. He had seen the pastor park his cars in the church parking lot instead of in his own driveway, and accused the pastor of trying to create the false impression of having more people at the church than they really did. The pastor calmly replied that he had moved his cars because of landscaping work at the parsonage—work that had been approved at a previous deacon's meeting. The music minister grumbled in retreat, but did not apologize.

After the meeting was over, Anne snuck back into her room. She heard her father come home soon after, and listened to her mother cry as he reported what happened at the meeting. She writes:

> I didn't sleep much that night. My heart was still racing, and my stomach felt a little sick from hearing people who were supposedly closest to my dad tear him apart and refuse to come to his defense. These were Christian men. I went to school with their children. We would eat at their homes, and they'd come over to ours.
>
> A little bit of my world crashed in on me that night.
>
> And I wish I would have known that this night was only the beginning.[2]

Many children of ministers, whether they lived in a parsonage or not, have had similar experiences. Little by little, they learned that the friendly faces they saw on a Sunday morning could mask other thoughts and feelings. They were exposed to tangled church politics that they were

2. Jackson, *Mad Church Disease*, 20.

too young to understand. Some grew up bitter and resentful of the church. One adult PK put it bluntly: "I hate church people. I hate what they did to my dad. He was never the same after losing the church."[3]

Thus, the burdens of ministry are not borne by the pastor alone; the spouses and children also struggle with the stressors that come with the role. But if families must share the burdens of the pastorate, they can also share the joys of living among a supportive church family. This doesn't happen by itself. Pastors must make the well-being of their families—and everyone's families—a top priority, and help the members of their churches to do the same.

That's not to make an idol of family life, as if domestic happiness were somehow more important than the progress of the gospel.[4] It's to remember that the never-ending demands of the ministry can tempt both pastors and congregations to forget that care for one's family is a godly vocation. Allison Moore writes:

> When vocation means only ordained ministry, and people seek to anchor their relationship with God primarily in activities that promote ordained ministry, their relationships with their families can suffer. . . . Vocation needs to be understood as the living out of a relationship with God in and through *all* the commitments into which God has invited us.[5]

Christians rightly make God's kingdom their first priority (Matt 6:33), but get sideways when they make a false dichotomy between this and all other commitments. For pastors, it's not either-or, but both-and: learning to recognize the presence of the kingdom in and through their commitment to the ministry *and* to their families.[6]

We're sure most Christians—pastors and congregations alike—would agree that strong families are important to the life of a church. It's a sin to take the well-being of one's spouse and children for granted. But that is precisely why we're grieved to see how often ministry demands are allowed to ride roughshod over the emotional and spiritual needs of clergy families. We should all know better. In this chapter, therefore, we'll review some of the key challenges. We'll begin with general concerns that affect the entire family, and then turn to the special concerns of spouses and PKs.

3. Quoted in Kinnaman and Ells, *Leaders that Last*, 39.

4. E.g., Lee, *Beyond Family Values.*

5. Moore, *Clergy Moms*, 14 (emphasis added).

6. Neuhaus, *Freedom for Ministry*, 92. See also Veith, *God at Work*, especially ch. 6.

The Challenges of Being a Clergy Family

In 1970, the United Church of Christ released a landmark study entitled *Ex-Pastors,* in which researchers asked over 200 male clergy why they had left the ministry. For those who were able to identify a "dominant reason" for leaving, 13.2 percent chose "problems of wife and children," and an additional 7 percent chose "divorce or separation." Other reasons, such as "money problems" (6.2 percent) or "unable to relocate when necessary" (14.7 percent), may also have had family implications. But even if these latter two reasons are not included, this means that at least one in five UCC pastors who left the ministry could clearly identify marriage and family concerns as their main reason for leaving.[7]

The researchers also asked these ex-pastors how leaving the ministry had impacted their families. The most common response (27.5 percent) was that family issues had not been the direct reason for leaving, but the family was happier anyway. Almost as many (24.4 percent) said that family problems *had* contributed to the decision (even if it wasn't the main reason), and that the situation had improved. Taken together, these findings suggest that over half of the pastors who left parish ministry experienced that decision as being good for their families, whether family problems were at the root of the decision or not.[8]

It seems little has changed since 1970. A more recent study targeted a larger sample of clergy, across five denominations, who had also left their pastorates. They gave a number of reasons for leaving; the most common was that they had other ministry opportunities to pursue. The other reasons were negative, and by now should come as no surprise: unreasonable expectations, burnout, and conflict. In numbers similar to the earlier study, 11 percent mentioned the "needs of family and children," and 6 percent cited "marital difficulties or divorce." Unlike the 1970 study, this one included female clergy, who were much more likely than men to cite the need to care for their families as a major motivation for leaving.[9]

For pastors who leave the ministry, therefore, family problems are a common reason. And we wonder how many more families regularly suffer the pressures of ministry but *haven't* left. What, then, are the family challenges that push some pastors out of the ministry? Many issues have been raised over the years; below are four of the most commonly cited.

---

7. Jud et al., *Ex-Pastors,* 50–51.
8. Ibid., 183.
9. Hoge and Wenger, *Pastors in Transition,* 35–39.

Boundaries and Time

As discussed in chapter 7, sometimes the social boundary between the congregation and the pastor's family needs to be more clearly defined. Most people expect to be able to leave their work at the office. If they bring work home, it's by choice. But that's not the case for many clergy, whose congregations expect 24/7 access. And again, the boundaries are even fuzzier in the case of parsonage life. What families do becomes even more visible when they live next door to the church. Parishioners may show up on the parsonage doorstep for any number of reasons. Or someone may notice that the porch light has been left on, and complain to the pastor about being careless with the electrical bill.

But a minister's family doesn't have to live in a parsonage to experience the problems of fuzzy boundaries. All that's required, for example, is a needy parishioner who knows the pastor's home telephone number: "When Mrs. Johnson calls to tell the pastor her sister just died and the pastor is not home, she tells whoever answered the telephone, whether it is the pastor's spouse or their twelve-year-old daughter."[10] It's not because Mrs. Johnson is a bad person. Under normal circumstances, she may understand perfectly well that it's not appropriate to unburden her grief to a twelve-year-old. But how many Mrs. Johnsons are there in a congregation? How many others wouldn't hesitate to call the pastor's home, at any hour of the night, without considering the impact on family members?

Perhaps the most common class of boundary issues has to do with the time needed for families to nurture their relationships. When it comes to pastors having time to spend with their families, there's both good news and bad news.[11] The good news: their schedules often allow more flexibility than typical jobs. That means, for example, that many pastors can attend school events in support of their children. The bad news: the family can't always count on having the time they want or need.

In most families, weekends and evenings are the best candidates for family time. But for pastors, weekends are the busiest days of the week, and family-friendly holidays like Christmas and Easter involve additional ministry responsibilities. Evenings are frequently co-opted by church events, committee meetings, and unexpected crises. All of this leaves the family feeling like they have to compete with the congregation for the pastor's time—a battle they frequently lose.

10. Hileman, "Unique Needs," 130.
11. Stalfa, "Protestant Clergy Marriage."

This may be particularly difficult for clergywomen, who often feel stuck in an either-or choice between ministry and motherhood.[12] Because they typically approach leadership more relationally, they may feel the needs of the congregation more keenly.[13] Add to this the expectations of what it means to be a devoted wife and mother—expectations that may come from the congregation, their husbands, or their own consciences— and it's easy to imagine how they can feel torn between their roles. Said one female pastor, "There's always more to do than can get done. . . . I feel guilty about not giving enough to the church and not giving enough to my family."[14] Another female minister agreed:

> The primary stresses I have encountered thus far in my ministry are within my family relationships. . . . I have struggled mightily to achieve some sort of balance [between ministry and family demands]. It is a never-ending, everyday, all the time struggle that may yet fail.[15]

Thus, the demands of ministry frequently make family together- ness more difficult. We remember one pastor's family that assembled in the living room for a long-awaited evening of fun and games. They had barely begun when the doorbell rang. The children listened at a distance as the pastor stood on the doorstep, dealing with a distraught parishioner. It soon became clear that game night had been pre-empted—again—and one by one they drifted away.

Even for the most sacrificial and ministry-minded of families, it's hard not to resent the loss, especially when there are no assurances of hav- ing other evenings together. Clergy families need the cooperation of their congregations to help them establish clear limits that protect the time the families need to nurture healthy relationships.

Frequent Moves

Who doesn't know how stressful moving can be? Here's one researcher's shortlist of the demands a relocating family faces:

12. E.g., Moore, *Clergy Moms*, 57.

13. Zikmund et al., *Clergy Women*, ch. 3; Frame and Shehan, "Care for the Caregiver."

14. Frame and Shehan, "Relationship between Work and Well-Being in Clergy- women," 13, 15. See also Moore, *Clergy Moms*.

15. Frame and Shehan, "Care for the Caregiver," 369.

disruption of family routines, the severance of support networks, potential loss of spouse's employment and thus income,
change in housing, new demands of work settings, and minor
hassles related to establishing oneself in a new community.[16]

Pastors in more congregationally oriented denominations may not have to
face this as often; some are able to stay leading the same church for many
years, sometimes even decades. But denominations with a more itinerant
system tend to relocate their clergy more frequently; their families have to
face the disorientation of being uprooted again and again.

There is some evidence that moving can be more stressful for family
members than for the pastor, who may have more to look forward to in
a new position.[17] Clergy also get social support from non-local peer networks that survive the move, while the spouse and children must find new
friends. And though pastors may need to throw themselves into their new
responsibilities, such busyness can be a way of coping with the change.
Family members, who may still be adjusting or even grieving, are left to
themselves to get their new home in order.

And sometimes, when congregations greet the families upon their
arrival, the stresses of moving and being in the fishbowl collide. One pastor, upon his retirement, told of his first day in one particular parsonage.
Dazed, dirty, and exhausted, he and his wife were standing amidst a chaos
of cardboard boxes when the doorbell rang. It was a woman from the
parsonage committee. Realizing the importance of the visit, the couple re-
luctantly invited her in. The woman welcomed them politely, then turned
to brush her gloved fingers over the top of the doorframe, clucking sym-
pathetically to the wife, "I can see, my dear, that you have not had time to
do your dusting."[18]

We doubt many pastors get the white-glove treatment these days! But
overeager parishioners can jump in too quickly, laying expectations on the
family before they've had a chance to recover from the move. The truly
hospitable congregation realizes that the pastor's family is in the midst of
a stressful transition, and looks for non-intrusive ways to welcome them
into the fold.

16. Frame, "Relocation and Well-Being," 416.

17. Frame, "Relocation and Well-Being"; Frame and Shehan, "Work and
Well-Being."

18. Joyner, Life in the Fish Bowl, 15.

Insufficient Income

Money can be a complicated issue in any calling, and the pastorate is no exception. Overall, pastors tend to be paid less than other professionals of similar levels of education and training. But there are many variables that seem to affect a pastor's salary.[19] Denominational polity, of course, is one. Church size is a key factor, with larger churches being richer in resources and paying higher salaries. This can be imbued with a secular aura of success, leaving many pastors (and parishioners!) feeling that their ministries have failed if the congregation doesn't show impressive growth in numbers. Megachurches (and their pastors) may get all the media hype, but they represent only a very small percentage of the total number of Protestant churches in the United States. The plain fact is that the vast majority of pastors serve small to medium churches, and many small churches struggle financially.

There are important gaps in salary patterns. African-American ministers earn less and are less likely to enjoy benefits like healthcare and retirement contributions. Women earn less than men overall, in part because they are more likely to be called to smaller congregations.[20] A United Methodist report found similar gender and race gaps in salary, but attributed most of the discrepancy to factors like church size and level of seniority, expressing optimism that the gender gap in particular would narrow over time.[21]

Even if this is so, money issues will continue to be a source of stress for many pastors, in two ways. First, in a market-driven society such as ours, money becomes a stand-in for value: to some extent, what a congregation pays symbolizes the pastor's worth. Granted, this is far from ideal theologically—though Paul suggests that those who minister to the church have the right to expect fair financial support (1 Cor 9:7–12; 1 Tim 5:17–18). The point is that because of its symbolic importance, money easily becomes a flash point in the tension between a pastor and congregation. One clergy husband, for example, lamented the way a church committee dickered over his wife's annual raise. In less than two years under her leadership, the church had enjoyed growth in numbers, giving, and

19. McMillan and Price, "How Much Should We Pay?"
20. Ibid.
21. Johnson, "Salaries."

enthusiasm. But when it came time for her salary review, a key board member stated outright, "She receives more than any woman should earn."[22]

The second concern is a purely practical one: does the minister's family have what they need to live in a way comparable to the bulk of the congregation? Do they have enough to pay the bills or be financially secure? As one recent report concluded, "the majority of clergy have bare minimum salaries and few fringe benefits."[23] The daughter of a Lutheran pastor recalls:

> My dad was the pastor at the biggest church in town, but unlike his peers in business or medicine, bigger didn't translate into more pay or other incentives either, if you don't count the clergy discount he received at the local 9-hole golf course. We were broke. Five kids and one small income will do that, even after the car allowance and parsonage are factored in. We often relied on the money my dad earned by officiating at funerals and weddings just to make ends meet.[24]

It's uncomfortable enough for pastors to speak openly of money, for fear of sounding worldly or materialistic. And the conversation can be complicated by misinformation. Some church members, for example, think of the parsonage as free housing, not understanding that the parsonage exists to make pastoral transitions more efficient for the *congregation*. The rental value of the parsonage is deducted from the pastor's compensation, and the family builds no equity, unless the church specifically sets aside funds for that purpose—meaning that some pastors can reach their retirement years with no home of their own.

Pastors, as a group, are not greedy people! They, and their families, understand that ministry entails sacrifice. But congregations that care won't take that sacrifice for granted. A careful and clear-eyed look at how congregational expectations affect the pastor's salary and expenses—including out-of-pocket ministry expenses[25]—is one tangible way to show support, for which pastors' families will be deeply grateful.

---

22. Anonymous, "I'm Ted."

23. McMillan and Price, "How Much Should We Pay?," 19.

24. Olson, "Reflections," 25.

25. E.g., does the congregation recognize/reimburse the costs associated with meeting parishioners for coffee, or taking the youth group to pizza? See Mickey and Ashmore, *Clergy Families*, 112–13.

The Family's Own Need for Pastoral Care

Eugene Peterson has emphasized the need for pastors to have spiritual direction.[26] They are rightly expected to be spiritual leaders in their congregations. But with that expectation comes the temptation to avoid pressure by hiding one's own spiritual struggles from the congregation or even from oneself. He writes,

> There is a saying among physicians that the doctor who is his own doctor has a fool for a doctor. . . . If those entrusted with the care of the body cannot be trusted to look after their own bodies, far less can those entrusted with the care of souls look after their own souls, which are even more complex than bodies and have a correspondingly greater capacity for self-deceit.[27]

Again, pastors are not alone in this. Because of a congregation's expectations, the members of the pastor's family can be caught between how they feel and how they believe they're supposed to act. Church conflict involving the pastor, for example, puts the family in a particularly precarious position:

> It may be especially hard on clergy spouses and children when the pastor is treated badly by members of the congregation because they must continue to attend worship services and church activities and socialize with the very people who are working against their mom or dad, husband or wife, all the while maintaining a sense of Christian charity and at least a facade of friendliness.[28]

In the midst of such a social environment, where do family members go for spiritual guidance? Who pastors the pastor's family? Clergy and their spouses, of course, guide their own children. But who pastors the pastor's spouse? Wendy Murray Zoba captures the difficulty well:

> Sometimes it is difficult when a wife hears her husband preach, to hear the "prophetic word" over the voice of the man who gets ticked off when she leaves the bathroom light on. Sometimes she can't get past the spot on his tie or the funny twirl in his hair. And she has heard that joke at least twice before.[29]

26. Peterson, *Working the Angles*, ch. 8.
27. Ibid., 165.
28. Hileman, "Unique Needs," 134.
29. Zoba, "Pastors' Wives," 23.

When things get tense in the church, the situation is more complicated. Spouses and children of embattled pastors are reluctant to add their own concerns about congregational politics to the pastor's load of cares. Pastors are reluctant to let their struggles be known to people in the denominational hierarchy, and sometimes even to other local pastors. And what if the problems are in the family itself? The pastor's spouse certainly can't go to the pastor for marital advice! As one minister's wife has written,

> When you are a pastor's wife, who is *your* pastor? I have not really had a pastor since we have been in the ministry. When your husband is the church pastor, it is difficult for him to be your pastor. Who helps *us* with *our* marriage? Sometimes, I wish we went to a different church. . . . At times, I truly feel alone and abandoned.[30]

In other words, parishioners have the pastor as a spiritual resource, and if that doesn't help, they feel free to try somewhere else. But the pastor's spouse and children may feel they have nowhere to go. And in many congregations, it would be unseemly for a pastor's spouse to seek counsel from anyone, especially another pastor.

It is right to expect spiritual integrity and maturity of pastors. But this should be expected of all Christians! Putting pastors and their families on a spiritual pedestal is dangerous: it invites play-acting to preserve the peace, which in turn cuts pastors off from the support they need to thrive.

Thus, congregations that understand their calling to live as the body of Christ also understand that clergy and their family members are not exempt from the need for pastoral care themselves. That compassionate recognition can help create a climate in which pastors' families are freer to be spiritually honest, knowing they have been embraced by a congregation that understands grace.

Married to the Minister

For well over a decade, statistics reported by George Barna's market research organization have repeatedly suggested that "born again Christians have the same likelihood of divorce as do non-Christians."[31] According to a massive study of over 4,500 clergy conducted by Hartford Seminary in the mid 1990s, the same may be true of pastors. The researchers found that

30. Diana Langford, quoted in Langford, *Pastor's Family*, 20 (emphasis in original).

31. Barna Group, "Born Again Christians." The finding has been disputed, often on the basis of what Barna means by "born again."

24 percent of the women clergy and 18 percent of the men had been divorced, compared to overall population statistics of 23 percent for women and 22 percent for men.[32] Veteran pastors H. B. London and Neil Wiseman claim that pastors have the "second highest divorce rate among all professions," and are just as likely as their parishioners to divorce.[33]

Part of the problem is an inherent competition of loyalties: pastors take ordination vows "that are not unlike the marriage vows."[34] When this gets out of balance, spouses feel like pastors are more committed to the church than to them. This creates a challenging context for the health of the marriage partnership; the competing pulls are always there, and must constantly be managed. Hoge and Wenger have warned:

> the ministry as a vocation seems to contain within itself some risk factors for divorce, among them emotionally demanding work, the obligation to be constantly "on call," and unspoken expectations from laity about the role of clergy spouses.[35]

We've seen some of the expectations of spouses in earlier chapters. Indeed, many books have been written by pastors' wives for the edification of their less experienced sisters.[36] But little has been written about the husbands of clergywomen, or the special challenges of couples in which both spouses are ordained. We'll examine each of these in turn, and include a reflection on the trials of being unmarried in the ministry.

The Wives of Male Pastors: A Two-for-One Deal?

In 1973, sociologist Hanna Papanek coined the phrase "two-person career" to describe the situation in which both partners in a marriage are drawn into the expectations of the husband's employer.[37] This is a good description of the traditional understanding of the role of the minister's wife. The man is interviewed and hired as the pastor, and it is assumed that his wife will automatically take on certain functions: teaching Sunday school, playing the piano, organizing church socials, and so on. She is expected to set an example for the congregation from her proper place in the

32. Zikmund et al., *Clergy Women*, 41.

33. London and Wiseman, *Pastors at Greater Risk*, 86.

34. Daniel and Copenhaver, *Odd and Wondrous Calling*, 179.

35. Hoge and Wenger, *Pastors in Transition*, 151.

36. E.g., Dobson, *More than the Pastor's Wife*; Floyd, *10 Things*; Hawkins, *One Ministry Wife*; McKay, *Cute Shoes*; Pannell, *Being a Minister's Wife*; Williams, *Piano*.

37. Papanek, "Men, Women, and Work."

front pew, managing her children and reverently taking in every word of her husband's sermons.

Some clergy wives know themselves to be called—in the same way that the pastor is called—to just such a role, or one like it, and are gifted accordingly. But many have neither the calling nor the gifts, and chafe under the way such role expectations are taken for granted by their congregations, their husbands, or both. Lorna Dobson suggests that this may be more of a problem in smaller and more tightly knit traditional congregations than in larger seeker-oriented ones; parishioners who have lived a largely unchurched life don't have the same expectations of clergy and their families.[38] Whatever the case may be, the women who must deal with such expectations often feel stifled by them. As one pastor's wife stated,

> This is not a two-for[-one] package. You are hiring him. My role is to be his spouse and to support him as any other spouse would support their spouse. And I will participate in the life of the church as any other member would based on my gifts and abilities. Please don't expect anything beyond that.[39]

What this woman and many others are asking for is the freedom to serve the church in a way that would be expected of *any* devoted member of the congregation—according to her gifts, not a preset list of expectations that are part of a package deal or established by how the previous minister's wife filled the role.

The problem with the two-for-one expectation, therefore, is not simply that the pastor's wife may be shoehorned into a role that doesn't fit. The larger issue is that her God-given gifts and unique contribution to the life of the congregation are wasted or ignored:

> The hardest thing for me is everyone wanting a piece of my husband and not acknowledging me in the least. . . . I feel like the person in the background who is only here to take care of the kids so he can be free to take care of everyone else.[40]

This woman lives in her husband's shadow, describing what Steinke calls a "clergy-focused" congregation, one that emotionally invests too much in the pastor and loses the sense of the whole.[41] This becomes even more

---

38. Dobson, *More than the Pastor's Wife*, 23–24.
39. McMinn et al., "Positive Coping," 452.
40. Quoted in McKay, *Cute Shoes*, 24.
41. Steinke, *Healthy Congregations*, 44–47.

complicated when the pastor's wife must deal with other women in the congregation who want her husband's individual attention:

> Many of your congregations have a Ms. Touchy-Feely. She's the one who is always trying to get a full-on pastor hug. Who always needs counseling. Who never comes close to your husband if you are near.[42]

In such situations, pastors' wives may need to help their sometimes oblivious husbands to better manage their interpersonal boundaries.[43] And they must take care lest they allow themselves to be victimized by women who befriend them just to get closer to the pastor.

Indeed, the possibilities and pitfalls of church friendships are a key concern for clergy wives. They are already more likely than their husbands to depend on relationships outside the family for social support.[44] But as discussed in chapter 8, friendships within the congregation may be avoided, leaving them feeling lonely and isolated. Even when such friendships are possible, the minister's wife may still feel that other women have difficulty relating to her as a person in her own right, apart from her role. For some clergy wives, the only viable alternative is to find solace in virtual networks, where they can safely share stories online and receive encouragement from their peers.[45]

On balance, though, the overall consensus is that it is possible for pastors' wives to have female friends among the congregation, as long as they avoid the perception of cliquishness and maintain some wise boundaries. Susie Hawkins, for example, recommends holding fast to two rules: "never share something with a church member that would affect how she would view your husband in the pulpit," and "never discuss 'church business' such as finances, staff relationships, or confidential matters."[46] Where careful limits like these are observed and expectations are realistic and appropriate to their giftedness, ministry wives can thrive.

---

42. McKay, *Cute Shoes*, 81.

43. This may include, e.g., staying close to the pastor before and after the service, participating in his counseling sessions with women, and working to keep the marital relationship strong. McKay, *Cute Shoes*, 81–82.

44. McMinn et al., "Positive Coping," 445–57.

45. See, e.g., Lisa McKay's blog/website at www.apreacherswife.com.

46. Hawkins, *One Ministry Wife*, 76.

The Husbands of Female Pastors: A Role Still under Construction

Though the number of ordained women has increased over the years, as of yet there's no stereotype of the clergy husband like there is of the clergy wife. This relative lack of role expectations can befuddle some congregations. "Some parishioners did not know at first how to treat me," mused one clergy husband.[47] Another reported that his wife's male colleagues were just as confused. "What is it like being married to a minister?" one male pastor asked of this clergy husband. "Why don't you ask your wife?" was his retort.[48]

Uncertainty and awkwardness abounds. Clergy husbands are frequently and unthinkingly introduced as the minister's "wife," to the embarrassment of all. Some church members make jokes at the husband's expense. If he attends conferences with his wife, others may assume that *he* is the pastor and she is the dutiful spouse. And at such conferences, he may find himself in meetings where he is the only male in a roomful of ministry wives—a humorous yet uncomfortable situation!

Occupying a role that's still under construction can have its advantages. A study published in 1986 suggested that clergy husbands were mostly exempt from the expectation of the two-person package deal so often placed on clergy wives.[49] Over two decades later, the same observation still rings true. Pastor Lillian Daniel's experience is worth quoting at length:

> The clergy husband, a relatively new character on the religious scene, gets a break from some of [the expectations of a two-for-one deal]. If there are role expectations, they are so new that they have less power. In some ways, the clergy husband is treated like a man who does something generous that is against gender type. Like the dad who shows up at school to volunteer, surrounded by volunteer mothers, he receives special attention for doing what women have done for years.

When a clergy wife misses church, people wonder where she is. The clergy husband can show up at church and hear, "How wonderful that you are so supportive." When a clergy wife chooses not to participate in a role that previous clergy wives have played, she runs the risk of disappointing the church. The clergy husband seems to get to choose his role, and given

47. Anonymous, "I'm Ted."
48. Quoted in Deming and Stubbs, *Men Married to Ministers*, 14.
49. Deming and Stubbs, *Men Married to Ministers*.

that most people do not know what to expect of a clergy husband, any interest he has in any aspect of the church is greeted with delight. "Your husband is really something," they tell me over and over again.[50]

Daniel is describing the upside of the lack of role definition: clergy husbands don't have stereotyped expectations to live up to, so anything they do to support their wives is received as a gift. There are exceptions, of course, as in the case of the husband who reported being expected to "vacuum the church, . . . prepare coffee, tea, and punch, type and print bulletins, keep up the church grounds, cut firewood, fix things, and help with sermons."[51] But for the most part, clergy husbands seem much freer than clergy wives.

This freedom, unfortunately, can be a source of strain in the marriage. It's long been assumed that clergy wives would function as their husbands' assistants, so their contribution has been taken for granted. Neither the congregation nor even the male pastor may be fully aware of just how much a devoted clergy wife can ease the burden of ministry. Female pastors, however, have no "wives" to help them in the same way.[52]

That's not to say that their husbands aren't supportive. But it's important to recognize how confusing the roles can be for both spouses. To say that the clergy husband's role is still under construction is the flip side of saying that the expectations of ordained women are unclear as well. How do two people, who may have grown up with traditional gender models, navigate a marriage in which the wife is a public authority figure? How do they divide up family and household responsibilities? Whose job is the "real" job? Is it the one that makes more money? Does the husband move to follow his wife's career, or does she move to follow his?

There are no easy answers; each couple will need to work out the balance themselves. But at the very least, congregations should be aware of the tension, and stay alert to the things they say and do that exacerbate the strain. Effusively praising the husband for his every contribution, for example, can rankle when the couple is trying to work out a more egalitarian compromise behind the scenes.

And even if a church has officially hired a female pastor, there are likely to be parishioners who are deeply ambivalent about being led by a woman. Some church members, for example, unhappy with something

---

50. Daniel, "Pastor's Husband," 29. An updated version is found in Daniel and Copenhaver, *Odd and Wondrous Calling*, 161–62.

51. Quoted in Deming and Stubbs, *Men Married to Ministers*, 12.

52. Cody-Rydzewski, "Married Clergy Women."

the pastor has said or done, will go to her husband with the implied expectation that he will straighten her out. Supportive clergy husbands have learned to straighten the parishioner out instead! But wise and supportive congregations, aware but not afraid of the differences within their own ranks, also work to eliminate that kind of inhospitality.

Two-Clergy Couples: When Both Spouses Are Ordained

When both spouses are clergy, there can be an added depth of mutual understanding and support within the marriage. Both understand the joys and burdens, the pushes and pulls. There is, as one couple put it, a sense of partnership in which "you have this shared Christian life, shared priorities . . . [and] shared values" that helps the spouses develop together as a ministry team.[53]

At the same time, however, another layer of complexity is being added to the pastor-congregation relationship. The spouses may serve different churches, or the same church in different capacities, or even share one position as co-pastors, in some combination of full- and part-time work. Each situation, in its own unique way, combines the challenges of being both clergy and clergy spouse at the same time.

Take the case of the two spouses serving separate congregations. Again, because clergy husbands have fewer expectations put on them, the man may not be expected to show up for functions at his wife's church. When he does, "he is greeted like a rock star, with comments like, 'How wonderful you could make it. We know you must be so busy!'" But when the situation is reversed, and the female pastor attends an event at her husband's church, the attitude of the members there is, "Well, it's about time"—suggesting that to some extent she is expected to carry the expectations of being the pastor in one church, and of being the pastor's wife in the other.[54]

Then there are the logistical challenges. If having time together as a family is difficult when one parent is a pastor, imagine what happens when both parents are pastors, serving churches with different or competing schedules. For example, who's on deck to take care of the children when both parents have ministry responsibilities at the same time? PKs can be left sitting around a church for hours, waiting for either Mom or Dad to finish talking to people.

53. Quoted by James, "Two Pastors under One Roof."
54. Daniel, in Daniel and Copenhaver, *Odd and Wondrous Calling*, 162.

What about working in the same church? On the positive side of the ledger, as Christopher James observes, clergy couples who co-pastor are good for the congregation because the mutual support the spouses give each other results in more hours of work than the church would get with one pastor. And the work can be of higher quality, when the spouses split the responsibilities according to their gifts. As one male pastor observed, "The parts that I don't like that [my wife] does get done immensely better. My stewardship campaign sucks, but [hers] doesn't . . . because she loves stewardship."[55] It's also a practical benefit for the spouses. It can be a blessing to have a spouse nearby who understands the responsibilities and has the gifts to help. As one pastor quipped, "If it's Saturday night and I don't have a sermon for Sunday or even an idea, there's someone just down the hall who might jump-start me."[56]

But again, there are challenges. Gender assumptions can play into the pastor-congregation relationship, as when the husband is accorded more respect or authority than his wife. Or a congregation may value the gifts of one spouse over the gifts of the other, as when one is clearly a better preacher. There are also practical matters: unlike unmarried members of the pastoral staff, one pastor can't cover for the other if they're trying to go on a family vacation![57] And with respect to the marriage partnership itself, one pair of researchers explicitly warns that highly competitive spouses should avoid co-pastoring altogether.[58]

Thus, whether they serve the same or different churches, there are advantages and disadvantages to a marriage between pastors. A family-centered congregation that hires one or both spouses can enjoy the benefits, while simultaneously understanding the practical challenges and adjusting their expectations accordingly.

The Unmarried Pastor

The apostle Paul treats singleness as a vocation in its own right, one which allows a person to be devoted wholeheartedly to kingdom work without the distractions that go with married life (e.g., 1 Cor 7). It's far from clear, however, that many others would agree. Some church members seem uncomfortable around unmarried clergy, as if an unspoken taboo were being

55. Quoted by James, "Two Pastors under One Roof."
56. Doug Earle, quoted in Stoeltje, "Clergy Couples."
57. James, "Two Pastors under One Roof."
58. Rallings and Pratto, *Two-Clergy Marriages*, 66.

violated. And as we saw in chapter 2, the fact that a minister has no family to go home to gives some congregations license to expect even more of their time!

Many clergy would pursue marriage if they could—but find dating to be a challenge. Barbara Zikmund and her colleagues, in the Hartford study cited earlier, asked single pastors whether their profession was an advantage or a disadvantage to forming "sustained intimate relationships." Nearly half of the men said it was a disadvantage, compared to 61 percent of the women. Time and opportunity were a concern for both genders; they were simply too busy to meet someone, let alone to have a serious relationship. The constant scrutiny of the congregation was another obstacle—imagine what happens when the pastor brings his or her "significant other" to church!

But for women, there was an added wrinkle. The most common explanation they gave was that men feel intimidated by their role. Said one clergywoman: "It is hard to date men as a single woman pastor . . . they are scared of you as a professional 'religious person.'"[59] From her study, Moore describes how awkward it is for female clergy "to tell a date what they do for a living." The reactions run the gamut of "incomprehension, rejection, confusion, expectations of prudery, or the need to 'behave' in the presence of a moral exemplar."[60] Dating is hard enough without such complications. With them, it requires more planning and persistence than a pastor may be able to muster.

Thus, pastors who do not see themselves as called to being single can face a congregational catch-22: parishioners would feel more at ease if the pastor were married, but may not understand how their own expectations make this more difficult. This is but one more reason for congregations to honor limits of time and privacy when relating to their pastors.

Growing Up as the Preacher's Kid

What is it about being a PK, a "preacher's kid" or "pastor's kid," that makes it worthy of its own acronym? The everyday doings of the children of cashiers, or accountants, or salespeople are not automatically gossip worthy. But pastors are necessarily public people, seen by many as religious celebrities holding people to a higher moral standard. What *their* children do is news.

59. Zikmund et al., *Clergy Women*, 34–35.
60. Moore, *Clergy Moms*, 76.

As Martin Copenhaver suggests, the role that comes with the label "PK" can constrain a child's developing identity:

> if you are a PK . . . try as you might at times, you never forget it. . . . I have found absolutely no one who grew up as the child of a minister who would say anything like, "Oh, it really wasn't a big deal. I don't think it had much of an impact on me." My own father has been dead for twenty-five years and I have been an ordained minister myself longer than that, and yet, to this day, I still think of myself as a PK.[61]

In part, that constraint reflects the existence of persistent stereotypes, especially among their own peers outside the church.[62] Some expect PKs to be goody-goodies, creating awkward moments when PKs overhear friends say, "Quiet! Here comes the pastor's kid." Others, ironically, expect them to be rebellious troublemakers—and many PKs have given them memorable reasons to believe it![63]

But even if PKs occasionally rebel, the question should be: against what? For some, it's a response to the relentless pressure to conform to the expectations of others. Here, for example, is a list of the kinds of expectations PKs routinely face: to act more maturely than other kids their age, to follow their parents into the ministry, to know more about the Bible than other kids in the youth group, to be more involved in the church's ministry, to be well-groomed in appearance (especially daughters), and generally to have it all together.[64] PKs may worry about disappointing the congregation, or disappointing parents who need PKs to toe the line so as not to rock the congregational boat.

For others, seemingly rebellious behavior is a response to the disillusionment that comes when their families are mistreated by Christians. PKs figure out early on that not everyone in the church is fond of their parents. One night at the dinner table, my (Kurt's) own daughter asked me, "Dad, how many people hate you?" That's not a question you want to hear from your daughter! I thought for a moment, and said, "About twelve," hastily adding, "You know, out of six billion people that's not too bad." She replied, "Yeah, but Dad, all six billion people don't know you yet."

61. Daniel and Copenhaver, *Odd and Wondrous Calling*, 119.

62. Stereotypes may be more prevalent among a PK's peers than in the congregation. Stalfa, "Protestant Clergy Marriage," 255.

63. On positive and negative stereotypes, see Lee, *PK*, ch. 4.

64. Adapted from ibid., 103.

In the more extreme case, PKs struggle to make sense of how their parents could devote their lives to serving God and yet get slapped down by the very people for whom they sacrificed, day in and day out:

> My Dad was fired today by his church. Their reason was because he didn't have the right attitude in the office. . . . I don't know what to do. I want to just give up on my calling of being a youth pastor because of everything I've seen my dad and my family go through. It's so hard to trust the ministry right now. . . . I'm barely holding on to God.[65]

It's no surprise that some PKs would turn their backs on the church, especially after what Josh Mayo calls the "train wreck" that comes with the failure of a ministry or a forced resignation.[66]

We're reminded of the story of Jay Bakker, the son of televangelists Jim and Tammy Faye. After his parents had been publicly disgraced, Bakker turned to a hard-partying, hard-drinking lifestyle. His memoir opens with these words:

> If anyone had an excuse to lose faith in God, it would've been me. I'd been beaten up so often by traditional religion that turning away from God, as so many others my age did, would have been the most natural reaction.[67]

Bakker neither ignores nor denies the problems in his family. But he also chronicles the excessive vendettas carried out against his parents, by people who seemed to be looking for a way to take personal advantage of the downfall of their media empire. Thankfully, Bakker's memoir ends on a positive note: God led him by winding paths to a ministry of his own. For pastors who are grieved when their own children seem to lose their way, his story offers hope. But happy endings can never justify how hurtfully some pastors are treated by their congregations, nor the devastating emotional consequences visited on the pastor's children.

It is a disservice to PKs to try to categorize them as saints or rebels according to some preexisting stereotype. They are kids like anyone else's kids. The difference lies not in their psychological makeup, but their social environment. And for the PKs who are born into that environment, their understanding of God, the church, their parents, and themselves is

---

65. Quoted in Josh Mayo, *Help!*, 163.

66. Ibid., ch. 11.

67. Bakker, *Son of a Preacher Man*, 3.

fundamentally molded—for good or for bad—by the pastor-congregation relationship.

For many pastors' kids, the experience is a positive one. Despite the occasional difficulties, PKs talk glowingly about the blessings of growing up in a pastor's family, including having beloved role models at home and in the church. They reminisce fondly about visiting missionaries who opened their eyes to the movement of God in the world beyond the parish. For these ministry kids, church was a warm and supportive extended family, replete with spiritual aunts, uncles, cousins, and grandparents. My (Kurt's) own experience, generally, was that my family was well cared for by the church family. They prayed for me, my wife, and for my kids. They took a genuine interest in my family and always wanted the very best for us.

Thus, when the congregation is supportive in ways that respect the family's boundaries and the PK's uniqueness as a human being, all is well. But some extended families can be intrusive. We've heard PKs say that the best thing about growing up in the church was having multiple "parents," and that the worst thing was . . . having multiple parents. The problem was most acute when other adults hypocritically applied a double standard:

> I think everybody older than myself in my dad's congregation felt it was their responsibility to act as my parents whenever my parents weren't around. They were constantly telling me how I should act. Even if their own children behaved outrageously, they would tell me how they felt a preacher's son should conduct himself.[68]

For the sake of their children, then, pastors and their spouses need to establish clear boundaries with parishioners. One pastor tells of how a member of the church found the pastor's son doing something that seemed mischievous (the man was mistaken) and took it upon himself to drag the crying boy to his father between services. The pastor decided then and there to make an announcement in the next service:

> I am the pastor of this church. My wife and my children are not the pastors of this church. My children are normal children, and I want to raise them as normal children. And if any one of you ever comes to me with a criticism of my kids and says, "After all, they are the pastor's kids," I'll nail you to the wall. I will not have my kids growing up to hate my job or my God.[69]

68. Daniel Aaron Langford, quoted in Langford, *Pastor's Family*, 36.
69. Quoted in Ulstein, *Pastors Off the Record*, 21.

Of course, the image of pastors nailing church members to the wall isn't one we'd advocate! There are less adversarial ways to say this. And we would hope that the pastor spoke first to the man who collared his son, instead of only dealing with the issue by public fiat. But his point is well taken. This pastor sent a firm and unambiguous message to the congregation that set a clear limit on behalf of his family. The congregation actually applauded, and that was the end of the matter.

And in case you were wondering: the boy grew up to become a minister.

The Family Within the Family

One of the greatest and most unfortunate ironies of the ministry is that many congregations expect clergy and their families to be exemplary Christians, model spouses and parents, and spiritually healthy kids—and yet unwittingly engage in behaviors that make this much more complicated than it needs to be. It's as if the family must always have its act together, whatever the circumstances, regardless of the impact of intrusive expectations or the lack of safely supportive relationships.

That, of course, is an intentional overgeneralization on our part. Not all congregations are like that; not all individuals within the same congregation are like that. Most people understand the issues when they're explained patiently and lovingly in a one-on-one conversation.

Most, but not all. And when anxiety mounts in the pastor-congregation relationship, it's discouraging to see how even people who know better fall silent in the face of congregational groupthink. The whispering of conscience, of the Holy Spirit—both can be drowned out when even a handful of upset but influential parishioners raise their voices.

For the sake of pastors, their families, and the church of Jesus Christ, we are calling upon congregations to proactively revisit their vision of who they want and are meant to be. Our message is not, "Be nice to pastors!" (though that might not be a bad place for some churches to start). Rather, the message is: be the church, a body of which Christ is the head, a family of brothers and sisters whose unity is a gift of his Spirit.

The Jesus we follow is the one who rebuked his disciples for keeping children away from him (Matt 19:13–15). Apparently, they thought their master too important, and too busy with God's work, to trifle with blessing a bunch of kids. His response must have surprised them. Jesus upbraided them not only for their attitude toward children, but their misguided understanding of his priorities.

What about the rest of us? Do our understandings of the work of the church bristle with adult self-importance, in ways that are inhospitable to kids and the families that are responsible for raising them? Mickey and Ashmore have said it directly and elegantly:

> Spiritual care of children is a vital part of one's ministry, and
> where a loving, nurturing relationship with children is avoided
> or neglected, whether in the pastor's family or with children in
> the church, we have a clear indication of spiritual breakdown.[70]

As we've suggested above, one indication of that breakdown is when congregations mistreat pastors with nary a thought given to what PKs are thereby learning about God and the church. But again, this isn't just about the happiness of pastors or their spouses or children, but the calling of the church as a whole to be a family that welcomes and nurtures all the smaller families within its midst.

It is right for congregations to expect exemplary behavior from their pastors. Of course, we imagine that most pastors are unwilling to be as bold as the apostle Paul in that regard; few would come right out and say, "I urge you to imitate me" (1 Cor 4:16)! At the same time, however, they understand that it's intrinsic to their vocation to model what it means to be a disciple of Jesus Christ, in thought, word, and deed.

But let's be clear. To be exemplary does *not* mean being at the beck and call of every congregational demand, especially if it entails neglecting one's family. It does not mean being a "perfect" husband or wife, father or mother, son or daughter. It does not mean that the pastor's spouse must make the coffee or mow the lawn. It does not mean that the pastor's children must never do anything, well, *childish*.

What *does* it mean to be an exemplary pastor? It means to demonstrate, in both one's ministry and family life, the constant need for God's grace and the knowledge of where to find it. And it means to encourage others to do the same, whether in their own families or the family we call the church.

So, yes, let's be nice to pastors' families. But let's do it because we want to help them help us—to be a people of love, patience, compassion, and hospitality. That's how family members should treat each other.

---

70. Mickey and Ashmore, *Clergy Families*, 116.

Postscript

To Pastors:

How is your family doing? If someone were to ask your spouse and children what they love or hate about the ministry, what do you think they would they say? And here's a harder question: how much of it would have to do with you and your priorities?

Does your spouse share your sense of calling? The mutual vocation that characterizes dual-clergy couples is missing in many marriages where only one spouse is ordained. One may feel exhilarated in doing God's work; the other feels like he or she is just along for the ride. Add to that the pressure of having to conform to congregational role expectations, and you have a situation ripe for spiritual stagnation, depression, or marital conflict. The choices can be difficult, requiring both wisdom and honesty. Here again is Lillian Daniel:

> In clergy marriages, we have to pick our battles. When do we ask our spouses to yield to our standards and when do we rejoice in letting them be themselves? While we might want to say that our spouses should be themselves, most of us occupy a more complicated middle ground. I have seen clergy couples in which the weight of expectation from the minister reduced the spouse to a bland and bored partner—such spouses dread church events because they cannot be themselves and therefore can never have any fun. I have heard from clergy spouses who find that the numerous role expectations even prevent them from worshiping.
>
> On the other hand, I have seen cases in which clergy spouses apply the highest standards to themselves, trying to be perfect but ending up isolated—perfect clergy partners with no real friends in the church.[71]

If you serve a congregation with multiple and stress-producing expectations, the temptation will be to pressure your spouse and children into cooperating just to keep the peace. You may give spiritual and scriptural reasons why they should do so, and there may be some truth in these rationalizations. But let God search your heart: is part of your motivation to make things easier for *you*? If so, what conversations with your congregation are you avoiding, and at what cost to your family?

We've noted above how ordination vows can compete with marriage vows. The reality, though, is this: although you may be called to a lifetime

---

71. Daniel, "Pastor's Husband," 30.

of vocational ministry, you are unlikely to serve the same church for a lifetime. Ministries come and go. Today you are the pastor of this congregation; tomorrow it will be another. That may even be the norm in your denomination.

But that's not God's intent for the vocation of marriage and family. Your marriage vow is for life. Though marriages, tragically, may end, it's not by denominational design (some pastors may want to argue that point). You might lead this church for three years, or five, or ten—but your children are your children forever. Take it from two men whose kids are now grown: those formative years in which they need you the most vanish quickly, evaporating like mist. It would be a shame to trade them for a building campaign.

This isn't meant to be an exercise in guilt mongering. We know that most of you already want the best for your spouses and children, even if you struggle to figure out how to achieve that in the face of the demands of ministry. Those of you who are learning to balance the roles of minister and mother feel the pulls particularly keenly.

What to do? There's no shortage of advice available for ministers' families, as documented in the footnotes for this chapter. A notable memoir by Josh Mayo, for example, has the unique distinction of being written by a PK for *pastors*, chronicling the wise ways his parents helped keep his love of God and the church vibrantly alive.[72]

For our purposes, nearly everything we've said in this book so far is relevant here. Revisit your calling: envision the kingdom importance of your commitment to your family. Embrace a Sabbath spirituality: rest regularly in the knowledge that the ministry is God's work before it is yours. Take care of your body: manage the stress that tempts you to get your priorities out of alignment.

Learn to appreciate and celebrate what your spouse contributes to the ministry; never take it for granted. Help your spouse and children to discover God's unique calling on their lives—even if it's not an extension of your own. Set wise limits with your congregation where needed, for the sake of the spiritual and psychological well-being of your spouse and children. Set limits on yourself. For example, don't tell stories about family members from the pulpit unless you have their clear permission to do so. If you're not sure what those limits should be, ask your spouse and children. Even if you think you *are* sure, ask them anyway—and be prepared to listen.

72. Mayo, *Help!*

To Congregations:

How important are family commitments to you? How important do you think they should be to any Christian? What would you think of church members who regularly put service to the congregation above their dedication to their spouses or the care of their children?

Would it make a difference if that church member was the pastor?

As Christians, we rightly love, value, protect, and sacrifice for our families. We look to our pastors to help prepare us for marriage, or to bring a sense of communal worship to the wedding ceremony itself. When our family relationships go awry, we look to clergy for spiritual counsel. In short, at some level, we hope that part of a pastor's ministry will be to help the rest of us figure out how to follow Jesus daily as spouses and parents.

Why, then, do so many churches seem to lack any explicit or sustained ministry to families? There are ministries to adults in which the topic of marriage rarely arises. There are ministries to youth and children in which youth pastors despair over what they see in parent-child relationships. And still, few seem to want to tackle the issue of parenting directly, or to address the implicit assumption of many parents in the church that it is the youth minister's responsibility to teach their kids what it means to be a Christian.

One provocative explanation for this state of affairs is that pastors are afraid that if they say too much about family life, the scrutiny of their own families will intensify.[73] If that's true, the implication is that congregations who don't put wise limits on their expectations of the pastor's family are shooting themselves in the foot. Supporting pastors means supporting their families. Long-term, pastors who are to be of any real use to the families in a congregation will need that congregation's help in turn.

What can you do? Take an honest look at your pastor's workload. Realistically, does your pastor have the time needed to nurture strong relationships? If you expect him or her to be at the office all day, out visiting or at the church for meetings every night, and preparing for or leading services every weekend, the answer is clearly no. Reevaluate whether all of these things are necessary. Create the alternative expectation that you *want* your pastor to spend time with family. That may even mean being gentle but firm with a workaholic pastor: "Go home and love on your kids for a while. We'll be fine."

73. E.g., Sell, *Family Ministry*, 14.

Also examine your expectations of the pastor's spouse and children. Has the two-for-one deal been taken for granted? Has anyone ever talked to the pastor's spouse to find out how he or she actually *wants* to be involved? Have the unique contributions and gifts of the spouse been acknowledged and celebrated? Are PKs expected to be something that they're not? Does being a preacher's kid in your congregation mean that you can't just be a kid?

The easy answer to such questions is, "No, we don't expect those things. Nobody's ever said it. It's not written down anywhere." Not officially. But the expectations are often communicated unofficially, by the words and behaviors of church members—in casual conversations in the parking lot, at the back of the church after the service, in emails and letters and phone calls. On a day-to-day basis, that's the contract that matters. Church members need to hold each other accountable for how pastors and their families are treated.

All of this means coming back to the refrain we've repeated over and over: the best thing you can do for your pastor is to be the church, to be a community of true love and grace. All of us, including the pastor, together with our families, are works in progress. By the grace of God and the power of his Spirit, we slouch slowly and awkwardly toward perfection. And by that same grace, we hold one another up along the way.

To Seminarians:

How will your marriage fare once you begin full-time ministry? If you're already married, take a look at what's happening in your relationship now. Is there an explicit or implicit assumption that your spouse's role is to keep the way clear for you to attend lectures and group meetings, write without distraction, read incessantly, study obsessively, and navigate the minefield of church internships?

It's nice to think that the stress of graduate school is just a temporary aberration: "If I can just get through this paper—or this exam, this course, this degree—then everything will be fine." But there's always something else to get through. Don't kid yourself: going from seminary to ministry is to trade one set of demands for another. If you've already made compromises in your marriage partnership in order to cope, those patterns won't change when you begin pastoring, not without a great deal of conscious effort.

The question is whether both of you share an equal sense of vocation to serve a local congregation. That doesn't mean you both have to be pastors. As we said earlier, in some couples, there is a complementary call—one is drawn to the pastorate, the other to the role of pastor's spouse (which usually means "wife," at least until the role of clergy husband becomes more commonplace). But often, only the one who is preparing for the ministry feels called, while the spouse remains ambivalent, taking a wait-and-see attitude. And when there is tension in the marriage, the seminarian is tempted to play the language of call as a trump card. After all, who wants to get in *God's* way?

If any of that sounds familiar, then ask yourself right now whether your marriage vow is as important to you as the ordination vow that you haven't even taken yet. The best time to get your priorities in order is now. Do it before you begin ministry, before you have children, not after. With those commitments firmly in place, you will be better prepared to ask the right questions and set the right limits while you are still interviewing with a church. Unanticipated expectations, of course, may still take you by surprise. But taking a stand for your present and future family up front will make the later conversations easier.

So put this book down, and spend some time with your spouse. God will be pleased, and so will your beloved.

Response Letters

IN THIS FINAL SECTION, we've gathered together a dozen letters from friends and colleagues in the ministry, who have all read the book and have agreed to give us their personal responses and reflections. We've given them the freedom to agree or disagree, add or correct. But we've asked them all to speak from their own experience. We hope their stories will be an encouragement to you!

Cameron & Kurt

Call and Complication

Mindy Coates Smith

Mindy Coates Smith is currently the Co-Director of Youth Discipleship at Bel Air Presbyterian Church in Los Angeles. Together, she and her husband lead the youth ministries for sixth- to twelfth-grade students, and love investing in families through their service to adolescents.

From a pastoral point of view, this book is quite compelling. Actually, as a youth director, I'm technically not a pastor. And as a female who works with her spouse, I don't really fit into a typical pastor category. But as this book alludes to, the face of the typical pastor is changing. In my case, I co-direct the youth programs at our church with my husband. We share almost everything: an office, a one-bedroom apartment, the same roll of toilet paper—you get the idea. Since we are on staff at a large church, our roster of students probably outnumbers the membership of most congregations in our denomination. That puts us in a unique position. We are a pastoral voice into the lives of the families we serve, but we lack structural authority within the organization, which has its perks and limitations.

My initial response to this book is one of comfort and validation. I am impressed with the realistic picture of the pastorate, captured within a sense of call, and the many layers of complication that accompany this life. Vocational ministry is not a job; it's a lifestyle. Several different parts of the book definitely resonate with my own experiences in ministry. At the same time there are a couple of areas that might have been overlooked and would be worth discussing. I'm grateful for the opportunity to share these thoughts with you.

The sections of the book that addressed gender roles and family life were of interest to me. My husband and I met while working together at a camp (yes, we are a camp couple) and since we are in the same field of youth ministry we find it better to work together than apart. There have been times when we worked for different organizations. Several years ago I was part of a ministry staff that was ninety percent male. On a staff retreat my husband was invited to participate in the program for the staff wives that included afternoon tea and shopping trips.

Having served in roles similar to those my husband has, I have noticed things that are more difficult for me as a female. One notable area is our outward appearance. When my husband gets dressed, he can pretty much wear the same outfit for almost every situation at work: khaki pants, collared shirt, and Chuck Taylors (we live in Southern California, so this is actually dressed up). He can wear this to a staff meeting, to speak in front of the congregation, or to play games with junior-highers. No one has ever had a concerned conversation with him about his clothes.

My wardrobe, however, is a constant chore. I have to think about how tight my jeans are, how high my heels are, and when I shaved my legs last (if I need to wear a dress). I've been spoken to about my choice of sweater and told that my hair was too pretty and was distracting from the message. Despite these superficial annoyances, I'm lucky that I have been fairly compensated for my work in comparison with my male colleagues. I know this is sadly not the case for many women in ministry.

Perhaps the most poignant theme of the book is the commentary on the call to selfless sacrifice juxtaposed with appropriate boundaries and self-care. Finding this balance is a constant and never-ending issue. Like many other helping professions, there is always more that can be done. Being a pastor is like a cross between being a small business owner and an emergency room doctor. A small business owner is the person that drives the vision, puts in the most sweat equity and is most disappointed if something goes wrong. ER doctors go from one crisis to another, and despite their best efforts, sometimes people die under their care. The pressure on a small business owner coupled with the emotional turmoil of an ER physician is sort of what it is like to be a pastor. A shut-off valve is needed that creates separation between work and home to have any hope of healthy boundaries.

Yet defining the difference between work and home can be surprisingly difficult. It gets tricky because as paid clergy there is a concern about perceived laziness and at the same time being misunderstood as a workaholic. I've heard comments from congregations wondering whether the pastors spend any time with their own kids. I've also been aware of search committees wary of hiring a pastor with small children because they might be too distracted by family life.

As a non-ordained member of a church staff, I can attest that the majority of the issues raised in this book do not apply just to pastors. Many staff members feel the same tensions, especially those in pastoral roles who do not have the notoriety or larger paychecks of those with the title of "pastor." Youth directors, children's ministers, small group coordinators, and other staff who have constant contact with the congregation might fit into this category. Sometimes members of the congregation have a sense of respect for the pastor's time but have no problem harassing his assistant for answers to their questions. I think it is worth pointing out that most people who work at a church have some sense of call to their roles. Otherwise, it's just a job that doesn't pay much, and people judge you for things like the emoticons you use in emails.

While the majority of this writing is spot on, I was surprised by a couple of topics that were not discussed in detail. A huge responsibility of a pastor is managing people, specifically employees and volunteers. While pastoral relationships were addressed in depth, the daily minutiae of overseeing a staff of people might have been overlooked. There are staff meetings, time cards, background checks, budgets, and a long list of other administratively intense tasks for which a pastor is held accountable. Besides the paperwork there is also the duty of appropriately training paid staff and volunteers, and then trusting them to carry out the vision of the church. Keeping everyone on the same page can be a full-time job in itself!

Another topic that could have been more intricately deliberated is the pastoral role in church politics. Many of the situations used to illustrate relational conflict most likely had deeper roots of a political nature. By "political" I mean situations in which one agenda seeks to be more important or powerful than another agenda, even if both proposals are beneficial to the greater whole. For example, person A wants to plan a worship night on the same date that person B wants to host a silent prayer retreat. If person A has more access to the pastor and utilizes the opportunity to advocate for a worship night, the pastor might be more inclined to approve the worship night over the silent retreat. Things only get more complicated when one party contributes a lot of time or money to the church or has a strong social influence amongst the congregation. Pastors must be able to make discerning decisions in the midst of competing well-intentioned agendas. Integrity can be seriously exhausting.

Possibly my favorite theme throughout the book is the overall tone of hope. I loved learning that pastors are happy and fulfilled in their work. I enjoyed the appreciation that Cameron and Kurt have for the pastorate. I am encouraged in my pastoral role. May God's redeeming grace continue to smother us together.

Why I Started Taking Care of My Body

Danny Martinez

Danny Martinez grew up in a Pentecostal church in Guatemala, joined the Evangelical Covenant Church in 1989, and was ordained in 2005. He pastored in Latino congregations until 2003, when he planted a multiracial church in South Central Los Angeles. Currently, he is Senior Pastor of Grace Covenant Church in Spring Valley, California. He is proud of his Latino heritage, but even more proud of being part of the kingdom of heaven, where all races matter.

The most meaningful chapter in the book for me was number 6. The issues raised in that chapter have haunted me all of my life. I have never been my ideal weight. Even as a child, I remember being called *gordito* or "chubby" as a normal part of life. As I entered ministry, I loved being able to just spend time with people and help them in their lives, as so many seem to have no direction or anyone who can help them. The majority of my ministry as a volunteer pastor has been in Latino contexts where there are big expectations of the pastor, his wife, his family, and his time.

Being an extrovert, my energy always came from people, from their acceptance, and relationship building. These would drive me to work hard. I finally decided to attend seminary, and experienced a big move from Chicago to Los Angeles to attend my denominational (Evangelical Covenant) seminary, called CHET, or the Hispanic Center for Theological Studies. I suffered a major loss in income, since I was attending school full-time and serving as a youth pastor part-time. This started to put a strain on my family. My weight, which had always been an issue, started to climb even higher.

After graduating from CHET, I was called to plant a church in South Los Angeles, while attending Fuller Seminary to finish my Master of Divinity. This was a very stressful time, which led me to gain even more weight. At the height of my weight—approximately 330 pounds—I started to suffer from high blood pressure, stomach problems, and diabetes. I began having problems singing due to acid reflux, and was later diagnosed with sleep apnea. I was a mess—but very determined to finish school and continue with my current church in San Diego. As my marriage started to deteriorate, I needed to make a change. I was at the end of my rope.

I was doing well in other areas. We had purchased a house with help from the church, and all three kids were thriving. But my body was not being respected nor appreciated. Sleep, exercise, and a regular diet were not in my schedule. I was probably sleeping an average of four hours a night, not exercising at all, and eating what I could in the middle of the turmoil that I called ministry.

Finally, while in the middle of a horrible depression due to the loss of my spouse to divorce, something clicked. If I did not do something about my weight, I would die a young death or live the rest of my years in a body that could not handle much. I'm afraid that it took a deep depression, in which I considered taking my life, to make me start taking care of my body as my first responsibility. I had made all the excuses that one can think of: it would take too much time, effort, money, etc. In the end, these excuses led me nowhere but packing on more pounds. I definitely was counted among the pastors surveyed that were way beyond their ideal weight.

I was busy running around taking care of everyone, excluding myself. After all, this is what good ministers are supposed to do, isn't it?

From a Latino perspective, many of the pastors that share the same experience see this as normal and as part of sacrificial ministry. We are to be ministers—servants of the kingdom—and our own peril is but a pearl of reward in the crowns we will receive in heaven. Heaven is when we will finally have the bodies that we desire, so we don't have to worry too much about these ones. I had to change this way of thinking if I wanted to change my habits.

As an educated man, I already knew what I had to do to take care of my body. It was not the lack of knowledge that bound me, it was the will and understanding that I am indeed a steward of this body and need to take care of it. It's the understanding of oneself as an example to others who struggle with the same things in our congregations due to sedentary lives and limited options for exercise.

I can happily report that I am on my way to my ideal weight. I have lost almost one hundred pounds, and my medications for high blood pressure, diabetes, and kidney stones have been reduced or eliminated. I have given away all the suits I used to wear—size 54—because I have no plans to use them ever again.

What happened? What was so drastic in my life that allowed me to have such a turnaround? Some attribute it to the divorce. I believe that it certainly helped me get to where I finally understood that God wants me to be healthy and that he does not want me to blame my former sedentary life, my lack of sleep, and my bad diet on my service for him.

I am grateful for the many good and godly friends around me, including my twenty-year-old son, Eric. They have all encouraged me and walked alongside me to recover and to develop a lifestyle that is conducive to a healthier outcome instead of returning to the same routine. My son Eric became my personal trainer, and has made me dislike him quite a bit at the gym! I am ever so grateful for his persistence and faith in me when I had none.

I also had to change my diet. Now I have four small meals a day rather than just a big one plus snacks. I watch what I eat but do not deprive myself of things I like. I visit the gym four to five times a week, doing a half-hour of weight training and another half-hour of aerobic exercise. Since I began weight training I have not lost as much weight, but have lost inches from my waist. I take my kids to the gym with me so that I can be a good example to them, and we enjoy the activities together. We do this as soon as they are out of school for the day.

Needless to say, my life has changed dramatically. I am currently visiting family in Guatemala, who did not even recognize me. I had to communicate to them that I do not eat certain foods in the same huge quantities that I did before. I had to be very sensitive since food is a big issue and relationships are built on sharing meals together. My whole experience has been liberating. I am still committed to losing an additional forty pounds, and maintaining this weight for my health and the example I provide my children, church, and colleagues.

My congregation has also noticed the incredible difference. Most members have congratulated me, and some continue to bug me to lose more! Overall, people assume that this has been due to the depression that I faced last year. But I can honestly say that I had planned to lose this weight when I was done with my doctorate degree. I'm glad that I did not wait any longer. I feel younger, look healthier, and project a better image of what a pastor is and should be. All of this can be done with a better perspective of who I really am.

A passage that has been very helpful to me in this journey is Mark 1:1–12, which describes John the Baptist and his role in the presentation of the forthcoming Messiah. John, dressed as he was and eating what he ate, confronted God's chosen people with repentance and invited them to be baptized. John knew who he was. He knew that he was merely "a voice that calls from the desert." His job was to simply present and prepare the way for the Lord Jesus. When asked if he was the Messiah, his answer was no; he was simply preparing the way. When Jesus came to him he introduced him to the world as the "Lamb of God who takes away all of our sin," thus removing himself from the middle.

I need to learn to be more like John the Baptist. Perhaps not in his diet or wardrobe, but in his humility and understanding that we are not the Messiah. We cannot save people nor can we pretend to walk on water. We are human beings, responsible for many—but it needs to start with ourselves. Our job is merely to point to the Master, as he is the only that can take the sin of the world.

I continue to serve my church with all my heart, but my efforts are limited to what I can do within a certain allotted time. I make time to go to the gym, to spend with my kids, to study and to do my doctoral work. The church understands that I cannot have any sweets and do not take it personally anymore. I communicate this from the pulpit and enforce it every time I am offered those incredibly good brownies our church is known for!

The best thing that has come from this kind of attitude is that more people are stepping up to plate to be trained to be ministers, to get fit, and to find a little balance in their lives through being able to love God with all of our heart, soul, mind, and strength, and to love our neighbor as we love ourselves—provided that we *do* love ourselves and are taking care of our bodies, not as a selfish act, but as one that is necessary to continue ministry in a consistent and holistic way.

We need to continue to hear what this book is saying, not because we don't know it, but because we need to be reminded how precious we are to God. And it starts in our body.

Minding the Gap

Becky and John Hart

John and Becky Hart are currently co-pastors of Liberty Presbyterian Church (PCUSA) in Columbus, Ohio. They met in college starting up a Young Life club, were married in 1979, and have served as co-pastors since 1982 in four different congregations.

This book hits the nail on the head of one of the primary themes of ministry as we have experienced it over the past two and a half decades: expectations. One of our favorite phrases from the book is that "ministry is messy." It is this mess of conflicting expectations from church committees, leadership, staff, visitors, professors, our families and, of course, our own sense of call that can make ministry so overwhelming. As a clergy couple who have shared a single position at four different churches over the past twenty-seven years, we have delighted in this unique calling. But too often, we've also found ourselves knee deep in the mess of tangled communication, hopes, dreams, and realities.

Living in Oxford for a few years, we came to love the metro system, and its ubiquitous sign: "Mind the Gap." It's a popular London phrase used to remind train passengers to watch their step as they enter or exit the train, being careful to mind the gap between the train and the platform.

Ministry is all about minding the gap between the real and the ideal, the high vision and the daily tasks, the infinite joys and the weighty burdens. Some days that gap is wide. Until her dying day, Becky's mother insisted that we should have Christmas Eve off: "You're going to work Christmas Eve—again? Really? Do you have to?"

As a clergy couple, and heads of staff, we have had to be quite intentional in bridging the gap in a number of areas. In response to some of Lee and Fredrickson's chapters, there are four practices we want to highlight and discuss through the lens of our own experiences. They are: (1) bridging the gap between the real and the ideal, (2) understanding stress and burnout, (3) embracing wise limits, and (4) practicing forgiveness.

Bridging the Gap between the Real and the Ideal

Being a pastor is just plain humbling. We study hard for three years learning about things like eschatology, ontology, and whole lot of other

-ologies, and people lay hands on us and declare that we have set aside our lives for the cause of Jesus Christ, and then . . . then we hit reality, which looks something like this:

- The sewer system backed up into the church nursery.

- A thirty-ish woman is meeting guys in bars and wonders why she has not yet met the perfect mate.

- Someone saw the thirty-ish woman in the bar and wants her taken off the deacon board;

- The former pastor wrote the most beautiful prayers ever written in the history of the universe (that person didn't want me to do anything about it, she just wanted me to know).

- "I know this is your day off, but could you just call Nancy/Edwina/ Mildred today? I know she'd really appreciate it."

- The pastor down the street has a hundred kids signed up to go on a mission trip, and they've bought a brand new church bus. What about us?

And that's just last week's hit list! New pastors are disillusioned by it all, whereas church members who have been out in the workforce for years often find pastors naïve and unrealistic about "what the real world looks like."

Two things that have helped us sort out this mess.

Make Meetings Ministry

As a clergy couple, we make all of our interior thoughts on the church— what we should be doing, why, how—exterior as we process them with one another. We pray together about vision and share inspiration. We have tried to become intentional about doing that with church leaders also: inviting them into discussions that are focused on the big issues, praying not just "God bless this meeting" but about real concerns, and diving deep into ministry instead of a to-do list. We also try to make meetings ministry by setting aside real time for quality devotions—not reading from that cheesy devotional book form the grocery store, but real faith sharing. Invite committee members to share a "God moment" from their daily lives. Make that group a little church—for yourself and others. The realities of church life are much less discouraging if you know that something spiritually significant will happen at that next gathering. Which leads to:

Take Time to Ask the Big Questions

As Lee and Fredrickson ask, "Why does this congregation exist at this time and place?" Or, as we ask our officers at our annual retreat, borrowing from Esther 4:14, *why has God put us here at such a time as this?* And *why has God put me here for such a time as this?* You may even want to drive out to some well-known spots in town (the library, the post office, the movie theater, the bars) and discuss how you as a church are caring for that population. These kinds of conversations are soul food for pastors and congregations alike. Creating intentional ministry out of meetings and events helps to bridge the gap between the real and the ideal.

Understanding Stress and Burnout

We were speaking at a pastoral conference recently, and when we paused for questions, the first response from a pastor was, "How do I make friends?" It wasn't the immediate topic, but it was on his heart, and heads nodded all around the room. Lee and Fredrickson name "isolation and loneliness" as one of the leading factors in pastoral stress and burnout. We all need support systems in life, places where we can be real and honest and even raw. In fact, we highly recommend being in several groups—a group of pastors, a group of peers you study and share with, and a group that has nothing whatsoever in any way to do with church (Becky's yoga buddies, John's golf guys). You will also want to find a mentor outside of the church staff. We senior pastors cannot be all things to all people! In chapter 8, Lee and Frederickson talk about nurturing healthy relationships. You can't nurture healthy relationships if you are not in them yourself.

This is probably the greatest gift of being a clergy couple. We have a built-in support system. Each of us understands what the other is dealing with perfectly, because we pastor together in the same situation. More than that, we have the immense joy and privilege of sharing and shaping our vision for the congregation together. But buyers beware: working together can also multiply stress if you are not careful, by bringing work home and talking church breakfast, lunch, and dinner. A former clergy couple (and we stress the word "former"!) described with gritted teeth hearing "the other's voice all day long through the walls." It's best to find out if you can work as a team together long before you serve a church. Volunteer, go on some mission trips, share leadership of an event—get some real-life practice before you involve a church and experience the pain of changing a call if it doesn't work out.

But whether you are a clergy couple or individual pastor, prioritize finding or creating several places where you can give and receive real support.

Embracing Wise Limits

Boundaries are a big topic these days with new pastors. Young pastors are starting out with strong boundaries (a good thing) and talking about them from day one on the job with everyone that they meet (a bad thing). Setting limits—whether social or emotional—is critical. But how you communicate those boundaries is just as important as what those boundaries are!

One area that challenges clergy is the boundary between family life and the church. Assumptions about the pastor's spouse and kids can be difficult. Sunday school teachers feel the need to check that their answers are correct with your children, and church members feel the need to announce, "That's the pastor's wife/husband" to everyone they meet. But from where we sit, there is no better place to raise your family than the church. It really does take a village to raise a child, and to have the church love your children through the years is a gift beyond measure. Our churches loved our kids through thick and thin and were truly extended family to them. Where else does that happen in the workplace?

In terms of emotional boundaries, clergy couples need to be particularly aware of the transference phenomenon. You look like Mom and Dad to people, and both staff and church members can expect you to function in that role for them. If they have rebellion issues with their parents, they may have authority issues with you. If they are used to constant self-esteem building from their parents, they may expect that of you. If they have a healthy relationship with their parents, you are in luck! You will want to be alert to this phenomenon so that you can clearly define your relationship with others.

And last but not least:

Practicing Forgiveness

If we were to add a chapter to the book, it would be this: practice forgiveness on a daily basis. The gap between the real and the ideal, between job and calling, can make pastors cranky—and congregations too! There is a great Reformation doctrine that we must believe with all our hearts: *simul iustus et peccator.* That is, Christians are always, at the very same time, righteous ones and sinners. *Both/and, all the time.*

One of the keys to dealing with disillusionment and hurt with the church—and with one another—is sharing the grace of a fresh start with one another. We need to wipe the slate clean on a regular basis. As Henri Nouwen writes, "Forgiveness is the name of love practiced among people who love poorly. The hard truth is that all people love poorly. We need to forgive and be forgiven every day, every hour increasingly. That is the great work of love among the fellowship of the weak that is the human family."[1]

Working as a clergy couple forces us to forgive each other on a regular basis. On our best days, all that spousal communication reminds us that if this person we love so much rains on our parade or lets us down, maybe others fall down on the job too and need a little grace. After all, in the messiness of ministry, everyone needs a fresh chance. And to be known as a pastor and congregation that practices forgiveness on a regular basis? You won't be able to keep the people from flooding in.

1. Nouwen, *Only Necessary Thing*, 153.

Of Pastors, Congregations, and Wholeness

Chuck Hunt

Chuck Hunt is the Associate Pastor for Youth, Family, and Mission at St. Peter's by the Sea Presbyterian Church in Rancho Palos Verdes, California. Though he grew up never wanting to be a pastor, he now has been involved in full-time ministry for fifteen years and ordained (PCUSA) for five. He speaks passionately about God, his Word, and the need for wholeness in relationship. Chuck and his wife Shannon have been married for twelve years, and have their hands full with their eight-year-old daughter, Rhyen.

Wholeness can never be considered a state in which one arrives; it must always be a direction in which one strives. It is encouraging to be reminded that along the way it is necessary to pick up your head in order to see where you are and in what direction you are headed. Cameron and Kurt do a great job of creating a space in which, as a pastor, I am reminded of my call. In almost twenty years of ministry, I find it amazing that I have repeatedly been consumed by the job of ministry and not living the joy of my call.

As I am writing this, the Tour de France has started. Over the last few years I have enjoyed getting up early and watching it on TV. It struck me one morning that a church staff can be like a team in a bike race. Each team has a chosen leader, and the rest of the riders are *domestiques*. According to Wikipedia, "A domestique is a road bicycle racer who works for the benefit of his team and leader. The French domestique translates as 'servant.'"

The call of the senior pastor is to be the lead domestique, who sets the pace, provides food, and works for the glory of the team leader (Jesus). The rest of the staff is there to assist in that work. The difficulty is when pastors forget their call and begin to believe that they are the leaders and should get the glory of winning.

I believe that it is when we are committed to our calling that we are able to remain fixed on serving Jesus and not performing for the paycheck. Our primary call is to the person and work of Christ, whether or not we are getting paid for it. Kurt and Cameron remind us that this is the case. We are called to the vocation of ministry, and they rightly reminded us, "When profession routinely supersedes vocation in the pastor's imagination, the life of ministry can become hollow and empty."

This is even more difficult for those who are in associate and assistant roles. At times those roles are more difficult to define, and many churches don't respect the boundaries of those roles. In my job description there is the line, "Conduct other duties as assigned by the Head of Staff." While the Head of Staff has not abused this reality in my current call, I have been in churches and heard of others where this is routinely used as the stick to require associate pastors to do more. In this and other ways the associate role is very different than that of the senior pastor. Associates are the domestiques of churches, being called to the work of supporting the team leader and senior pastor. It is difficult and sometimes thankless work. But as many have said, "It is amazing what one can accomplish when one does not care who gets the credit."

I have worked as an associate pastor and primarily with adolescents for most of my career and I continue to love ministering to adolescents and their families. Recently I heard a colleague say, "Youth ministry isn't a job; it's a lifestyle." This has proven true in my experience, though I have taken on different lifestyles over the years. The ministry that I did fifteen years ago does not look like the ministry that I am doing right now. Fifteen years ago, I immersed myself in the lives of teenagers, taking every opportunity to be where they were. Though my desire to be where adolescents are has not changed, my time and my ability to always be there has. The job of ministry has gotten larger. My family has gotten larger. My income has gotten larger (barely). The demands on my time have increased. In order to continue to be a healthy and whole person I have had to make some sacrifices.

The problems came when the sacrifices I made were to my detriment. Early in my ministry I remember coming home from a camp or retreat and wanting to just be alone. I really valued the time just learning how to recuperate without any distractions. After I got married that strategy didn't work so well. My wife was not so excited about me being away then not being present for a day after I got home! I have had to learn a different way. I wish I could say that it happened once and then we figured it out. Instead, it took about four years for us to figure out a good way to be connected while I was trying to recuperate, and honestly, it doesn't always work. But that has been part of the journey to wholeness.

I write this because in this book I found myself reading about all of the external pressures that are placed upon me and my family. Though those can be really complicated, it is the internal pressures that may be more important. I know I have to go to camp. I know that I have to preach.

I know that I have to be at late night meetings. But I also have a say in how I reengage my family after any of those things. The church has nothing to do with that. I am 100 percent responsible for the way that I connect with my family.

I was pretty impressed with Cameron and Kurt's chapter on taking care of the body that God gave you. As a pastor I have been very aware of the challenges of trying to remain healthy when almost every meeting has some sort of food—and rarely are there veggies! As an African American I am also cognizant of the health challenges that are a greater risk for me, including high blood pressure and heart disease. Given the stresses of ministry, it is vitally important that I take care of myself, making time to eat correctly and exercise. I have been blessed to have not had to deal with significant health issues during my ministry. I have always found time to exercise. I have surfed, cycled, run, and most recently started triathlons as a way to keep in shape and provide some more structure and discipline to my workday.

What I have not been able to do is convince my friends and colleagues of the importance of taking care of their health. Recently I was speaking with one of my mentors. I have known this person for almost twenty years, and he has been a pastor and a church planter for the whole time I have known him. When we first met, he surfed a bunch and made sure to get out on his bike. But as ministry increased his participation in these activities decreased.

When we talked, he told me that he was taking a sabbatical for the first time in his career, which surprised me. But what left me almost breathless was when he said that he saw his declining health as a badge of honor, and held theologians who had died young (such as Jonathan Edwards) in high esteem. I said that I didn't think that was what Bonhoeffer meant when he said, "When Jesus calls a man, he bids him come and die." He agreed, and that is why he was on sabbatical. He was being cared for by his church, but there are many others that allow their health to fail in the name of dying to self. It takes courage to commit to caring for oneself—but it is necessary.

I was so grateful to be reminded of these truths and ideals. Currently, our church is in the midst of saying goodbye to our senior pastor and beginning to transition to a new pastoral leader. This book has been so helpful in reminding me of things that I know but are not always at the forefront of my mind. It has helped and will continue to help as we progress through the transition. I am also going to encourage the people who will eventually search for a new pastor to read this book as a way of processing how they will care for the incoming pastor. The sections that speak to the congregations are thought provoking for those who serve churches in any lay ministry capacity. The ability to think through how a church cares for its pastoral staff is vital; some do it well, while others need some help. Even the congregations that do it well can use an occasional reminder about the importance of setting realistic expectations, respecting boundaries, and helping pastors thrive so that they can serve the team leader and the church the way in which they were gifted.

The book has been a gift and I intend to use it as a gift and a tool. The gift is in the thoughtful and reflective reading of the book, which allowed me to honestly take an inventory of where I am. It is not often that I get the opportunity to take a broad look at the state of my ministry and life. More depth would have been nice, but the breadth and brevity were life-giving. The tool is the ability to encourage others to use the book as a discussion starter. More importantly, I am going to read this again with my wife, so that we can have a discussion instead of doing this on my own. It is not easy, but it is necessary. As Roy Oswald says, "There are no shortcuts to wholeness, and the process toward health never ends in this life."[2]

2. Oswald, *Clergy Self-Care*, 20.

The Invitation of Gratitude

Jeanie Thorndike

Jeanie Thorndike, a former pastor and a clinical psychologist, and is an ordained minister in the Presbytery of Los Ranchos (PCUSA). She enjoys discovery and learning, whether through reading the latest marital therapy book or hiking in the national parks.

I have a series of photographs I took hanging on the wall of my den at home. They are for me more than pictures of beautiful places I've hiked to; they are living memories, memories of truths about life I've discovered on my hikes. One frame contains two photographs. The bottom one shows a set of rocky switchbacks leading to Blue Lake, which is shown in the top photograph. Whenever I look at these two pictures I think to myself, "Life is a lot like that." Let me tell you what I mean.

A number of years ago, I read up on different trails in search of a good beginning hike that would help me get acclimated and conditioned for a longer fifteen-mile hike. Thus, I was looking for a day hike that was not too long, about six to eight miles round trip; at not too high of an elevation, 9,000 feet or below; with not too much elevation gain, about 500 to 750 feet; and with a pretty destination. After all my reading, Blue Lake, in the Sierra Nevada Mountains behind Bishop, seemed the perfect conditioning hike.

Well, it was probably the most difficult hike I'd ever been on! There was an error in the trail description. The elevation gain on the three miles to the Blue Lake was not 500 feet, but *1,500*. That meant a serious climb over three miles. It also meant that the elevation was over 10,000 feet— 10,388 feet to be exact—which brings its own set of challenges. A leisurely hike this was not! Nevertheless, off I set on my warm-up hike. Sure to be a confidence builder, I thought, but not in the way I'd imagined. The trail would bring me to my knees.

Up I climbed, and climbed, and climbed. The trail was composed of what I call "giant steps," cut out of the rock by trail crews that must have been Amazons. Two and a half miles into the climb, I rounded a bend in the trail and saw a towering set of switchbacks up a canyon wall of giant boulders.

The good news is that at this point I met the Gardner family, a mother and father with two children, a boy and a girl. The family was on the verge of mutiny, ready to throw Dad overboard for bringing them on this hike. I walked in on their argument. Dad had read the same guidebook that I had. It was their first family backpacking trip and it was not turning out well. They were exhausted and disheartened, their spirits already dashed by the boulders ahead of them.

I gladly sat down with them. We shared out fruit, commiserated about the trail, and plotted possible means of torturing the authors of the guidebook. Our spirits were just beginning to perk up when a man appeared, jogging up the trail! It seemed like a group hallucination. He was wearing black running shorts, a black tank top, black jogging shoes, and a black fanny pack, and he had a black dog with him. He paused by us, still jogging in place, and said something about being a high-altitude runner. He grinned at us and then took off up the trial, sprinting over the boulders. The little girl turned to her mom and asked, "Mommy, who was that?" The mother replied without a pause, "Satan."

After a bit we all got up and began our final climb. The steepness of the trail made it impossible to see how far you had to go to reach the top. It was one of those trails where you put your head down and simply go one step at a time.

The exhilaration on arriving at Blue Lake was incredible. The Gardner family and I hugged each other with joy. My sack lunch seemed like a feast. I framed the photographs of the rocky switchbacks and the alpine Blue Lake, and titled the composition: "The Invitation."

I believe that the life of ministry is full of many seemingly simple hikes to Blue Lake that turn out to hold invitations to enormous challenges. Where do we find the strength to meet them?

When I say to myself, "I'm having a Blue Lake kind of day," I'm saying a lot to myself about what's happening for me and about what I anticipate will happen. I remember the unexpected challenge of that day, the toil of the trail, the unexpected companions along the way, the reward of the journey's end—and most of all, the gratitude such a trip produced in me.

Christians have long believed that gratitude lies at the heart of a believer's life. I find it interesting that psychologists have recently discovered that gratitude may lie at the heart of emotional well-being. Researchers describe a grateful disposition as one that focuses on the positive outcome of daily life events. The positive appraisal of life events takes place in a two-step process. First, a person is aware of receiving a positive consequence, and second, the positive outcome is attributed to a source outside of them.[3] A person with a grateful disposition recognizes and appreciates the selfless gift of another.[4]

To me, one of the most exciting aspects of the research on gratitude is the finding that a conscious and intentional focus on what we are grateful for each day fosters emotional and relational benefits.[5] For example, a study of participants who kept a gratitude log reported higher levels of positive well-being, and found they were more likely to offer help to another.

Not surprisingly, then, research on positive emotions following the aftermath of terrorist attacks on the United States on September 11, 2001, suggested that positive emotions buffer people against depression and stimulate thriving.[6] Out of the ten positive emotions assessed, the three most frequently experienced were gratitude, interest, and love. Thus, although crises can deplete people's psychological resources, it appears that positive emotions such as gratitude foster thriving after a crisis. In my own research, I've found that pastors who obtain a high score on resilience may be inclined to use gratitude to cope with the demands of ministry.[7]

What is gratitude? It's a choice about how I look at my life. It's a way to see how God is at work in my life, in the world, and in others. In the Judeo-Christian tradition, gratitude and its expression are represented by the Greek noun *eucharistia*, which means the "act of thanksgiving." As Henri Nouwen has suggested, the great mystery celebrated in the Lord's Supper, or Eucharist, is one that all people are invited to live in the midst of our daily life.[8] Whatever the vicissitudes of life in the ministry, it is possible to find a gift from God and to experience gratitude for that gift.

The Eucharist prompts us to invite Jesus into the circumstances and events of our daily life in the ministry. When I was ordained in 1985, though I did not fully understand it at the time, to be a woman who is a minister in the Presbyterian Church (USA) was to participate in a social statement about the equity of God. At the time of my ordination, my heart and mind were full of excitement about counseling, small groups, and equipping ministries. Becoming the focus of social change had not entered my mind. My first call as an associate pastor was to a large congregation in

3. Weiner, "Attributional Theory."
4. Roberts, "Blessings of Gratitude."
5. Emmons and McCullough, "Counting Blessings."
6. Fredrickson et al., "Positive Emotions."
7. Thorndike, "Gratitude and Human Flourishing."
8. Nouwen, *Burning Hearts.*

the South where I was the first ordained female joining a staff of thirteen male pastors. I remember with great clarity the first Sunday when Communion was served. As I stood to serve, a significant number of people left in protest. But what I remember more vividly was a prominent family in the church leading just as many people forward to receive Communion from my side of the Lord's Table. It strengthens my heart just to remember. It was the Sunday that I discovered a solidarity with others that transformed my sense of being "the first female pastor" into an embodiment of the community of Christ.

Gratitude connects me to God as the source of my life and ministry. Gratitude helps me to see others as God's blessings to me. When I am thankful for the action or presence of another person in my life, I am also giving thanks to the God who made them and has moved through them to care for me. Gratitude invites me to entrust myself, as a minister, and my life in the ministry, to the never-failing love of God.

Pastoring and Mutual Submission:
Working Together, Trusting the Spirit

David Fitch and Matt Tebbe

David and Matt (together with Geoff Holsclaw) co-pastored Life on the Vine Christian Community (Christian and Missionary Alliance), located in the northwest suburbs of Chicago. David is also on the faculty of Northern Seminary in Lombard, Illinois. His most recent book is The End of Evangelicalism? *(Cascade, 2011). Matt Tebbe is now associate pastor for spiritual formation at River Valley Church in Mishawaka, Indiana.*

We have pastored together and feel like we have learned firsthand many of the things Cameron Lee and Kurt Fredrickson write about in this book. We co-pastored the Life on the Vine Christian Community in Chicago's northwest suburbs together with Geoff Holsclaw. Matt was the preacher and the pastor. Dave preached and pastored too, but was more often the apostle-gatherer-prophet. Geoff was the teacher-administrator.

From our different perspectives, we learned firsthand the importance of nurturing healthy relationships as pastors. As Kurt and Cameron articulate well (in chapter 8), this means handling conflict incarnationally, i.e., taking a posture of being among, with, and in submission to those we live the gospel with. We learned this first, however, through cultivating our relationships as pastors with each other. Only in working out our own co-pastor relationship did this truth work its way into the many relationships with and among the congregation of Life on the Vine.

For a church to be healthy, the pastors must be healthy. Often (though not necessarily), the church structure can calcify the unhealthy emotional systems of pastors—especially senior pastors. The senior pastor in particular can set the "temperature" of the congregation; as the main leader, the congregation (and associate pastors) will submit to his or her decisions and way of handling difficulties and conflict. But this means that the emotional health of a congregation is tied to one man or woman; they are subjected to his or her character deficiencies, weaknesses, and blind spots. His or her sensitivities, ways of discerning, reactions to conflict, and approaches to handling crisis become how the church operates.

When we first started co-pastoring together, we brought to our relationship a complex arrangement of ideas, visions, agendas, and hopes. Throw in another co-pastor (Geoff), and it was a recipe for a power struggle. Two dominant leadership options were available to us: Geoff and I (Matt) could submit to Dave as the lead and founding pastor of Life on the Vine; we could give him input, but he would make final decisions. Or we could have a democracy: there were three of us and each would have an equal vote. Or we could have discrete areas of ministry where we took each other's input but ultimately had the final say.

We all knew, based on previous church experience and a growing sense of self-awareness, that there existed in each of us a capacity for self-deception, egocentric leadership, and our own unhealthy emotional responses, which would set the temperature of our church. So, with Dave's encouragement and careful leading, we decided it was better for our church to enter into a relationship of mutual submission as co-leaders, as the best means to invest in the health of our congregation.

This was the most difficult and most fruitful relationship I (Matt) ever entered into. There were two characterological postures we learned in this relational commitment: 1) trust in the Spirit vs. one's own self-willfulness as pastor, and 2) viewing conflict as a process of sanctification vs. as something to be minimized, managed, or leveraged for the "health" of church.

Trust vs. Self-Willfulness

Because of our experiences and spiritual giftings, Dave and I would often see the same situation in two completely different (and sometimes in competing) ways. Training leaders, leading meetings, scheduling and planning church events, handling conflict—all of these created tension and brought our divergent personalities into focus. The relational matrix of mutual submission among us as pastors became the means God used to "strengthen our congregational immune system" (chapter 8).

Dallas Willard is often quoted as saying, "What God gets out of me isn't what I do, it's the person I become."[9] We would say that what God got out of us as pastors was the people we became, in mutual submission to his work in each other. The same goes for the entire congregation at Life on the Vine. As we lived into the reality of mutual submission in co-pastoring, we found this to be the best stance for our congregation and for our spiritual formation as pastors.

But how could we pay attention to the kind of persons we were becoming as pastors and not become self-preoccupied, egomaniacal narcissists?

9. For the original quote, see Willard, *Divine Conspiracy*, 285.

The answer, we discovered, was trust—submitting ourselves to each other in love and vulnerability. We learned to trust that the Spirit speaks and works not just in each person individually but in his church. We learned to test our agendas, preferences, opinions, and sensitivities based on giftings to the Holy Spirit. Through the discipline of mutual submission we found ourselves becoming the kinds of people who increasingly trusted the Holy Spirit and each other. This vulnerability and trust became the posture and attitude out of which we sought to lead our congregation into health and wholeness.

Conflict as Sanctification vs. Something to be Minimized, Managed or Leveraged

As Cameron and Kurt say in chapter 8, "In the end, what makes for a healthy church is not just how we respond to the conflicts that erupt, but the kind of relationships we cultivate before an eruption happens." Conflict—among the three of us and by extension in our congregation—went from something we sought to manage or minimize to an opportunity to grow, learn, submit, love, die, and rise to new life. Conflict became ground zero for the seed to find fertile soil in our pastoral relationships—and then, with that imagination, in the life of our church.

We have learned that conflict is the means by which God moves a congregation deeper into his mission. In order for conflict to be used by God however, we as pastors cannot control it. Instead we as pastors must become vulnerable, carrying a posture of submission always as a model to one another, following Matthew 18. In so doing, we allow conflict to ferment in the Spirit. If the conflict is about us (which, as pastors, it will be many, many times) we must listen and submit. We must reflect back what we have heard, and then give our observations, and then submit by asking, "Is this how you see it?" We might describe how we see the way forward, how we see Scripture on this, or what we hear the Spirit saying. But we will always then submit these affirmations to the one we sit with. What do you see? In your prayer what are you hearing God say to us? In this place of mutual submission, a coming together happens. Jesus becomes present and a "binding and loosing" is shaped where we discern together where to go from here (Matt 18:15–20). It is the very kingdom of God breaking in.

When we as pastors find ourselves participating in such relationships, the burden of managing conflict is taken from us. The power relationship is put into the hands of God. The act of submission places one into God's power, what the Spirit is doing . . . and asking everyone else to test it. This is at the very heart of what we have learned together about pastoring in Christ's authority instead of our own—what Kurt and Cameron call "healthy relationships."

May God bless this book in guiding many pastors, leaders, and disciples of all kinds to this place of putting the power relationship into the hands of God. In so doing, God's power will be unleashed in his church.

From One Preacher's Wife to Another

Lisa McKay

Lisa McKay is a mom of four and wife to Luke, a senior pastor who shepherds a thriving church in northern Alabama. They have served in various pastoral and parachurch ministry roles over the past eighteen years. Lisa is the author of You Can Still Wear Cute Shoes . . . and Other Great Advice from an Unlikely Preacher's Wife *(2010).*

It is with great delight that I offer my perspective—that of a senior pastor's wife—on this book. I am incredibly grateful that Cameron and Kurt have gracefully tackled practically every topic we find difficult (or impossible) to address with the people Luke and I are privileged to serve. I wonder if our church members will be suspicious if a copy shows up in all of their Christmas stockings with the "To Congregations" sections brightly highlighted?

I take very seriously my role as Luke's wife and my call to uphold him as he shepherds the various congregations God has entrusted to our care. I have shared many times and in many settings that when someone blesses Luke, they've blessed me; when they've broken his heart, they have broken mine. I've been a witness to his elation when someone comes to him asking for biblical advice and then, for heaven's sake, does what Scripture says! I've seen him come home and sit down a little heavier than usual, put his head in his hands, and let out that long sigh that says that church just flat out hurt that day. Or that week. Or that year.

I offer as a complement to this book a few things that male pastors need to know (or be reminded of) from the women who love them most.

His "Success" Rests in His Obedience, Not in the Spiritual State of His Congregation

It is a given that most pastors are constantly assessing the effectiveness of their ministries. I believe this is healthy in right measure, but often the responses and service (or lack thereof) of congregation members are weighted too heavily in the self-evaluation. It's incredibly easy to allow waning commitments and petty conflicts to reflect on our leadership when, actually, we are told to expect these:

> Preach the word, be ready in season and out of season; reprove, rebuke, and exhort, with complete patience and teaching. For the time is coming when people will not endure sound teaching, but having itching ears they will accumulate for themselves teachers to suit their own passions, and will turn always from listening to truth and wander off into myths. As for you always be sober-minded, endure suffering, do the work of an evangelist, fulfill your ministry. (2 Tim 4:2–5)[10]

I am in no way suggesting that a loss of influence or wandering church members is never a part of the Lord's confirmation that it is time to move on, but don't discount Satan's work in causing us to perceive there is a loss, when in fact cold hearts are simply a very sad sign of the times.

Often, when our husbands are dismayed, we are the first and sometimes the only ones to know. Do you recognize a particular pattern in his discouragements? Does it seem to come in the summer when attendance is naturally off? Is it during times when he is pleading for positions of service to be filled with no response? When he's preached his heart out only to look onto a crowd of glazed eyes and an occasional snore?

So what's the minister's wife to do? In times like these the Lord has called me to be an encourager and gently offer perspective shifts. Just as Paul exhorted Timothy to always be "sober-minded," Peter also reminds us to set our thoughts in healthier places when he says to "prepare your minds for action, and being sober-minded, set your hope fully on the grace that will be brought to you at the revelation of Jesus Christ" (1 Pet 1:13).[11] We have to remember that Jesus himself had a hard time winning over a crowd when he was speaking truth rather than feeding or healing them.

Satan would have us believe that it is every person in the pews who has gone astray, when in reality he has exaggerated the minority. Remind your husband of the bright spots, of those who are new converts, who are growing in their faith, and who are serving with all their hearts. As I make a mental note of the Body we serve, there are so many more faithful than not. And yet when discouragement comes, Satan would blind us to those who are devoted to their shepherd and the selfless acts they have offered to Christ.

Ultimately, our husbands will be called to give an account based on faithfully proclaiming the truth, sounding the gospel call, and equipping the saints for acts of service. You can give a football player shoulder pads,

10. ESV, emphasis added.
11. ESV.

a helmet, and a playbook, but you can't run the ball for him. Sometimes there is nothing more to do but look at him with eyes of love and let him know that you—the person on earth who loves him most—see his faithfulness. "As for you . . . fulfill your ministry," Paul said. And leave the response of people to God.

His Congregation Is His Heritage

A pastor never wants to catch himself uttering the phrase, "Well, now I've seen it all," because that is just asking for some new form of madness to break loose in your church. We've not seen it all yet, but I'm ashamed to say that when a season of calamity blows in, we are no longer shocked. Saddened beyond words—but not surprised. As much as no one wants to admit it, there are crazy people in church. Sometimes it's a crazy pastor, and sometimes a crazy parishioner, and sometimes it's both doing and saying things that don't deserve to be uttered here. I've asked Luke many times, "Does God hate us or what? Have we not done our time with the outrageous?" (Somehow I'm certain some of you have asked that very same question.)

Could the answer be that he doesn't hate us at all, but rather, he is confident? That he knew before the foundation of the universe that this body of believers would be facing this situation and that when his eyes roamed throughout the earth to seek out that one who would be faithful he chose your family for such a time as this? First Peter 5:3 reads, "nor yet as lording it (i.e. the pastor's position as shepherd) over those allotted to your charge, but proving to be examples to the flock."[12]

Distinct congregations are allotted to a pastor as his inheritance. That means this wasn't accidental. The groups of people we serve are carefully and purposefully given us as a heritage so that they may be presented to Christ at his revealing. You may be feeling like the red-headed stepchild if you are comparing the inheritance you ended up with that of the pastor across town, but hear me well: if your heritage does not look like a crown now, it will be the means by which you earn many. I need to know that and be reminded of it on a regular basis. I'll bet your husband does too.

12. NASB, emphasis added.

His Family Is His Safe Place

At the risk of sounding like a June Cleaver wannabe from decades long past, more than anything I desire to have an excellent family. I want Luke to feel that his spouse and children are spiritually and emotionally healthy and that his home is a refuge. The primary responsibility of creating that environment rests with me, as wife and mom. When Luke reads this, he will laugh his head off—because my running through the house yelling at the kids before school, "Get in the car NOW or we are going to be late again!" isn't exactly restful, and the nights he has come home to my serving him Hamburger Helper in my yoga pants/tee shirt ensemble are innumerable, and I'm afraid slightly unsatisfying.

Do you know what else? My kids fight, we struggle finding the right family devotional formula, my house isn't always spotless, and there are days Luke and I are lucky to get fifteen minutes of real conversation. It may not be perfect, but it's our family and I'm one blessed woman to be able to report that it is a happy one. However, that hasn't happened by accident, but rather because my husband and I have marked firm boundaries around our marriage. When the pressures of life and/or ministry have taken their toll, we have remembered that our relationship is the first priority and have taken necessary steps to protect it.

We've gone to great pains to make certain our kids are given the same grace as others. This required my once visiting a teacher and intensely "speaking the truth in love" when she suggested to my son that he should be careful in all he said and did because he was a PK. She went on to remind him how badly he would feel if he embarrassed his parents by acting foolish like the other nine-year-old boys. (Can a nine-year-old be anything but foolish!?) I will never forget the relieved look on his face when I looked him dead in the eye, told him how wrong she was to place that burden on him, and that we would always be on his side whether he did right or wrong. That child has never given us a second of trouble, and as of this writing our PKs, without any undue pressure from us because of those dreaded initials, have guarded well the family name, which remains—for the most part!—intact.

The writers have stated the sentiment of excellent family more eloquently than I ever could:

> To be exemplary does not mean being at the beck and call of
> every congregational demand, especially if it entails neglecting
> one's family. It does not mean being a "perfect" husband or wife,
> father or mother, son or daughter. It does not mean that the

pastor's spouse must make the coffee or mow the lawn. It does not mean that the pastor's children must never do anything, well, childish. What does it mean to be an exemplary pastor? It means to demonstrate, in both one's ministry and family life, the constant need for God's grace and the knowledge of where to find it. And it means to encourage others to do the same, whether in their own families or the family we call the church.

No ministry family is perfect, but we have to be certain that our quirks work. It is a devastation to me to learn of struggling marriages and the fallout on the home. Sweet ministry wife, if your home isn't the safe place it needs to be, seek wise counsel and be willing to do whatever it takes for your relationship to model that of Christ and his bride, the church.

How I wish we were across the table from one another so we could continue discussing all the things we certainly have in common! In the meantime, take the words of this needful work, learn from them, and be encouraged that they were written with great affection for you, the minister's family.

On Life as a PK

Lindsay Sturgeon

The following two letters were written by PKs who grew up as siblings in the Evangelical Covenant Church. They are the children of one of the authors of this book (hint: it's not Cameron). Lindsay is currently self-employed as a marriage and family therapist. She loves being involved in the church, and is married to Chris, the minister to students at Menlo Park Presbyterian in California.

As a pastor's child you get used to being a little bit in the limelight. In the church world, it feels a bit like being famous. You get mentioned in sermons a lot (my dad owed me $5.00 for every mention), so people know about your life. As a child, that's where you start to build some of your identity—as the "daughter of" instead of just "Lindsay." I remember when I went to college and people didn't know my dad or my mom. It was such a different experience to become known just for *me* and not for my parents or my role as pastor's kid.

Let me get some of the negative aspects out of the way. One interesting/difficult part about being a pastor's kid is knowing that my dad's salary came from the people in the church and therefore was based upon how much people gave. I remember times when I would overhear my dad telling my mom about a board meeting where finances were tough. Hearing this made me nervous. It was strange to know that the people I loved and cared about essentially determined my dad's salary.

At our church we had a quarterly open house for new members. I remember one open house where someone commented, "Oh, you got a new couch." The underlying tone of this statement was not, "How nice, congratulations!" It was more of a raised-eyebrow kind of disapproval, as if to say, "so *this* is where our tithe money is going." That may or may not be what this person meant—but as a child that is how I received it. What I really wanted to say at that moment was, "Hey, my mom works too! And even if she didn't, my parents are allowed to spend their money as they please!" Little things like that stood out to me. I remember that when I decided to go to Pepperdine University (which is a pretty expensive school) I felt like I had to justify my going with, "But I got really good scholarships!" There was often somewhat of a need to defend decisions that included money.

I remember times when people chose to leave the church, or when I found out certain people disliked my dad. That was a hard feeling. I like being liked, and I liked my family being liked. I imagine it's similar to being in a politician's family, where because of the role you are in some people will absolutely love and agree with you and others absolutely will not. I had to work to be okay with this as well as not automatically dislike the people who left or didn't like my dad.

There were and continue to be so many joys to being the daughter of a pastor. I felt like I had this huge family who knew me and loved me. I enjoyed going to church and having people say hello to me, hug me, and look glad to see me. It created a church environment for me that was very welcoming and happy. I am a person who tends to be open and loves to be known, so this was a really good thing for me. I could see how for more private people this could be very difficult.

One thing that I feel spared from as a pastor's child is that my dad stayed at one church his entire career. I am very grateful for this. I know this is rare and not the norm. Because of this, I got to have relationships with people in the church that continued to grow, instead of having to start over as I know a lot of pastors' kids have to do. I was able to stay at my school, in my neighborhood, and with my friends instead of moving around a lot.

Another thing I really liked about my parents in particular is that they were—in my eyes and in my friend's eyes—"normal." I liked that my dad didn't look or act like some people's stereotypes of a pastor. He told funny jokes. He wasn't stiff and unapproachable. Sometimes when I would tell friends my dad is a pastor I'd imagine them thinking, "Your dad must be dull, not open-minded, and maybe a little weird." I would always follow up by saying, "But you'd never know it! He's really cool and normal!"

I felt comfortable inviting my friends over—no matter what their faith beliefs were. I liked this—this made me feel proud and happy. I remember going out to lunch with my dad and two guy friends who were atheists. I liked that my dad didn't make them feel like horrible people or sound judgmental but instead listened well, shared in a truthful but respectful way, and that those two guys liked him! I liked being able to be a part of shattering some people's image of what a pastor's family had to be like.

It's not all a walk in the park, but I wouldn't at all trade being a pastor's daughter. Mainly, that's because I wouldn't trade being my dad's daughter, but also because of the joy that came from being a part of community that knew me, loved me, and walked with me through my childhood and now my adulthood. There have been times in my life where I've been sheltered in the loving arms of my church family, and for that I am so grateful. They have been my second family—surrogate grandparents and parents and brothers and sisters. There is no substitute for that type of community.

The Church Behind the Scenes

Daniel Fredrickson

Daniel is an attorney, serving as Associate General Counsel at Tendril, an energy management company. He and his wife Malia live in Boulder, CO.

I am a pastor's kid . . . a "PK," I suppose. I grew up in a fantastic congregation. I was loved, nurtured, and cared for on a constant basis—so much so that it was almost suffocating at times. In all honesty, I find it hard to imagine a better church family for a PK to be raised in.

Still, I must admit that I identify with many of the pressures and heightened expectations that seem to be inherent in the role of a PK: I was singled out when my group of friends got into trouble because I was the pastor's kid, I was expected to take on leadership roles in youth group because I was the pastors kid, and of course I was expected to follow in my dad's footsteps and become a pastor as well. I'm not a pastor.

Overall, though, being identified by others as a PK really had only a minor impact on me. Sure, at times I would feel compelled to act out simply because I was told that a PK shouldn't do this or that (almost like a "do not touch" sign at a museum). The real impact, though, came from seeing the church, not for what it can be or for what it is intended to be, but as an organization that is imperfect despite all of the best intentions.

Parts of this book describe how congregants may not see all of the work that pastors do behind the scenes. Pastors have hard jobs, and all too often their work is taken for granted. It makes sense that churches, as a whole, could be healthier if congregants understood the time, effort, and emotional strain that pastors deal with on a regular basis.

The same is not true for PKs. We are, as a rule, overexposed to the inner workings of the church. It is unavoidable. We go to church on Sundays and are surrounded by church business during the rest of the week. More often than not our experiences on Sundays and our experiences throughout the rest of the week convey a mixed message about what the church is. We are taught on Sundays about loving and supporting each other and the community around us, yet the church business we are exposed to through the week can seem like anything but loving and supportive. The message on Sundays tends to reflect what the church is meant to be, and often that message is inconsistent with what a PK observes from behind the scenes.

Even now, in my late twenties, it can be difficult to reconcile the difference between what the church is meant to be and the reality of church—and as an adolescent it was nearly impossible. How can a church aim to change a community for the better when the church itself can seem so broken? Today I can recognize that these differences exist because the church is imperfect, and I see that the church strives to positively impact its community despite its imperfection. As a child, though, these conflicting messages were incompatible, and the realities of church life diminished my view of what the church strives to be. I think it is important to recognize how difficult it can be for a child to accept what the church is meant to be, when he or she has a front-row seat to congregational realities that others may not see.

To be clear, I think that churches do amazing things, and being a PK has not scared me away from staying involved in the church. I see how churches impact their communities and how church members rally around each other in times of need. I watched how that happened in the life of our family. I also know that the displays of love and compassion within churches vastly outweigh instances of cruelty or unkindness. This was certainly true in my home church, where I found a second family that I love to this day.

The Nurturing of Calling and Development

Efrem Smith

Efrem Smith was ordained in both the National Baptist Convention and the Evangelical Covenant Church. In 2003, he founded The Sanctuary Covenant Church in Minneapolis, Minnesota. Currently, he is the Superintendent of the Pacific Southwest Conference of the Evangelical Covenant Church. He is an itinerant speaker with Kingdom Building Ministries, and his most recent book is The Post-Black and Post-White Church: Becoming the Beloved Community in a Multi-Ethnic World *(2012).*

In this very important and needed resource, I appreciate the authors' focus on "Being a Pastor: The Calling and the Job." It is indeed both. As I think about my years as a pastor, I realize how blessed I've been to have such great local churches in which to discover my sense of calling and grow in my professional development. I must say that I am somewhat concerned today about local churches intentionally nurturing the call of pastors, as well as being a place of intentional professional and spiritual development for emerging pastors. My thoughts and theology on this subject are connected to my being nurtured within both the African-American and urban church. I believe the way these churches have historically nurtured the calling and development of pastors can be a blessing to the broader church.

I would point to two reasons for why this isn't already the case. One, we are still in a very race-based and class-based society. On a global scale, we experience tribalism and ethnocentrism as well. The issue of race, for instance, causes us to believe that what is going on in the African-American church is relevant only for African-Americans. The issue of class causes us to believe that what is going on in the urban church is only for the urban community. But the models and theologies going on in the European-American and European churches are seen as normative for all churches. When this is the case, we lose the importance of contextualization as well as the opportunity for cross-cultural blessings.

This is connected to the second reason why the broader church is missing the blessing: the African-American and urban church tend to be marginalized. Many conferences focused on pastoral development and leadership either have no focus on African-American and urban church approaches, or they marginalize these approaches by having what comes across as one token speaker from this context, or a separate "track" that keeps these unique approaches from blessing the broader body. Because of this, African-American and urban church approaches are not widely accepted by denominations, at leadership conferences, and in seminaries as having the merit to impact the broader church (which is another way of saying the European-American and European church).

I believe that there are theologies and ministry practices within the African-American and urban church that are meant to be a blessing to the broader church. I believe this is true of Asian American and Hispanic churches as well. Because this is a personal response, based on my ministry experiences as a pastor, I will be dealing with the blessings for the broader church body coming from the African-American and multiethnic urban church.

As a pastor and regional denominational leader, I owe my development on so many levels to the African-American and urban church. I grew up in the African-American church, specifically the churches of the National Baptist Convention USA. It is important to understand the historic role the African-American church has played not only in nurturing the calling and professional development of pastors, but also of African-American leaders beyond just church positions. During slavery and Jim Crow segregation, the African-American church was the premier leadership development institution for African-Americans. When African-Americans weren't able to be CEOs, mayors, governors, or president, the African-American pastor was the frontline theological, intellectual, and executive leader. This meant that the church had to be an innovative center around the discovery of calling and the journey of development in various pastoral areas. Even though I am of the post-civil rights, hip-hop generation, as a pastor, I am still a product of this heritage and legacy.

Growing up in the African-American church, I was in awe of the African-American pastor, who played the roles of preacher, shepherd, and community leader. My awe didn't immediately lead to my having a sense of call, though it did lead me to desire a life of purpose, making a difference in my community and beyond. But whether someone senses a call to the pastorate or not, the church should foster an ethos that calls people to a priesthood of all believers.

Tabernacle Missionary Baptist Church (now called Redeemer Missionary Baptist) was that kind of church in my life growing up in Minneapolis. People within the local church should be lovingly and proactively equipped to live lives of purpose and kingdom advancement. Because I was in a medium-sized African-American church, I was blessed to have interaction with the senior pastor, Reverend Stanley King, and associate pastors such as Jerry MacAfee.

While in high school, I had a friend named Joey, who invited me to attend youth group with him at a multiethnic urban church, Park Avenue United Methodist. I began to attend youth group with Joey on Wednesday evenings, while still attending Tabernacle Missionary Baptist on Sundays. Though Park Avenue was predominantly European-American, the youth ministry was very multiethnic. Associate Pastor Art Erickson was a former area leader for Young Life. His role was to not only oversee the youth ministry of the church, but also to lead community development and outreach models as well. These initiatives are what attracted youth such as Joey and myself. I realize today that the culture and community involvement of the African-American church as well as the community engagement of an Urban Methodist Church played a key role in my discovery of calling and my development as a leader.

These churches supported me in going to college and seminary. While I was in college, I worked every summer at Park Avenue, getting not only experience in youth ministry, but community development work as well. The church must be proactive in the leadership development and discovery of calling with young people. A contemporary "priesthood of all believers" approach is key. This approach has been innovated in unique ways within the African-American and urban church and could be a blessing to the broader church body.

Another important part of my discovery of calling and my pastoral development was the apprenticeship I received in the African-American church. During my senior year in college, I developed a strong sense of calling. At the time I was going to church with my fiancée, Donecia Norwood, who is now my wife. Her grandfather, Dr. Edward Berry, was the senior pastor of Rising Star Missionary Baptist. After one Sunday morning service, I approached him and said that I thought I might be called into the ministry. I was hoping to be able to have a longer discussion with him later that week. He simply looked at me and said, "Well, we're about to find out if you're called." After saying that, he walked away.

The next Sunday, before he preached the sermon, he mentioned what I had said to him the Sunday before. Then he said, "We're going to find out if Brother Efrem is called to the ministry. Three weeks from today Brother Efrem is going to preach his initial sermon and then we're going to vote as a congregation as to whether he's called or not." Wow, I couldn't believe what he had just said. I thought we were going to have a conversation. Instead, I had to prepare to preach my first sermon!

Three weeks later I preached that sermon and the congregation voted to license me. For the next few months, I was in what I would call an "old-school apprenticeship" to Pastor Berry. When he went to visit someone in the hospital, I was with him. When he went to visit the sick and shut in at their homes, I was with him. I met with him in his office on Saturday mornings, gaining wisdom on the call of a pastor. He let me preach on a monthly basis.

I am so grateful for this trial-by-fire approach. He was my pastor and mentor in the ministry. With his guidance and the support of the church, I was ordained into the National Baptist Convention USA a year later. During this time I also began seminary. Seminary was a significant part of my development as a pastor, but the mentoring I received from Pastor Berry was even more significant. I also am so grateful to the congregation of Rising Star for loving me and giving me the opportunity to fail, grow, and nurture my calling.

When Pastor Berry retired, I returned to Redeemer Missionary Baptist and put myself under the coaching and mentoring of Pastor Gerald Joiner. To this day I call Pastor Joiner my "father in the ministry." I have not made any major decisions in ministry without talking to and praying with Pastor Joiner.

During my time as senior pastor of The Sanctuary Covenant Church, I felt it was important to move beyond just leaning on my father in the ministry for coaching, mentoring, and accountability. I now have a team of brothers and sisters who play an important role in my journey of living into my calling and continuing my pastoral development. Pastor Keith Johnson of North Carolina, Pastor Elwood Jones of Maryland, Dr. Brenda Salter-McNeil of Washington, and Dr. Robert Owens of Georgia are some of those who pray for me, speak into my life, and provide me with the healthy relationships needed for healthy ministry.

In short, the calling and development of a pastor should not happen in isolation. The church must continue to play a crucial role in affirming and nurturing what the Lord is doing through called-out men and women. I feel blessed to have had so many friends and mentors who have walked with me in the journey, and pray for a similar blessing for pastors throughout the broader church.

From PK to Clergy Couple with PKs

Andy Mattick

Andy Mattick, a storyteller, musician, and keynote speaker for youth events, is currently the Lead Pastor at Simi Valley United Methodist Church, Simi Valley, California. Having grown up as a Methodist PK, he is now in his twelfth year as a Methodist minister, and has served churches ranging from fourteen to three hundred in attendance. Andy and his wife, Camille, an ordained deacon, are raising two young PKs of their own.

The story I know best is my own, so I want to chance that there might be touchstone points between my story and yours, and with the work of Kurt and Cameron. My story is a lifelong transition from pastor's kid to a pastor in a clergy couple relationship with two children of my own.

I was born in my dad's last semester of seminary, and at three months old moved for what would become the first of thirteen times before my eighteenth birthday. As the son of a Methodist elder, my own experiences as a PK mirror some of the praises and concerns that Kurt and Cameron raise up. My dad is well liked as a pastor, an excellent preacher, and gifted care provider. Having these gifts for ministry meant they were cherished—if not craved!—in the local church, and my dad found himself in popular demand. He could schedule to make some of my unique events (an afternoon volleyball match or a lunchtime recital) a priority, but I struggled with a sense that he seemed to be more regularly present to the life demands of the local church. I believe that he shared this struggle given that he took what would become a sabbatical from local church ministry to better provide for our family and to be available more consistent hours. He found his way back into local church ministry, and my siblings and I all acknowledge that he is better for it, serving as God has called and intended him to.

I fought my own call into ministry. In my youth, well-meaning members of my dad's church tried their hands at lay prophecy. They observed my participation in youth group or the choir, would gently pat my shaggy head, and say things like, "Well, the apple did not fall far from the tree." What they could not know was that this apple was striving to roll as far from the tree as he could. I saw ministry as "my dad's business." Having seen the struggles of scheduling and family life and living with the fracture of my parent's divorce, I began to assert that the ministry was *not* for me.

I moved away from home for college, got a scholarship to study computer science (that seemed like a comfortable buffer), and prepared myself for a decidedly non-pastoral adult life.

My own call into ministry happened in the midst of that tumult. I share it here briefly only because I am confident that an assurance of call is the bedrock of health and vitality in ministry. It is assurance of God's presence and providence in your ministry that will carry you through many of the pitfalls described in this book and call you to the disciplines that promote personal and congregational health. Simply put, I clarified my call when a dear friend asked me to describe how I *knew* I wasn't called into ministry. "Tell me what you mean by that and then I will never bring it up again." I sat in the silence of an awaited answer for about five minutes, and then I spoke a phrase that has since transformed my purpose. "Oh my God!" I said with the utmost reverence, "I *am* called into ministry!" Your body can be an excellent barometer for truth and I felt at my core that I had never said a truer phrase. God had revealed to me that I was not to be about "my dad's business," but was being called and equipped to "God's business."

By September of 2000, I had started my first year in ministry as a student pastor, gotten married to Camille, and celebrated my twenty-third birthday. In my first year, I was learning on the fly how to be a pastor, a husband, and most days a grown-up. The gift of that church setting was their clear identity of being a teaching congregation. They knew who they were and in some part what they were getting and could expect of me. I remember their willingness to live into an identity that did not overextend their self-worth or my potential. It was a church of much grace and forgiveness. I wish that every church had a clear sense of its present reality with the wisdom to be honest about their gifts, potential, and pitfalls. That transparency allows for both pastors and laity to strive toward a common sense of purpose and hope without being mired in the memories of what used to be, or lost in the ether of what ought to be.

To date, I have served in four local church settings, which included a student pastorate described above, a six-year appointment as an associate at a large suburban church, a three-year appointment at a small but vibrant beach community, and my current appointment as lead pastor of a multi-staff church in a community that is bridging the gap between rural and suburban living.

One thing that I have come to learn through the transitions is the necessity of the disciplines of self-care. As Kurt and Cameron point out, incarnational living must honor the relationship between our bodies and work with and for the body of Christ. For me, this involves regular exercise (cycling is a new favorite), regular sleep, and attention to diet. As a lifelong "food addict," the last is certainly the most taxing for me. But experience has taught me a twofold reality: first, the regular rigor of "normal" ministry will wear you out without this attention to bodily health, and second, times of crisis become almost unmanageable without these disciplines. The demands of local ministry following the national tragedy of 9/11 were further complicated by my own sedentary lifestyle and poor eating habits.

I have also seen the power and gift that pastoral health can provide to a local congregation. In 2007, I was assigned to Malibu UMC and arrived at 365 pounds. After watching a triathlon at a local beach, I decided that I wanted to attempt it myself the following year. The next morning I walked to work, a mile and a half, which nearly did me in. A month later I was up on a bike. A year later, I did that same race at just under 300 pounds. However, that achievement pales for me in light of my challenge to the church to rise to the occasion and address their disciplines of health and fitness. The next year, 14 members of that church (including an 83-year old-woman who did the swim leg) joined me in that race. And in my current setting, my regular Saturday morning bike rides have developed into a small group ministry of fellow riders from the church.

I have spent these eleven years in ministry with my wife, Camille. She and I met in seminary and married knowing full well that each was pursuing a God-called and God-directed life in ministry. We have unique and different skill sets that we honor in one another. My gifts are primarily in worship leadership and preaching, hers in Christian education and creative arts. Within our denomination that has meant that our ordinations have followed separate but parallel tracks as I am an ordained elder and she is an ordained deacon. For those unfamiliar with our polity, a significant implication of that has been my call to itinerant ministry. Camille's ministry is ever contextual and her appointments are affirmed in any given setting. Two truths emerge for us. First, our cabinet is only accountable to discerning for my appointment in how it matches my gifts and graces with the present needs and potential of a local church. Second, we have had to address this prayerfully in our private life, striving to honor the full value and commitments of her ministries with the trust that the Spirit's providence is ever at work in the discernment of mine.

Being a clergy couple has been a real gift to us. Maintaining the sanctity of that gift has required clear boundaries on our part with both our congregations. One truly rung bell from Kurt and Cameron's reflection was on the disparity of expectations between our local churches. Camille's work also requires a commute, as we live in the community my church serves. As such, her church honors the times I can be there but treats them as a welcome rarity. As both a pastor's wife and ordained spouse, her relationships to my local churches have varied. One layperson recently asked if her church would consider giving her one Sunday a month off so she could worship in my local church setting. I have yet to be asked the same.

That we might reframe the conversation about her work, I consistently highlight in my context the value and fruits of her ministry. We have prayed about the possibility of working at the same church. We realize that Camille may someday make a great associate pastor in a multi-staff local church where I serve as senior pastor. But because of overlapping schedules and demands—vacations, church crises—it wouldn't be suitable for her to be the only associate pastor in that church. Given her present commute, each church is clear on our hopes and needs related to care for our family as a part of their ministry.

Now having children of my own, I am keenly aware of the dynamics of my own relationship with my dad. Camille (who is also a PK) and I set clear boundaries of time and obligation in regards to our children (now eight and five). My daughter and son are the children of two churches, participating in family ministries in each setting freely and regularly. They are likely to someday face choices about their involvement and investment in a church setting, but we do not anticipate forcing the issue.

I choose one other word to describe my family to compliment what Kurt and Cameron use in chapter 9: *stewardship*. I believe that my spouse and children are tremendous gifts that I have stewardship over, not unlike being given stewardship of my body in self-care or a congregation in the practice of ministry. I did not have children in order to benefit my ministry as sermon illustrations or as tokens of my ability to attract families to a church. God expects faithful shepherding of these relationships from me. As such, my ministry will not and cannot come at their expense.

I am grateful to Kurt and Cameron for their faithful and fruitful look at the life of the pastor. As a young clergyperson, I have found their insights poignant and helpful. I join their prayer for all who are a part of this tremendous work of God's kingdom building.

Holy Permission

Anonymous

The final response letter was written by a pastor's wife who has chosen to remain anonymous.

There are a few books that seem to meet you at a point in your journey where you feel they were written just for you. That's how I felt when I read this one. I graduated from seminary thinking I was going to change the world. I had no idea about all the lessons that ministry in the local church would teach me.

Six years ago, my husband was appointed to the pastorate of a small urban church that was about to shut down. At the time, we had just graduated from college and were only dating. The church seemed to think that a young, enthusiastic bilingual pastor would somehow fix decades of dysfunction. We were in our early twenties, and being asked to minister to a handful of elderly couples who were holding on to the good old days when the church thrived. The congregation was English-speaking, but the surrounding neighborhood had changed to become a predominantly Latino immigrant community. The church had barely enough money to keep the lights on, and a meager salary for one staff person only.

In almost three years of marriage and six years of ministry, it's been a major challenge to figure out my role as a wife, let alone a *pastor's* wife. I won't go into all the details, but the Lord has comforted and upheld us through the many times when we wanted to give up. Here are a few of the lessons I learned; I hope they will be an encouragement to those of you who identify with the challenges of being married to the pastor of a small urban church.

One major lesson I am continuing to learn is to protect myself from taking on too much. No one else will say no for me. There will never be an end to the needs around me, especially in a small congregation with no resources and no paid staff besides my husband. When we first started, my husband and I were doing everything in the church. I was leading worship, running the children's ministry, helping with the youth ministry, hosting a small group in our home, starting a women's ministry, and coordinating special events. I was also finishing graduate school, working full-time, and trying to be the perfect newlywed wife by making nice meals and keeping the house clean! I had no time for myself, was isolated from friends, and was burning out quickly. But I felt like I had no choice. I had the capacity to lead, and compassion for each area—and there was no one else to take on the roles. Plus, I wanted to support my husband so he didn't have to carry everything alone.

But I was giving so much of myself away that I had nothing left to give to him. He had little left to give to me either. We both felt empty and exhausted. We didn't know what our roles were supposed to be; there was no direction from the church or the denomination, and no clear mission statement. There was little feedback from the people we were serving, except for criticism. I felt like I was never doing enough, even though I was doing more than any sane person should.

One morning I answered the phone and the woman on the other end said, "Oh, you're probably still sleeping—because you sleep in a lot, don't you?" It was 10 a.m.; she thought all I did was lounge around the parsonage. I bit my tongue and explained I had actually been up for hours. It hurt to be so badly misunderstood when I was trying to serve with all my heart and strength. But there would always be people who thought I should be doing more, or tackling projects more directly related to their needs.

When our district superintendent came to see how we were doing, he took us into the office, sat us down, and said, "I knew something was going to have to die in this congregation before it came back to life—I didn't know it would be you two." He laughed heartily and slapped us on the back, but gave not one word of the encouragement we desperately needed. I felt overlooked and used, and irate that he had not acknowledged my husband's hard work. I wanted to give him a slap myself—of a different kind!—but I held back and gave a forced smile instead. What else could I do? Where was the support from the denomination? Where would we get encouragement if not even from my husband's supervisor?

One of my greatest strengths became one of my greatest weaknesses. As a child of a well-known pastor and missionary, I grew up in the limelight with the constant pressure of performing for the expectations of others. I am keenly sensitive to the cultural expectations of each environment. In a positive sense, this means I can adapt quickly to different types of people; however, this has also made me hyper-vigilant to the expectations of others. Everyone seems to have an opinion about how I should dress, behave, and relate in the church. I have lived with the "walk-on-water syndrome" most of my life—but I am subject to the same laws of gravity as everyone else, and can therefore sink. My stress level has been chronically high trying to please everyone; I put so much pressure on myself to analyze and meet others' needs.

For example, I remember one Sunday a little girl from the neighborhood pulling on one side of my dress literally asking me to be her mom, while on the other side a lady was tapping me on the shoulder waiting to talk with me about her husband's infidelity. If I ignored the little girl, who was neglected in her own family, then I would fail her because she was coming to the church to find a second home. If I didn't talk to the woman, she might leave depressed, with the impression that God didn't care about her. Trying to be all things to all people at all times made me feel like I constantly fell short. I had always heard it was impossible to please everyone, but had succeeded in the past. I finally realized for myself that it really *is* impossible. And I have also recognized that many times my perceptions of what people are expecting of me are inaccurate.

Isolated from real friendships, I was truly burning out. I was slipping into a mild depression and had no one to talk to. Once I asked an older lady in the church to have coffee with me so I could share with her about what I was going through. She seemed motherly and kind so my hopes were high, and I took the risk. But instead of listening with compassion, she told me that my struggles were nothing compared to what she went through when *she* was my age. She cut me off and talked for the rest of the time about her troubled childhood. I quickly packed away my heart and put on my pastoral counseling hat to comfort her instead. Even though she was at least twice my age she couldn't see that I just needed a space to be heard.

Since that time I have sought out safe people that will truly listen and encourage me. I now meet with a spiritual director, and I am also in therapy once a week. These resources, which are outside my marriage, my family, and most importantly outside of our congregation, have been a major life source for me. If you don't have a safe place to discuss your struggles, please don't wait. Find someone safe to help carry your burdens. I was forced to realize that I am just as human and broken as everyone else. It took humility and courage to admit my need for accountability, and it's helped me to better relate to those who come to me in their own brokenness.

The "subversive act" of Sabbath talked about in this book is a helpful antidote to battling the people-pleasing/performance syndrome. My own theology has been twisted: I had bought into the lie that it was up to me to make the kingdom of God a reality. In my head, I knew it was about

God ushering in the kingdom, but somewhere in my subconscious I felt a great weight of responsibility to help people change and heal through *my* efforts. Eugene Peterson's idea of the "two-beat rhythm"—that God begins to work creatively before we even lift a finger—is a core truth that I long to grasp in a deeper part of me. He invites me to participate in what he is doing but is not asking me to make it happen on my own. I long to internalize the words of Walter Brueggemann, quoted in this book: "the Sabbath announces that the world is safely in God's hands." Even when I stop to rest, the world will not stop being under God's great care. My work is important, but never ultimate; the world is in God's hands and not my own. I am a child of God before I am a servant, a performer, or a producer of anything. I can trust that he is the one who ultimately carries his people, not me. What a wonderful, liberating truth! This frees me from the weight of worrying about what will happen if I don't do everything perfectly, and allows me to take time to rest and discern the one or two things that God is inviting me to do with him. What can I do out of sincere love, and not out of an obligation to keep people happy?

My frenzied activity also created a passivity among the other members of the church. They assumed I was willing to do everything, so why should they get involved? Now that I have begun saying no, I have noticed people slowly taking on more active roles. As I trust God's ability to carry our church, I notice the people around me seem to be less stressed, and more relaxed. We can look to God together, instead of them looking to me or to my husband to provide their emotional and spiritual needs.

I have finally given myself permission to first be a child of God. I have never had the title or calling to be a pastor, nor have I ever been paid to be one, even though I have been working under the weight of the "two-for-one special." But now I will let myself be a support to my husband and find my role as an active church member just like everyone else. I am already working full-time to support us as a family, and I need to remind myself that this contribution in itself allows my husband to finish graduate school and be involved in a congregation with a very limited budget. This change of perspective may seem simple, but it has been monumental for me and has freed me from a destructive cycle of unrealistic expectations and poor boundaries.

My husband and I are both making efforts to practice better self-care. We are meeting with our spiritual directors regularly, working out several times a week, and making our own emotional, physical, and spiritual connection with one another a top priority. We protect Fridays for our date nights (youth group had to be moved to another night!). My husband took ordination vows before we took our marriage vows—but we are realigning our priorities so that church responsibilities do not disintegrate our marriage covenant. This is a daily battle and takes constant open communication between us, as well as accountability to others who love us and want to see our marriage succeed. The first few years of marriage have been challenging, but I am so grateful we are learning these lessons now so that our marriage won't turn into another sad statistic. I can honestly say that by the grace of God I am more in love with my husband today than on our wedding day.

So wherever you are as you are reading this, my prayer is that you would find a way to see yourself as a beloved child of God, someone who is treasured by your Father in heaven. He wants you to rest, and to live life in abundance in him, not scraping the bottom of the barrel. Taking care of yourself is something that delights his heart, because he cares about you just as much as any of his other kids that you are serving. The compassion you have for others, have for yourself. This is not selfish; it is godly. When you are a good steward of your health emotionally, spiritually, and physically, you will also have something to give to your own family, and you can overflow into the lives of those around you. Instead of modeling a life characterized by the striving emptiness of good works and a burned-out and unhappy soul, you will model what it means to have a life that is characterized by the goodness and grace of God!

Take courage; you are not alone.

Bibliography

Aldwin, Carolyn. *Stress, Coping, and Development: An Integrative Perspective.* New York: Guilford, 1994.

Alter, Robert. *Genesis: Translation and Commentary.* New York: Norton, 1996.

American Society of Plastic Surgeons. "National Clearinghouse of Plastic Surgery Statistics: 2010 Report of the 2009 Statistics." Online: http://www.plasticsurgery .org/Documents/Media/statistics/ 2009-US-cosmeticreconstructiveplasticsurger yminimally-invasive-statistics.pdf.

Anderson, Ray S. *The Soul of Ministry: Forming Leaders for God's People.* Louisville: Westminster John Knox, 1997.

Anonymous. "I'm Ted and I'm Married to Your Minister." *Grow* (Summer 1992) 21–23. Online: http://www.whwomenclergy.org/articles/article57.php.

Baab, Lynne. *Sabbath Keeping: Finding Freedom in the Rhythms of Rest.* Downers Grove, IL: InterVarsity, 2005.

Bakker, Jay. *Son of a Preacher Man.* New York: HarperOne, 2001.

Barcomb-Peterson, Erinn. "K-State Finds that Healthier Pastors Lead to More Health Programming at Churches, Where Wellness Messages Can Reach as Much as 60 Percent of Americans." January 14, 2010. Online: http://www.k-state.edu/media/ newsreleases/jan10/chrchhlth11410.html.

Barna Group. "Born Again Christians Just as Likely to Divorce as Non-Christians." September 8, 2004. Online: http://www.barna.org/barna-update/article/5 -barna-update/194-born-again-christians-just-as-likely-to-divorce-as-are-non -christians.

Bass, Dorothy. *Receiving the Day: Christian Practices for Opening the Gift of Time.* San Francisco: Jossey-Bass, 2000.

Berry, Bill. "One Pastor's Story." December 22, 2009. Online: http://healthypastor .com/?p=74.

Bird, Warren. "Teacher First: Leadership Network's 2009 Large-Church Senior Pastor Survey." July 14, 2009. Online: http://leadnet.org//resources/download/teacher_ first_2009_survey_large_church_senior_pastors.

Bloesch, Donald. *The Church: Sacraments, Worship, Ministry Mission.* Downers Grove, IL: InterVarsity, 2005.

Bonhoeffer, Dietrich. *Letters and Papers from Prison.* New York: Touchstone, 1997.

Brown, Chris. "Sacred Space: Why I'm Bivocational." Online: http://presbymergent. org/2009/ 08/13/sacred-space-why-im-bi-vocational/.

Brueggemann, Walter. *Genesis.* Atlanta: John Knox, 1982.

Buchanan, Mark. *The Rest of God: Restoring your Soul by Restoring Sabbath.* Nashville, TN: Thomas Nelson, 2006.

———. *Spiritual Rhythm: Being With Jesus Every Season of Your Soul*. Grand Rapids, MI: Zondervan, 2010.

Buechner, Frederick. *The Longing for Home*. San Francisco, CA: HarperSanFrancisco, 1996.

———. *Wishful Thinking: A Theological ABC*. New York: Harper and Row, 1973.

Callahan, Kennon. *Effective Church Leadership: Building on the Twelve Keys*. San Francisco, CA: Jossey-Bass, 2007.

Carroll, Jackson A. *God's Potters: Pastoral Leadership and the Shaping of Congregations*. Grand Rapids, MI: Eerdmans, 2006.

Centers for Disease Control and Prevention. "Fact Sheet for Health Professionals on Physical Activity Guidelines for Adults." 2008. Online: http://www.cdc.gov/nccdphp/dnpa/ physical/pdf/PA_Fact_Sheet_Adults.pdf.

Chandler, Diane J. "Pastoral Burnout and the Impact of Personal Spiritual Renewal, Rest-Taking, and Support System Practices." *Pastoral Psychology* 58 (2009) 273–87.

Christensen, Andrew, and Neil S. Jacobson. *Reconcilable Differences*. New York: Guilford, 2000.

Clapp, Rodney. *Tortured Wonders*. Grand Rapids, MI: Brazos Press, 2004.

Cloud, Henry, and John Townsend. *Boundaries*. Grand Rapids, MI: Zondervan, 1992.

———. *Boundaries in Dating*. Grand Rapids, MI: Zondervan, 2000.

———. *Boundaries with Kids*. Grand Rapids, MI: Zondervan, 1998.

Cody-Rydzewski, Susan. "Married Clergy Women: How They Maintain Traditional Marriage Even as They Claim New Authority." *Review of Religious Research* 48 (2007) 273–89.

Constantine, Mark D. *Travelers on the Journey: Pastors Talk About their Lives and Commitments*. Grand Rapids, MI: Eerdmans, 2005.

Cordeiro, Wayne. *Leading on Empty*. Minneapolis: Bethany House, 2009.

Cosby, Bill. *Bill Cosby: 49*. Kodak Video, 2002.

Cosden, Darrell. *The Heavenly Good of Earthly Work*. Milton Keynes, UK: Paternoster Press, 2006.

Covey, Stephen R., A. Roger Merrill, and Rebecca R. Merrill. *First Things First*. New York: Fireside, 1994.

Currie III, Thomas W. *The Joy of Ministry*. Louisville: Westminster John Knox, 2008.

Daniel, Lillian. "The Pastor's Husband." *The Christian Century* 126 (July 14, 2009) 28–31.

Daniel, Lillian, and Martin B. Copenhaver. *This Odd and Wondrous Calling: The Public and Private Lives of Two Ministers*. Grand Rapids, MI: Eerdmans, 2009.

Deming, Laura, and Jack Stubbs. *Men Married to Ministers*. Washington, DC: Alban Institute, 1986.

Department of Health and Human Services. "Be Active Your Way: A Guide for Adults." ODPHP Publication No. U0037 (October 2008). Online: http://www.health.gov/paguidelines/pdf/adultguide.pdf.

Dobson, Edward G., Speed B. Leas, and Marshall Shelley. *Mastering Conflict and Controversy*. Portland, OR: Multnomah Press, 1992.

Dobson, Lorna. *Caring for your Pastor: Helping God's Servant to Minister with Joy*. Grand Rapids, MI: Kregel Publications, 2001.

———. *I'm More than the Pastor's Wife*. Revised ed. Grand Rapids, MI: Zondervan, 2003.

Dulles, Avery. *Models of the Church.* New York: Image, 2002.

Easum, Bill. "On Not Being Nice for the Sake of the Gospel." No pages. Online: http://churchconsultations.com/community/articles/view-articles/?tx_ttnews%5Btt_news%5D=474&cHash=e4c4879dc5bf126732603c08efa9f10f.

Ellison, Christopher G., et al. "Religious Resources, Spiritual Struggles, and Mental Health in a Nationwide Sample of PCUSA Clergy." *Pastoral Psychology* 59 (2010) 287–304.

Ellison Research. "Just How Healthy is the Typical Pastor?" August 1, 2003. No pages. Online: http://ellisonresearch.com/releases/20030801.htm.

Emmons, Robert A., and Michael E. McCullough. "Counting Blessings Versus Burdens: An Experimental Investigation of Gratitude and Subjective Well-Being in Daily Life." *Journal of Personality and Social Psychology* 84 (2003) 377–89.

Epstein, Lawrence J., and Steven Mardon. *The Harvard Medical School Guide to a Good Night's Sleep.* New York: McGraw-Hill, 2007.

Evers, Will, and Welko Tomic. "Burnout Among Dutch Reformed Pastors." *Journal of Psychology and Theology* 31 (2003) 328–38.

Floyd, Jeana. *10 Things Every Minister's Wife Needs to Know.* Green Forest, AR: New Leaf Press, 2009.

Focus on the Family. "Pastoral Ministries 2009 Survey." Online: http://www.parsonage.org/images/pdf/2009PMSurvey.pdf.

Frame, Marsha Wiggins. "Relocation and Well-Being in United Methodist Clergy and their Spouses: What Pastoral Counselors Need to Know." *Pastoral Psychology* 46 (1998) 415–30.

Frame, Marsha Wiggins, and Constance L. Shehan. "Care for the Caregiver: Clues for the Pastoral Care of Clergywomen." *Pastoral Psychology* 52 (2004) 369–80.

———. "The Relationship between Work and Well-Being in Clergywomen: Implications for Career Counseling." *Journal of Employment Counseling* 42 (2005) 10–19.

———. "Work and Well-Being in the Two-Person Career: Relocation Stress and Coping Among Clergy Husbands and Wives." *Family Relations* 43 (1994) 196–205.

Francis, Leslie J., et al. "Clergy Work-Related Satisfaction in Parochial Ministry: The Influence of Personality and Churchmanship." *Mental Health, Religion & Culture* 11 (2008) 327–39.

Fredrickson, Barbara L., et al. "What Good Are Positive Emotions in Crises?" *Journal of Personality and Social Psychology* 84 (2003) 365–76.

Friedman, Edwin. *Generation to Generation: Family Process in Church and Synagogue.* New York: Guilford Press, 1985.

Galindo, Israel. *The Hidden Lives of Congregations.* Herndon, VA: The Alban Institute, 2004.

Galli, Mark. "The Most Risky Profession." *Christianity Today* (Web only) 55 (July 14, 2011). No pages. Online: http://www.christianitytoday.com/ct/2011/julyweb-only/mostriskyprofession.html.

General Assembly Mission Council (PCUSA). "Tentmaking or Bi-Vocational Ministers." No pages. Online: http://gamc.pcusa.org/ministries/ministers/tentmaking-or-bi-vocational-ministers/.

Gilbert, Barbara G. *Who Ministers to Ministers?* Herndon, VA: The Alban Institute, 1987.

Gilbert, Roberta M. *The Eight Concepts of Bowen Theory.* Falls Church, VA: Leading Systems Press, 2006.

Bibliography

Guder, Darrell, editor. *Missional Church: A Vision for the Sending of the Church in North America.* Grand Rapids, MI: Eerdmans, 1998.

Guinness, Os. *The Call.* Nashville, TN: W Publishing Group, 2003.

Halaas, Gwen Wagstrom. *The Right Road: Life Choices for Clergy.* Minneapolis: Fortress Press, 2004.

Halverstadt, Hugh F. *Managing Church Conflict.* Louisville: Westminster John Knox, 1991.

Hancock, Elizabeth Emerson. *Trespassers Will Be Baptized.* New York: Center Street, 2008.

Hart, Archibald D. *Adrenaline and Stress.* Dallas: Word, 1995.

———. *Sleep: It Does a Family Good.* Carol Stream, IL: Tyndale, 2010.

Haugk, Kenneth. *Antagonists in the Church.* Minneapolis: Augsburg, 1988.

Hawkins, Susie. *From One Ministry Wife to Another.* Chicago: Moody, 2009.

Heller, Alfred L. *Your Body, His Temple.* Nashville, TN: Thomas Nelson, 1981.

Hernandez, Edwin I., et al. "Strengthening Hispanic Ministry Across Denominations: A Call to Action." *Pulpit and Pew Research Reports*, 2005.

Heschel, Abraham. *The Sabbath.* New York: Farrar, Straus and Giroux, 2005.

Hileman, Linda. "The Unique Needs of Protestant Clergy Families: Implications for Marriage and Family Counseling." *Journal of Spirituality in Mental Health* 10 (2008) 119–44.

Hoge, Dean R., and Jacqueline E. Wenger. *Pastors in Transition: Why Clergy Leave Local Church Ministry.* Grand Rapids, MI: Eerdmans, 2005.

Hotchkiss, Dan. "Why Pay the Preacher?" *Clergy Journal* 85 (Nov/Dec 2009). Online: http://www.alban.org/conversation.aspx?id=8796.

Hulme, William E. *Managing Stress in Ministry.* San Francisco, CA: Harper and Row, 1985.

Jackson, Anne. *Mad Church Disease: Overcoming the Burnout Epidemic.* Grand Rapids, MI: Zondervan, 2009.

James, Christopher B. "Two Pastors under One Roof and Steeple: Clergy Couples Talk." No pages. Online: http://www.jesusdust.com/2008/01/two-pastors-under-one-roof-and-steeple.html.

Jinkins, Michael. *Letters to New Pastors.* Grand Rapids, MI: Eerdmans, 2006.

Johnson, Ben Campbell. *Hearing God's Call.* Grand Rapids, MI: Eerdmans, 2002.

Johnson, Eric B. "Salaries for United Methodist Clergy in the U. S. Context." Online: http://www.gbhem.org/atf/cf/%7B0bcef929-bdba-4aa0-968f-d1986a8eef80%7D/DOM_SalaryStudy Packet.pdf.

Jones, Kirk Byron. *Rest in the Storm.* Valley Forge, PA: Judson, 2001.

Jones, L. Gregory. "Take This Job." *The Christian Century* 119 (August 14-27, 2002) 35.

Jones, L. Gregory, and Kevin R. Armstrong. *Resurrecting Excellence: Shaping Faithful Christian Ministry.* Grand Rapids, MI: Eerdmans, 2006.

Joyner, F. Belton. *Life in the Fish Bowl.* Nashville, TN: Abingdon, 2006.

Jud, Gerald J., et al. *Ex-Pastors: Why Men Leave the Parish Ministry.* Philadelphia, PA: Pilgrim Press, 1970.

Kantor, David, and William Lehr. *Inside the Family.* New York: Harper Colophon, 1975.

Katz, Daniel, and Robert L. Kahn. *The Social Psychology of Organizations.* 2nd ed. New York: Wiley and Sons, 1978.

Kerr, Michael E., and Murray Bowen. *Family Evaluation.* New York: Norton, 1988.

Kinnaman, David, and Gabe Lyons. *Unchristian.* Grand Rapids, MI: Baker Books, 2007.

Kinnaman, Gary D., and Alfred H. Ells. *Leaders that Last*. Grand Rapids, MI: Baker Books, 2003.

Krakow, Barry. *Sound Sleep, Sound Mind*. Hoboken, NJ: John Wiley, 2007.

Krause, Neal, et al. "Church-Based Emotional Support, Negative Interaction, and Psychological Well-Being: Findings from a Nationwide Sample of Presbyterians." *Journal for the Scientific Study of Religion* 37 (1998) 725–41.

Krejcir, Richard J. "Statistics on Pastors." 2007. No pages. Online: http://www .intothyword.org/apps/articles/default.asp?articleid=36562.

Kung, Hans. *The Church*. New York: Sheed and Ward, 1967.

Langford, Daniel L. *The Pastor's Family: The Challenges of Family Life and Pastoral Responsibilities*. New York: The Haworth Pastoral Press, 1998.

Lazarus, Richard S. *Stress and Emotion: A New Synthesis*. New York: Springer, 1999.

Lee, Cameron. *Beyond Family Values: A Call to Christian Virtue*. Downers Grove, IL: InterVarsity, 1998.

———. "Dispositional Resiliency and Adjustment in Protestant Pastors: A Pilot Study." *Pastoral Psychology* 59 (2010) 631–40.

———. "Patterns of Stress and Support Among Adventist Clergy: Do Pastors and their Spouses Differ?" *Pastoral Psychology* 55 (2007) 761–71.

———. *PK: Helping Pastors' Kids through their Identity Crisis*. Grand Rapids, MI: Zondervan, 1992.

Lee, Cameron, and Jack Balswick. *Life in a Glass House: The Minister's Family in its Unique Social Context*. Grand Rapids, MI: Zondervan, 1989.

Lee, Cameron, and Judith Iverson-Gilbert. "Demand, Support, and Perception in Family-Related Stress among Protestant Clergy." *Family Relations* 52 (2003) 249–57.

Lehr, Fred. *Clergy Burnout*. Minneapolis: Fortress, 2006.

Lewis, C. S. *The Magician's Nephew*. New York: Harper, 1955.

London, H. B., and Neil B. Wiseman. *Pastors at Greater Risk*. Ventura, CA: Regal Books, 2003.

Long, Thomas G. "Of This Gospel..." In *Awakened to a Calling*, edited by Ann M. Svenningsen and Melissa Wiginton, 37–44. Nashville, TN: Abingdon, 2005.

Lott, David B., editor. *Conflict Management in Congregations*. Washington, DC: Alban Institute, 2001.

Mahler, Margaret S., et al. *The Psychological Birth of the Human Infant*. New York: Basic Books, 1975.

Maslach, Christina. *Burnout: The Cost of Caring*. Englewood Cliffs, NJ: Prentice-Hall, 1982.

Maslach, Christina, and Michael P. Leiter. *The Truth about Burnout*. San Francisco, CA: Jossey-Bass, 1997.

Maslach, Christina, Wilmar B. Schaufeli, and Michael P. Leiter. "Job Burnout." *Annual Review of Psychology* 52 (2001) 397–422.

Mayo, Josh. *Help! I'm Raising My Kids while Doing Ministry*. Longwood, FL: Xulon Press, 2007.

McDuff, Elaine M., and Charles W. Mueller. "Social Support and Compensating Differentials in the Ministry: Gender Differences in Two Protestant Denominations." *Review of Religious Research* 40 (1999) 307–30.

McKay, Lisa. *You Can Still Wear Cute Shoes*. Colorado Springs, CO: David C. Cook, 2010.

Bibliography

McMillan, Becky R. "What Do Clergy Do All Week?" No pages. Online: http://pulpitandpew.org/what-do-clergy-do-all-week.

McMillan, Becky R., and Matthew J. Price. "How Much Should We Pay the Pastor?" *Pulpit and Pew Research Reports* (Winter 2003). Online: http://www.pulpitandpew.org/sites/all/themes/pulpitandpew/files/salarystudy.pdf.

McMinn, Mark R., et al. "Positive Coping among Wives of Male Christian Clergy." *Pastoral Psychology* 56 (2008) 445–57.

McNeal, Reggie. *A Work of Heart: Understanding How God Shapes Spiritual Leaders.* San Francisco, CA: Jossey-Bass, 2000.

Mickey, Paul A., and Ginny W. Ashmore. *Clergy Families: Is Normal Life Possible?* Grand Rapids, MI: Zondervan, 1991.

Minuchin, Salvador. *Families and Family Therapy.* Cambridge, MA: Harvard, 1974.

Moltmann, Jurgen. *The Church in the Power of the Spirit.* New York: Harper and Row, 1977.

Muller, Wayne. *Sabbath.* New York: Bantam Books, 1999.

National Institute on Alcohol Abuse and Alcoholism. *Alcohol Alert* 41 (July 1998). No pages. Online: http://pubs.niaaa.nih.gov/publications/aa41.htm.

National Sleep Foundation. "One-Third of Americans Lose Sleep Over Economy." Online: http://www.sleepfoundation.org/sites/default/files/2009%20NSF%20POLL%20PRESS%20RELEASE.pdf.

———. "2009 Sleep in America Poll Summary of Findings." Online: http://www.sleepfoundation.org/sites/default/files/2009%20Sleep%20in%20America%20SOF%20EMBARGOED.pdf.

Neuhaus, Richard John. *Freedom for Ministry.* Revised ed. Grand Rapids, MI: Eerdmans, 1992.

Newbigin, Lesslie. *The Church in a Pluralist Society.* Grand Rapids, MI: Eerdmans, 1989.

———. *The Household of God: Lectures on the Nature of the Church.* Eugene, OR: Wipf and Stock, 2009.

Ngo, Hang-Yue, et al. "Work Role Stressors and Turnover Intentions: A Study of Professional Clergy in Hong Kong." *International Journal of Human Resource Management* 16 (2005) 2133–46.

Niebuhr, H. Richard. *The Purpose of the Church and its Ministry.* New York: Harper and Row, 1977.

Niebuhr, Reinhold. *Leaves from the Notebook of a Tamed Cynic.* New York: Harper, 1929.

Nordland, Frances. *The Unprivate Life of a Pastor's Wife.* Chicago: Moody, 1972.

Nouwen, Henri. *The Only Necessary Thing: Living a Prayerful Life.* Edited by Wendy Wilson Greer. New York: Crossroad, 1999.

———. *With Burning Hearts.* Maryknoll, NY: Orbis, 2004.

Oden, Thomas C. *Pastoral Theology: Essentials of Ministry.* San Francisco: HarperCollins, 1983.

Odom, Emily Enders. "A Two-Way Street." Online: http://gamc.pcusa.org/ministries/ministers/two-way-street/.

Olson, David. "Clergy Sometimes Neglect Their Own Needs While Helping Others." *The Press Enterprise* (September 26, 2010). Online: http://www.pe.com/localnews/religion/stories/PE_News_Local_D_clergystress27.2b7d011.html.

Olson, Suzanne. "Reflections of a Preacher's Kid." *The Clergy Journal* 82 (April 2006) 25.

Oswald, Roy M. *Clergy Self-Care.* Washington, DC: Alban Institute, 1991.

Palmer, Parker. *Let Your Life Speak: Listening to the Voice of Vocation*. San Francisco: Jossey-Bass, 2000.

Pannell, Nancy. *Being a Minister's Wife and Being Yourself*. Nashville: Broadman, 1993.

Papanek, Hanna. "Men, Women, and Work: Reflections on the Two-Person Career." *American Journal of Sociology* 78 (1973) 852–72.

Peterson, Eugene. *The Pastor: A Memoir*. New York: HarperOne, 2011.

———. *Practicing Resurrection: A Conversation about Growing Up in Christ*. Grand Rapids: Eerdmans, 2010.

———. *Under the Unpredictable Plant: An Exploration in Vocational Holiness*. Grand Rapids: Eerdmans, 1994.

———. *Working the Angles: The Shape of Pastoral Integrity*. Grand Rapids: Eerdmans, 1987.

Pollan, Michael. *In Defense of Food: An Eater's Manifesto*. New York: Penguin, 2008.

Postema, Don. *Catch Your Breath*. Grand Rapids: CRC Publications, 1997.

Potter, Beverly. *Overcoming Burnout: How to Renew Your Enthusiasm for Work*. Berkeley, CA: Ronin, 2005.

Proeschold-Bell, Rae Jean, and Sara H. LeGrand. "High Rates of Obesity and Chronic Disease among United Methodist Clergy." *Obesity* 18 (2010) 1867–70.

Rallings, E. M., and David J. Pratto. *Two-Clergy Marriages: A Special Case of Dual Careers*. Lanham, MD: University Press of America, 1984.

Raymond, Erik. "So Why are Pastors Fat?" October 13th, 2010. Online: http://www.irishcalvinist.com/?p=5158.

Rediger, G. Lloyd. *Clergy Killers: Guidance for Pastors and Congregations under Attack*. Louisville: Westminster John Knox, 1997.

Rediger, G. Lloyd. *Fit to Be a Pastor*. Louisville: Westminster John Knox, 2000.

Reiser, Paul. *Couplehood*. New York: Bantam, 1994.

Research Services, Presbyterian Church (USA). "Findings: 2008 Survey of Presbyterian Church (USA) Pastors." Online: http://www.pcusa.org/media/uploads/ research/ pdfs/bopfindings2008.pdf.

Richardson, Ronald W. *Becoming a Healthier Pastor*. Minneapolis: Fortress, 2005.

Roberts, Robert C. "The Blessings of Gratitude: A Conceptual Analysis." In *The Psychology of Gratitude*, edited by Robert A. Emmons and Michael E. McCullough, 58–78. New York: Oxford University Press, 2004.

Roof, Wade Clark. *Spiritual Marketplace: Baby Boomers and the Remaking of American Religion*. Princeton, NJ: Princeton University Press, 1999.

Sanford, John A. *Ministry Burnout*. Louisville: Westminster John Knox, 1982.

Sapolsky, Robert M. *Why Zebras Don't Get Ulcers*. 3rd ed. New York: Henry Holt, 2004.

Scazzero, Peter. *The Emotionally Healthy Church*. Grand Rapids: Zondervan, 2003.

Schlosser, Eric. *Fast Food Nation*. New York: HarperCollins, 2002.

Sell, Charles M. *Family Ministry*. 2nd ed. Grand Rapids: Zondervan, 1995.

Shelley, Marshall. *Well-Intentioned Dragons: Ministering to Problem People in the Church*. Minneapolis: Bethany House, 1994.

Smith, Tom W. "Job Satisfaction in the United States." Online: http://www-news.uchicago.edu/releases/07/pdf/070417.jobs.pdf.

Stalfa, Frank. "Protestant Clergy Marriage in the Congregational Context: A Report from the Field." *Journal of Pastoral Care and Counseling* 62 (2008) 252–56.

Stein, Jeannine. "Some Clergy May Have Higher Obesity and Chronic Disease Rates than their Congregations." *Los Angeles Times*, May 14, 2010. Online: http://

latimesblogs.latimes.com/ booster_shots/2010/05/clergy-obesity-rates-north-carolina.html.

Steinke, Peter L. *Healthy Congregations*. Herndon, VA: Alban Institute, 2006.

———. *How Your Church Family Works: Understanding Congregations as Emotional Systems*. Herndon, VA: Alban Institute, 2006.

Sternberg, Esther M. *The Balance Within: The Science Connecting Health and Emotions*. New York: W. H. Freeman, 2001.

Stoeltje, Melissa Fletcher. "Clergy Couples Do It for Eternity." *San Antonio Express-News*, June 6, 2004. Online: http://www.casparstartribune.net/articles/2004/06/06/news/ community/8e5bac761207332f87256eaa00129d1d.txt.

Stone, Charles. *5 Ministry Killers and How to Defeat Them*. Minneapolis: Bethany House, 2010.

Susek, Ron. *Firestorm: Preventing and Overcoming Church Conflicts*. Grand Rapids: Baker, 1999.

Swenson, Richard A. *Margin: Restoring Emotional, Physical, Financial, and Time Reserves to Overloaded Lives*. Colorado Springs, CO: NavPress, 2004.

Taubes, Gary. *Why We Get Fat*. New York: Borzoi Books, 2011.

Taylor, Shelley E., et al. "Biobehavioral Responses to Stress in Females: Tend-and-Befriend, Not Fight-or-Flight." *Psychological Review* 107 (2000) 411–29.

Thomas à Kempis. *The Imitation of Christ*. London: Penguin, 1952.

Thorndike, Jean M. "Gratitude and Human Flourishing: Examining the Benefits of Gratitude on Effective Coping, Resiliency, and Well-Being." PhD diss., Fuller Theological Seminary, 2007.

Trihub, Bobby L., et al. "Denominational Support for Clergy Mental Health." *Journal of Psychology and Theology* 38 (2010) 101–10.

Uchino, Bert N., et al. "The Relationship between Social Support and Physiological Processes: A Review with Emphasis on Underlying Mechanisms and Implications for Health." *Psychological Bulletin* 119 (1996) 488–531.

Ulstein, Stefan. *Pastors Off the Record*. Downers Grove, IL: InterVarsity, 1993.

Van Gelder, Craig. *The Essence of the Church*. Grand Rapids: Baker, 2000.

Veith, Gene Edward, Jr. *God at Work: Your Christian Vocation in All of Life*. Wheaton, IL: Crossway, 2002.

Vitello, Paul. "Taking a Break from the Lord's Work." *New York Times*, October 2, 2010. Online: http://www.nytimes.com/2010/08/02/nyregion/02burnout.html?_r=1&emc=eta1.

Watson, David. *I Believe in the Church*. Grand Rapids: Eerdmans, 1979.

Weiner, Bernard. "An Attributional Theory of Achievement Motivation and Emotion." *Psychological Review* 92 (1985) 548–73.

Wells, Bob. "Which Way to Clergy Health?" Online: http://www.divinity.duke.edu/programs/spe/resources/dukediv-clergyhealth.html.

Willard, Dallas. *The Divine Conspiracy: Rediscovering our Hidden Life in God*. New York: HarperCollins, 1998.

Williams, Joyce. *She Can't Even Play the Piano!* Kansas City, MO: Beacon Hill, 2005.

Willimon, William H. *Calling and Character: Virtues of the Ordained Life*. Nashville: Abingdon, 2000.

———. *Clergy and Laity Burnout*. Nashville: Abingdon, 1989.

———. *Pastor: The Theology and Practice of Ordained Ministry*. Nashville: Abingdon, 2002.

Wilson, Michael Todd, and Brad Hoffman. *Preventing Ministry Failure.* Downers Grove, IL: InterVarsity, 2007.

Wood, David. "'The Best Life': Eugene Peterson on Pastoral Ministry." *The Christian Century* 119 (March 13–20, 2002) 18–25.

Wright, N. T. *Surprised by Hope: Rethinking Heaven, the Resurrection, and the Mission of God.* New York: HarperOne, 2008.

Yancey, Philip. *Church: Why Bother?* Grand Rapids: Zondervan, 1998.

Zikmund, Barbara Brown, et al. *Clergy Women: An Uphill Calling.* Louisville: Westminster John Knox, 1998.

Zoba, Wendy Murray. "What Pastors' Wives Wish Their Churches Knew." *Christianity Today* 41 (April 7, 1997) 20, 22–23, 25–26.

Name and Subject Index

conflict in ministry (*continued*)
150, 152, 158, 159–65, 166,
168, 173, 179, 202, 220–23,
224
principles for handling, 164
Constantine, Mark D., 65n2
Copenhaver, Martin B., 7n5, 8n10,
49n3, 82n34, 156n18,
181n34, 185n50, 186n54,
189
Cordeiro, Wayne, vii–x, xiv, 10n14,
22–23, 33, 37n28
Cosby, Bill, 110
Cosden, Darrell, 87
couples, two-clergy, 16, 67, 181,
186–87, 194, 207–11,
238–41
Covey, Stephen R., 142
Currie III, Thomas W., 15, 61
Daniel, Lillian, 7n5, 8, 49, 82, 156,
181n34, 184–85, 186n54,
189n61, 194
Deming, Laura, 184n48, 185n51
Department of Health and Human
Services, 124n46
diet/eating habits, 114–15, 119–22,
126, 127, 203–5
divorce, pastors and, 173, 181, 204,
238
Dobson, Edward G., 160n28
Dobson, Lorna, 67n7, 167n38,
181n36, 182
Doctor of Ministry, 103, 104, 157
Dulles, Avery, 50
Easum, Bill, 137
Ellison, Christopher G., 156n17
Ellison Research, 114n17, 116n20
Ells, Alfred H., 51n6, 108, 139n15,
154n8, 172n3
Emmons, Robert A., 218n5
emotional exhaustion, 23, 40–41,
93, 95, 96
Epstein, Lawrence J., 116n21,
116n23, 117n26
Evers, Will, 41n42
exercise, physical, 113, 114, 115,
117, 122–24, 126, 127, 204–
5, 214, 240

federal guidelines for, 123
recommendations for getting
more, 123–24
Floyd, Jeana, 181n36
Focus on the Family, 8
Frame, Marsha, 39n35, 175n13,
175n14, 175n15, 176n16,
176n17
Francis, Leslie J., 8n9
Fredrickson, Barbara L., 218n6
Friedman, Edwin, 159
Galatia, churches in, 5–6, 8, 149
Galindo, Israel, 14n22, 163n32
Galli, Mark, 154n7
General Assembly Mission Council
(PCUSA), 14n24
Gilbert, Barbara G., 155n9, 155n11,
155n13, 156n19
Gilbert, Roberta M., 159n26
Guder, Darrell, 73n20
Guinness, Os, 75
Halaas, Gwen Wagstrom, 113, 120,
123, 124n45
Halverstadt, Hugh F., 160n28, 161,
164
Hancock, Elizabeth Emerson, 153,
154n5
Hart, Archibald D., 22, 26n10, 27,
30n17, 117n26, 118, 127n50
Haugk, Kenneth, 160n28
Hawkins, Susie, 181n36, 183
health statistics, pastoral, 112–15
Heller, Alfred L., 108
Hernandez, Edwin I., 14n26
Heschel, Abraham, 91, 96, 98,
100n23
Hileman, Linda, 174n10, 179n28
Hoffman, Brad, 140n18, 143
Hoge, Dean R., 35n24, 42n43,
160n27, 173n9, 181
Hotchkiss, Dan, 12n16
Hulme, William E., 41n41
husbands of female pastors, 181,
184–86
"immune system," congregational,
151–52, 161, 164, 221
intrusions of ministry into private
life, 33–35, 129–30, 131–37

Scripture Index